Michael Reeves

MANCHESTER
UNIVERSITY PRESS

BRIAN MCFARLANE, NEIL SINYARD *series editors*

ALLEN EYLES, PHILIP FRENCH, SUE HARPER,
TIM PULLEINE, JEFFREY RICHARDS, TOM RYALL
series advisers

**BRITISH
FILM
MAKERS**

already published

Jack Clayton   NEIL SINYARD

Lance Comfort   BRIAN MCFARLANE

Terence Fisher   PETER HUTCHINGS

Launder and Gilliat   BRUCE BABINGTON

J. Lee Thompson   STEVE CHIBNALL

Michael Reeves

BENJAMIN HALLIGAN

Manchester University Press

MANCHESTER AND NEW YORK

distributed exclusively in the USA by Palgrave

The right of Benjamin Halligan to be identified as the author of this work
has been asserted by him in accordance with the Copyright, Designs and
Patents Act 1988.

Published by Manchester University Press
Oxford Road, Manchester M13 9NR, UK
and Room 400, 175 Fifth Avenue, New York, NY 10010, USA
www.manchesteruniversitypress.co.uk

Distributed exclusively in the USA by
Palgrave, 175 Fifth Avenue, New York, NY 10010, USA

Distributed exclusively in Canada by
UBC Press, University of British Columbia, 2029 West Mall,
Vancouver, BC, Canada V6T 1Z2

British Library Cataloguing-in-Publication Data
A catalogue record for this book is available from the British Library

Library of Congress Cataloging-in-Publication Data applied for

ISBN 0 7190 6350 7 *hardback*
     0 7190 6351 5 *paperback*

First published 2003

11 10 09 08 07 06 05 04 03   10 9 8 7 6 5 4 3 2 1

Typeset in Scala with Meta display
by Koinonia, Manchester
Printed in Great Britain
by Bell & Bain Ltd, Glasgow

In memory of Lucy Bamonte

Contents

List of illustrations

Series editors' foreword

The aim of this series is to present in lively, authoritative volumes a guide to those film-makers who have made British cinema a rewarding but still under-researched branch of world cinema. The intention is to provide books which are up-to-date in terms of information and critical approach, but not bound to any one theoretical methodology. Though all books in the series will have certain elements in common – comprehensive filmographies, annotated bibliographies, appropriate illustration – the actual critical tools employed will be the responsibility of the individual authors.

Nevertheless, an important recurring element will be a concern for how the oeuvre of each film-maker does or does not fit certain critical and industrial contexts, as well as for the wider social contexts, which helped to shape not just that particular film-maker but the course of British cinema at large.

Although the series is director-orientated, the editors believe that a variety of stances and contexts referred to is more likely to reconceptualize and reappraise the phenomenon of British cinema as a complex, shifting field of production. All the texts in the series will engage in detailed discussion of major works of the film-makers involved, but they all consider as well the importance of other key collaborators, of studio organisation, of audience reception, of recurring themes and structures: all those other aspects which go towards the construction of a national cinema.

The series explores and charts a field which is more than ripe for serious excavation. The acknowledged leaders of the field will be reappraised; just as important, though, will be the bringing to light of those who have not so far received any serious attention. They are all part of the very rich texture of British cinema, and it will be the work of this series to give them all their due.

Foreword
Philip Waddilove

Over the years, several people have approached me for help in writing biographies or magazine articles on my late friend and colleague, the young British movie director Michael Reeves who died tragically in 1969 at the age of 25. The people who contacted me had their own – mostly respectable – agendas with regards to Michael's story. My desire was to dispel the inaccurate report in so many movie guides and reference books, that Michael committed suicide. Without denigrating the work of the other writers, I believe that Benjamin Halligan is the first who, after exhaustive research of Michael's short but extraordinary life, has been able to write an accurate yet fascinating account of it. Ben also went to considerable lengths to obtain original documentation, including a copy of the coroner's report on Michael's death in which, as you will see, the recorded verdict states that his death was accidental.

When Ben asked me to consider writing the foreword to his book, I did not know where to begin or end and was therefore hesitant to accept the honour. However, during my three-year e-mail and telephonic relationship with him, I was given the opportunity to read a large amount of material and to hear many anecdotes about Michael of which I was previously unaware. Also, in Ben's book, you will find a lengthy and articulate letter that Michael wrote in early 1968 regarding gratuitous violence on the screen. The letter was to John Trevelyan, head of the British Board of Film Censors after they demanded that sweeping cuts be made to our movie *Witchfinder General*. Rereading Michael's letter after all these years persuaded me that I should attempt to write the foreword.

I first met Michael socially just over a year before I found myself working with him on the movie, so I may be forgiven for not immediately recognising his genius – a word that I would hear repeatedly over the years to describe him. Indeed, just recently here in Los Angeles – more than thirty-three years after Michael's untimely death – I watched the first American Movie Channel national television network screening of *Witchfinder General* (under its inappropriate title in the United States of *The Conqueror Worm*) and was immensely gratified to hear it introduced as a movie directed by the young genius Michael Reeves 'that many critics today consider a masterpiece'.

After a career engaged mostly in what was commonly known as 'light entertainment', my somewhat unusual introduction to the world of motion picture making would change my life radically. Michael Reeves – fifteen years my junior – was the person most responsible for the change. He taught me what I know about moviemaking and gave me all my enthusiasm for it. A single area of concern to me was the direction in which he was leading me on the subject of gratuitous violence. Indeed, when I read the first draft screenplay of *Witchfinder General*, I realised that I would have to come to terms with its extremely violent content. But first it was necessary to immerse myself in the physical production of the movie, and there was little time for introspection regarding the morality of what we were about to accomplish.

After watching every frame of the movie being filmed and after seeing it innumerable times during post-production, I perhaps became somewhat immune to its violence. Certainly, as Michael's producer, I found myself supporting him wholeheartedly and unreservedly in his drawn-out battle with the British Board of Film Censors over the cuts they were demanding that we make to the movie.

At the premiere and first public screening of *Witchfinder General* at the Carlton Cinema in the West End of London, I was too excited by the enthusiastic reception that the movie was given to have any pangs of conscience with regard to its content. However, a few days later, I decided to return on my own to the Carlton Cinema for a matinée performance of the movie. At two o'clock on a mid-week afternoon the audience was sparse, but a more worrisome aspect of my visit was that practically all the people present belonged to the lunatic fringe who cheer and even laugh at every violent moment on the screen. I thought to myself: what have we done? After all our efforts, have we in fact ended up producing nothing more than a display of gratuitous violence? I did not then and do not now believe so.

Luckily for my psyche, at the time I had already begun development work on *The Buttercup Chain* – a movie for Columbia Pictures with a considerably less violent theme. Conscious of the gentle side of Michael Reeves's nature, my co-producer and I had witnessed Michael's talents as a moviemaker at close quarters. After we gave him our screenplay to read, he enthusiastically authorised us to put his name forward to Columbia Pictures executives as the prospective director of our movie and he contributed vitally to its planning. Unfortunately, after several months of lobbying, my partner and I failed in our attempts to convince the Columbia executives that Michael was the right director for the movie. Gracefully, both Michael and his agent told us that he had no option other than to retire from the project.

Although Michael and I parted as colleagues, we hoped earnestly that we would make another movie together, and we remained close friends. But my making another movie with him it was not to happen. The evening before my departure for Sweden on a location search for *The Buttercup Chain*, my wife told me the dreadful news that Michael had passed away. Professionally and personally, it was the unhappiest moment of my life.

Now, when I reread Michael's letter of all those years ago to John Trevelyan, I realise that I could never have described my philosophy regarding violence in the cinema more succinctly or in greater depth than Michael does in his letter. As Ben Halligan puts it so accurately in his book, it is in fact 'Reeves's manifesto for film-making'.

Los Angeles, California

Acknowledgements

This story draws on the memories of many of Mike Reeves's friends, associates and relatives. In a way, this book has been a 'Leith Production' too. I thank them for their welcomes, recollections and good humour. They are: Gillian Aldam; Nick Alexander; Michael Armstrong; Robert Armstrong; Tom Baker; Jane and Peter Barrett; Lars Bloch; Peter Bowles; John Burke; Richard Campling; Cherida Cannon; Jack Cardiff; Simon Clark; Zara Clark; Julie Cracknell; Patrick Curtis; Ralph Ferraro; Susan George; Charles B. Griffith; Michael Gross; John Hall; Ernest Harris; Hilary Heath; Gordon Hessler; Louis M. Heyward; Dennis Hopper; Euan Houstoun; Miles Huddleston; Christopher James; Alf Joint; Howard Lanning; Christopher Lee; Stanley Long; Jack Lynn; Robert Mackenzie; Digby Mackworth; Paul Maslansky; William Maxwell; Brian McAlpine; Michael Motley; Toby Motley; Frederick Muller; Ian Ogilvy; Euan Pearson; Richard Poore; Peter Raby; Ian Rakoff; Edward B. Randolph; John Sellers; Sarah Sesti; Laurie Shane; Alfred Shaughnessy; Ralph Sheldon; Anton Brooke Shellim; Iain Sinclair; Peter Sowerby; Hugh Strain; Tony Tenser; Diana Tetlow; Alex Waye; Mel Welles; David Woodward.

My thanks also to those who helped in the preparation of this book: Julian Bamford; Charles Barr; David Barraclough; Erika Bond; Kevin Brownlow; David Cairns; Wasel Chemij; Alex Cox; Ray Durgnat; Tony Earnshaw; Jay Fenton; James Ferman; Robert Fuest; John Hefin; Lee Hill; Jim Hillier; I. Q. Hunter; Peter Hutchings; Troy Howarth; Alexei Jankowski; Aled Llewelyn Jones; Sara Karloff; Ted Keeble; Magdalena Kožená; Craig Lapper; George Long; Tim Lucas; David Maxwell; Clive Meachen; Marc Morris; Jock Mullard; John B. Murray; Ken Russell; Mike Shaw; Antti Suonio; Sue Sutton; Kris Tabori; Jeremy Thomas;

Julian Palacios; Julian Petley; David Pirie; Derek Prior; David Prothero; John Stuart Roberts; David Del Valle; Tom Weaver; Christopher Weedman; Tony Whitehead.

Special thanks to those who went before me in this endeavour, and were then so generous with their archives: Lawrence French; Tim Hodgson; Christopher O'Brien; Chris O'Loughlin; Pete Tombs; Diana Tetlow; Lucy Chase Williams.

The following organisations and institutions have also provided support: the British Film Institute; BOUM Productions; Chelsea Reference Library; Em Gee Film Library; Ghoul Britannia; Heavenly Records; National Library of Wales; the Old Radleian Society; Pagan Films; Radley College; Redemption Films; Salvation Films; Sinister Cinema; Seaford Museum and Heritage Society; University of Wales, Aberystwyth; York St John College.

Particular thanks must go to Philip Waddilove, who helped enable both *Witchfinder General* and this book.

Epitaphs   1

Take me to your goddamn young genius!
(Vincent Price to *Witchfinder General* producer Philip Waddilove)[1]

Michael Reeves did not live long enough to shore up a reputation as an important film-maker, but nor did he live long enough to tarnish such a reputation. And, like the best of his contemporaries, he did not much care for a reputation – beyond something that would enable him to make further films. So when Mike died, his reputation was up for grabs and would come to be a way of understanding the loss. The common knowledge about the nature of the death of Michael Reeves was founded on the despair in his films, and that his life mirrored his art, tragically and finally, in one, last, despairing act: suicide. The beauty of the despair in his films lends itself to the beguiling myth of a young and talented film-maker, who only ever directed three films, before dying at the age of 25.

In his 1973 study *A Heritage of Horror: The English Gothic Cinema 1946–1972*, David Pirie opens his discussion of the life and work of Michael Reeves by evoking the lives of Byron, Shelley and Polidori, united in the 'aura of melodrama or even tragedy [that] surrounds the lives and careers of many of those involved in Romantic/Gothic literature'.[2] The consideration of 'Gothic cinema' is then unavoidably along the same lines:

> it should be observed that something of the same intensely tragic atmosphere pervades the world of the horror films and those who

create them. The point was made originally by Peter John Dyer in *Sight & Sound*, Autumn 1968, when he listed a number of horror names (Lon Chaney Sr, Laird Cregar, James Whale, Bela Lugosi, etc) who had died in tragic circumstances. Then, only weeks after Dyer's article appeared, Michael Reeves, one of the most remarkable young English film-makers of the 1960s, who had pioneered a new approach to British horror, was found dead in his flat of a barbiturate overdose.[3]

It is a persuasive association and Pirie goes one further, likening Reeves to Keats in his conclusion.[4] It is also a useful idea. Dead before 1970, Reeves easily comes to represent a new dawn that faded – not a wounded foot soldier left behind, but a potential general. British film production slid into the doldrums in the 1970s, not only because the dollars suddenly vanished (*Easy Rider* and *The Graduate* furnishing proof for the majors that films were not necessarily better if shot in London, and signalling a renewed interest in American material) and not only because cinema audiences in the UK continued their decline, but also because of a wider sense of uncertainty on the part of European auteurs, in the wake of the failure of 1968. Reeves came to represent what could have been.

This would have been immediately grasped in some quarters (in his summation of the state of British film at the turn of 1968, 'Case histories of the next renascence', David Robinson considers Reeves alongside Ken Loach, Ken Russell and Lindsay Anderson[5]), but the full extent of the potential that would remain unfulfilled could not have been apparent at the time, or for a while to come. The loss was most keenly felt by critics who championed genre film as the way ahead at this juncture, particularly Robin Wood. He started his obituary–career overview piece in *Movie* with an apology – that the one film-maker who had done just what *Movie* called for had been roundly overlooked:

It seems nicely ironic, when one looks back over the history of British film criticism in the last decade, that the director who perhaps came nearest to fulfilling the wishes of *Movie* for a revival in the British cinema – a director working at the heart of the commercial industry, making *genre* movies without apparent friction or frustration – should have been discovered by 'Films and Filming' and the associate editor of 'Sight and Sound.' I came out of *Witchfinder* telling myself that the next time a Michael Reeves film appeared I would review it for *Movie* and try to secure an interview with its director. Now there will be no interview, and *Witchfinder General* will have no successor ....[6]

The real irony is that the only interview proper would appear in the UK *Penthouse* (and a couple of quotes in a UK *Vogue* piece) – 'Reeves, a tall long-haired guy who surrounds himself with Presley sounds and Turner prints'.[7] Pirie provided the answer to Robinson's anticipation of the British cinema of the 1970s in the 1971 *Sight & Sound* piece 'New blood'. After a breeze through mostly forgotten films and film-makers, he concludes 'if only a few directors can emerge to continue the sort of work that Michael Reeves began, we could yet see the British cinema rejuvenated from its humblest roots'.[8] Perhaps it is precisely because this failed to happen that Reeves earned his subsequent period of marginalisation, a necessity for any true 'cult' figure. Perhaps because the seeming contradiction in terms of Pirie's 'pioneered a new approach to British horror' remains unresolved, Reeves's marginalisation has, by and large, continued. He sits uneasily, if at all, in histories of British film. He remains, if anywhere, in the 'underground British cinema' (and is claimed for this by his friend Iain Sinclair), that which William Johnson defines in relation to David Lean's *Great Expectations*; as Magwitch arrives in Pip's London chambers, Johnson finds in this rude intrusion that 'Such forces from the underworld can be found at work throughout the history of the British cinema ...'.[9] Reeves's unwanted presence in the industry that mostly revived itself through a dry but comfortable heritage cinema can be accounted for in terms of his cinematic imagination, audacity and transgression. Of his period, Anderson and Russell were certainly guilty of as much, but precious few others. In this critical biography, to understand how this came about, and in doing so to regroup the diaspora of Reeves's reputation, it has been necessary to return to the beginning.

After his death, Reeves's stock rapidly fell. Charles Barr reports that *Witchfinder* was rejected by the Selection Committee for the

National Film Archive,[10] and Reeves and his films are mostly absent from histories of British cinema written in the 1970s. His legacy was mangled upon its slight return. Roy Armes, in his 1978 volume *A Critical History of British Cinema*, lumps Reeves in with the casualties of 'a process of virtual self-destruction' (the others being Robert Hamer and Seth Holt: in these cases, the bottle).[11] More recently, *Witchfinder* is mentioned once in Brian McFarlane's *An Autobiography of British Cinema*, by Kevin Brownlow, and then in relation to how *not* to shoot period drama.[12] Elsewhere, when Reeves and *Witchfinder* do make an appearance, it is inevitably in studies of British horror films – or in the sections devoted to horror in wider studies of British film.[13] In this respect, *Witchfinder* remains almost entirely considered alongside films without ambivalence about their status.[14] The strategies in the film against such a generic horror status have been routed by the simple equation, first made by American International Pictures (the bigger of its two production companies), that Vincent Price equals horror. This is doubly problematic because, as Peter Hutchings argues,[15] the study of the British horror film has been beset with problems to begin with; fault lines of commonly held prejudices and erroneous generalisations across the critical discourses. But this horror context has also gone some way to keeping the myth alive in the face of academic insouciance; Reeves is a favourite of limited-circulation 'cult' film magazines. And, also, outside academic writing, is John B. Murray's oral history of Mike's life, published in 2001.[16]

For later purveyors of the 1960s, it was a wider sense of bad karma – or that which Lachman refers to as 'the dark side of the age of Aquarius'[17] – that would seem to have ensnared Reeves: 'Michael Reeves, director of *The Sorcerers*, took the suicide option in 1969 at the age of twenty-five (appropriately enough, drugs were the chosen method: a dose of unhip barbiturates) ... he chose his exit in February of the final year of that psychedelic decade, slipping away from the party without many people noticing ...'.[18] In this way, Reeves could join the Syd Barrett, Brian Epstein (also perceived to have had an 'ambiguous' end, also via barbiturates), Jimi Hendrix (he and Mike shared the same pathologist, the busy

Dr Donald Teare) and Brian Jones casualties group; those lightly sporting extraordinary talent, whose influence is difficult to over-estimate, but who did not quite make it through. Likewise, the first full retrospective piece on Reeves in North America concluded by likening him to James Dean.[19] It seems to have been as frustrating for those who knew Mike to see him reimagined in a Pop Art Houseman manner as surprising, for those who worked with him, to understand the 'mystique that has grown up around him'.[20]

Yet the idea of suicide did not originate from reports at the time. Mike's friend, the *Films and Filming* critic David Austen, en-sured that the magazine recorded that he had 'died accidentally'.[21] The *Chelsea News* recorded, in detail, the verdict of accidental death.[22] However, rumours of suicide did the rounds among friends and associates on the outskirts of his group. Those in the know could confirm his precarious and worsening mental state throughout 1968 and 1969. He had dropped out of film projects, was undergoing clinical treatment for depression, threw back pills, had been found unconscious only months before. It made more sense – Reeves caught up in the nihilism and death drive of his final film in which the very opening credits read like a suicide note: a frozen litho of a screaming face behind 'Directed by Michael Reeves'. And even Mike seems to have liked the idea; visiting his composer Paul Ferris in hospital after Ferris' unsuccessful suicide attempt, Mike joked about a bet as to which of them would suc-ceed in suicide first.[23] When introduced by Austen to another aspiring, young, British horror film-maker also working for Tigon and American International Pictures, Michael Armstrong, he showed him his involuntarily shaking hands and quipped 'This is what the film business has done to me',[24] before launching into a checklist of everything that had and would go wrong ('Don't make the mistake that anyone in the company knows how to look at the film. Show them the fine cut') and stories of how dreadful it had been to work with Vincent Price, tempered with general advice ('Tell the crew to tear down a wall to keep them busy if you need time to think'). Self-pity or self-diagnosis? Even a couple of years before Mike had talked of 'the infallible lullaby of my own neuroses'.[25]

The chief witness himself was unequivocal. Just as Vincent Price had been used to sell *Witchfinder,* so too he came to sell the myth. During interviews with Lawrence French some years later, Price recalled Reeves in a way to sustain the conventional wisdom: as highly talented, certainly; impossible, perhaps ... but troubled, depressive, suicidal, someone on borrowed time. Price, aware of the stories of their on-set friction, presents himself as the reasonable party. This seems to have begun during the post-synching of *Witchfinder General,* once Vincent was away from Mike (still filming), and rarely let up thereafter:

> Well he hated me. He didn't want me at all for that part. He wanted some other actor, and he got me and that was it. I didn't like him, either, and it was one of the first times in my life that I've been in a picture where really the director and I just clashed [twists his hands], like that. He didn't know how to talk to actors, he hadn't had the experience, or talked to enough of them, so all the actors on the picture had a very bad time. I knew though, that in a funny, uneducated sort of way, he was right, in his desire for me to approach the part in a certain way. He wanted it very serious and straight, and he was right, but he just didn't know how to communicate with actors. Actors are very sensitive people. I'll never forget one time he came up to me and said, 'don't shake your head.' I said, 'what do you mean, I don't shake my head.' He said 'yes, you do.' So we didn't get along at all. He was a funny young man, brilliant, but he had a lot of problems. Really mixed-up problems. One of them being dope, another being an unhappy romance, and he killed himself. It was a great loss to the cinema, because had he been disciplined he could have become a very good director. Believe me, this profession takes enormous discipline. You're out there at six in the morning, and you're up till midnight, and back at six the next morning, so there's no fooling around. If you want to last, you're disciplined ... he had this terrible problem of suicide. He tried about four times, and finally they thought they had him cured, but when we started to do costume tests and all the preparations for *The Oblong Box,* he tried it again, and they just said, 'he's too unstable'. It was a shame. He couldn't control himself, and he was on the flip, and then his girlfriend ditched him, because she couldn't put up with him. He was just completely determined to destroy himself ... he showed great promise. He was a wonderful

director, but these problems he had. He called me after [*sic*] *The Witchfinder General* was released in England, and it got very good notices. It was really a hit for him. He said, 'there, you see, I told you so!' It was a mad kind of thing to do. Then when we got together on *The Oblong Box*, I said, 'well, I think you were wonderful, you made a marvellous picture, now let's get along on this one,' but we didn't because he got sick again and killed himself.[26]

And, elsewhere:

[Working with Michael Reeves] was a very sad experience. He was a boy who had a lot of problems. Terrible problems, which nobody seemed to know about. He was very unstable ... difficult but brilliant. He was about twenty-seven when he committed suicide. He was very difficult to work with because he didn't know how to tell an actor what he wanted. It was sad ... he communicated the wrong way, and he rubbed everyone the wrong way. But we knew he had a tremendous talent, so we tried to overlook it.[23]

It is a heavy-handed and calculated character assassination, long after the event – Mike as a Byronic, tragic figure whose suicide was inevitable. It casts Vincent as the innocent and it made good copy. It also suggests that Vincent, a lifelong purveyor of fine art, understood something the academics and film historians did not; that Reeves's legacy was worth fighting over.

Notes

1 Philip Waddilove, interviews with author, across 1999–2002. All subsequent remarks are taken from this source.
2 D. Pirie, *A Heritage of Horror: The English Gothic Cinema 1946–1972* (London, Gordon Fraser, 1973), p. 145.
3 Pirie, *Heritage of Horror*, p. 145.
4 Pirie, *Heritage of Horror*, p. 155.
5 D. Robinson, 'Case histories of the next renascence', *Sight & Sound* (winter 1968/69) 36–40.
6 R. Wood, 'In memoriam Michael Reeves', *Movie* (winter 1969–70) 2.
7 Anon, 'Shows – horror clicks', *Penthouse*, 3: 10 (UK edition, undated) 12.
8 D. Pirie, 'New Blood', *Sight & Sound* (spring 1971) 75.
9 W. Johnson, 'A walk on the wild side', *Sight & Sound* (spring 1986) 124.
10 C. Barr, '*Straw Dogs, A Clockwork Orange* and the critics', *Screen: The Journal of the Society for Education in Film and Television*, 13: 2 (summer

1972) 30. Jim Hillier recalls that the reticence on the part of the Committee would have been over the issue of 'quality', particularly in relation to anything that was both popular and had attracted critical attention; Jim Hillier, interview with the author, 31 May 2002.

11 R. Armes, *A Critical History of British Cinema* (London, Secker & Warburg, 1979), p. 335.

12 B. McFarlane, *An Autobiography of British Cinema* (London, Methuen, 1997), p. 98.

13 For example, as considered under 'Hammer's competitors' in R. Murphy, *Sixties British Cinema* (London, British Film Institute, 1997), pp. 186–94; or in S. Street, *British National Cinema* (London and New York, Routledge, 1997), p. 94.

14 For example, David Sanjek considers the film in relation to the monsters-on-the-London-Underground *Death Line* in W. W. Dixon, *Re-Viewing British Cinema, 1990–1992: Essays and Interviews* (Albany, State University of New York Press, 1994), pp. 205–6.

15 P. Hutchings, *Hammer and Beyond: The British Horror Film* (Manchester, Manchester University Press, 1993), pp. 3–23.

16 J. B. Murray, *The Remarkable Michael Reeves: His Short and Tragic Life* (London, Cinematics Publishing, 2001).

17 G. V. Lachman, *Turn off Your Mind: The Mystic Sixties and the Dark Side of the Age of Aquarius* (London, Sidgwick & Jackson, 2001).

18 M. Jones, *Psychedelic Decadence: Sex, Drugs, Low-Art in Sixties and Seventies Britain* (Manchester, Critical Vision/Headpress, 2001), p. 8.

19 B. Kelley, 'Filming Reeves' masterpiece: *Witchfinder General*', *Cinefantastique* 1 (1991) 45. *Video Watchdog* editor Tim Lucas puts Reeves's low US profile down to the shoddy video presentations of *Revenge of the Blood Beast* (badly panned and scanned), *The Sorcerers* (cut) and *Witchfinder* (with the wrong score) over the years; Tim Lucas, interview with author, 28 June 2000.

20 Mel Welles, interview with author, 1 April 2002. All subsequent remarks are taken from this source.

21 Anon., 'Obituary', *Films and Filming* 15:8 (May 1969) 91.

22 Anon., 'Film director's death from pills was accidental', *Chelsea News* (28 February 1969) 7.

23 Murray, *The Remarkable Michael Reeves*, p. 306.

24 Michael Armstrong, interview with author, 8 May 2002. All subsequent remarks are taken from this source.

25 This is taken from an entry from the few surviving pages of Mike's diary, mostly a list of appointments, reproduced in Murray, *The Remarkable Michael Reeves*, p. 110.

26 L. French, 'An interview with Vincent Price', conducted in 1979 and 1985, unpublished. Parts of the interview appear throughout G. J. Svehla, and S. Svehla (eds): *Midnight Marquee Actors Series: Vincent Price* (Baltimore, Maryland, Midnight Marquee Press, Inc., 1998).

27 W. W. Dixon (ed.), *Collected Interviews: Voices from Twentieth-Century Cinema* (Carbondale and Edwardsville, Southern Illinois University Press, 2001), p. 205.

'Displaced Person English' **2**

The King's Mead magazine from the 1950s reads, in part, like medical dispatches from the Crimean War. Terms are denoted by the onset of new diseases and the imposition of quarantines, the characteristics of which become more the measure of the year's passing than the commentary on the weather (inevitably extreme during the winter months) and the gifts donated to the school by leavers (invariably furnishings). Other sections are narratives of broken limbs and notable afflictions, reported with news-item detail – 'Disaster on the Tennis Court': '… he fell heavily on his left arm and broke it. He had previously broken his arm in the same place … [and was] taken to hospital in agony'; 'Yet Another Casualty': 'Another injury so soon after James' accident was very bad luck … But it was not better that evening, or the next morning. Then, as most of us know, Bannerman's arm was reset and at the moment he is convalescing'; 'Mackenzie ma[jor] has another of those arm injuries. We are told that he did it trying to jump over a wall'; 'Great disappointment to all boxers was caused by the inevitable postponement of this year's boxing tournament on account of the chicken-pox scourge'; 'Owing to Asian 'flu there was no play in 1957 …'.

But young boys tend to break things and these incidents were cast as the exceptions that proved the rule since the prep school itself was first imagined, in 1914, as a fortress against illnesses. King's Mead was positioned in ozone-rich Seaford, in Sussex, on the South Coast where, from October to May, the weather was uniformly and bracingly cold and wet. It retained this 'taking the airs' ambience in the 1950s. The school was a robust, ivy-clad country manor in extensive grounds. Inside was polished oak panelling and high ceilings, armchairs in the library ('a distinct lack of exciting literature ... mostly novels by G. A. Henty with titles like *With Clive to India*[1]) and the day's newspapers in the Billiards Room (from where the boys followed the developments in Suez while Mike would study the film reviews). King's Mead was regimented; boys would be assigned to 'Patrols' for the duration of their time at King's Mead and life was governed by bells: morning exercises on 'the tarmac' ('ten minutes, jumping up and down, led by the boys',[2] possibly a cold bath too), then breakfast, lessons, lunch, games, high tea, prep, supper, hobbies, bed, lights out. The Sunday night evensong in the gloomy chapel, with the hymns 'For Those in Peril on the Sea', 'Through the Night of Doubt and Sorrow' and 'The Day Thou Gavest Lord has Ended' and the wind howling outside ('Our shelter from the stormy blast'; 'The darkness falls at Thy behest'), made for a definitive end to the limited freedoms of the weekend. Those who had been out, with parents or the parents of friends, were to have returned, and to be in place in their uncomfortable wooden seats in time for evensong, at 6 p.m.

Such character-building minimalisations of creature comforts, however, did not detract from the undoubtedly warm, and slightly bohemian, and certainly eccentric atmosphere in King's Mead, in the manner of most such prep schools, barely changing for the majority of the century. Looking back, headmaster Peter Barrett recalled 'A high standard of living – it was a happy school' and Old Boys agree, citing in particular the choice of meals as the height of luxury. The classes were small and the formal education far from the *raison d'être* of the school; emphasis was given to full and productive activity during free time. Boxing, archaeological digs and model-making were particularly encouraged; a retired brigadier taught carpentry and responsibilities were doled out – mowing the lawns was a sought-after privilege. Staff lived locally or on the site and all mucked in. In a way, the chapel embodied the King's Mead life and ethos; it had been constructed by pupils in the late 1920s, chairs donated by Old Boys over the years (plaques affixed, name and years), and faced west (so that the congregation would have to turn around and face the back of the chapel for the recitation of the Creed). One likes to think the one hundred or so pupils were left unchecked and made this blunder, misreading the sketches of a local architect; a 'creative atmosphere', one of the goals of King's Mead, can also have its hazards.

The academic and sporting endeavours were lightened by the annual calendar highlights: the bonfire night, the school fête, theatre trips, talks by the RAF, dancing lessons (including the occasional female to practice on, brought in from the locale), school matches (those not playing were required to spectate and cheer in an orderly fashion, and, after cricket matches, compulsory score cards would be inspected for accuracy), visits to galleries and museums, the fathers vs. sons cricket match, the school play. The whole was tempered by weekly treats: Sunday walks on the South Downs or Beachy Head, *The Goon Show*, eleven pence of 'shop' a week (principally liquorice shoelaces and balsa wood), gramophone recitals on Saturdays (requests in by Wednesday; rock 'n' roll records had little chance, yodelling cowboys did, but only after negotiations). The masters would read stories to the boys in the library, who could sit or lie on the floor and eat tuck as they listened. Sherlock Holmes and Blackbeard are well-remembered favourites. Older boys would join one of the two headmasters, Paul Holmes ('Pathy', a chain-smoking Wykehamist) for soirées in his study, where he would recount well-worn yarns about his escape from an Italian POW camp, over gin and Guinness. Television arrived in time for Christmas 1953 and was permissible only on Sunday nights. Punishment was infrequent and relatively mild: a miniature cricket bat from Barrett (pupils would bend over the arm of his office sofa) and orthodox cane from Pathy (kept, in the time-honoured fashion of prep school headmasters, in the top drawer of the desk). Pathy also used a cricket bat on occasion, autographed by the England team during a tour of India, across the bare buttocks. The painful wait for a beating which had taught Hitchcock (he claimed) so much about suspense, was practised in King's Mead too: the unfortunates were called from their places at some unspecified point during prep. For minor dormitory offences, one was given 'state' – lying motionless, hands by sides, for five to ten minutes, depending on the nature of the misdemeanour.

Such an atmosphere would allow Reeves (no longer 'Mike') to reconfigure himself in the wake of his father's death – two days before he was due to start the prep school, at the age of 8, in May 1952. Mike had literally gone straight to King's Mead from his father's funeral. For Mike's mother, Elizabeth, this day was a double loss and therefore would have tested her considerable skills of outward control. She had first met Mike's father when she was playing piano in the Savoy Hotel (she was the relief pianist for Carroll Gibbons and his Savoy Hotel Orpheans). Some comfort would have been afforded by her own proximity to the school, and that she knew the Barretts well. Elizabeth, or Betty to the wider family, would have busied herself with the details of Mike's departure during the painful days in between: 'Boys should have a pencil box or case and a supply of pencils'; 'He should have a pad of lined writing-paper and envelopes'; 'Parents are asked to ensure that the books boys bring back to School are suitable reading. Please see that all books are marked. The only 'comics' allowed are *The Eagle* and *The Ranger*'.

She did not forcibly sever the second umbilical cord as some parents will do as the child, in new blazer and with full tuck box, says a stiff upper-lipped goodbye on the railway station platform. Elizabeth remained on hand, visiting and dining with the Barretts (judging an art competition provided an excuse for one such call), becoming a regular for their sherry nights. She would invite Mike and his friends out to lunch when she visited, one summer holding a picnic for the whole gang on the South Downs. Or Mike would join his friend Mike Gross and his parents for lunch at the Grand in Brighton, followed by a trip in a speedboat.

After depositing Mike at King's Mead for the first term, she would have set her thoughts down in a letter, which he would have read over breakfast in the noisy dining hall, and then later, alone, in the Baden-Powell dormitory for new boys. He was to be brave, to enjoy life at King's Mead (and he *would*, she knew it), to do all the activities he wanted, that other boys too had lost their fathers, in the war, and that he should not hesitate to talk about things with

Mr Barrett if he needed anything – anything at all. And that she was only a telephone call away.

Betty was tall and elegant, remembered as domineering and grand – but utterly likeable – and had a demi-American accent which wowed the other boys (her own mother was from Boston). She had met her husband late and had Mike when she was in her early forties. The nature of her husband's death could well have added trauma to Betty's burdens. He had died from a heart attack, 'in the marital bed' (as was confided to only the closest members of the family). Noël Coward noted the unruffled demeanour of Carroll Gibbons and the Savoy band – not missing a beat as the bombs fell[3] – and such stoicism in the face of adversity would have served Elizabeth well; her social skills and focus on her outward demeanour – 'she was a great one for covering things up'[4] – would have held her together during that week in May 1952. It is unlikely that Mike ever knew about the exact nature of his father's death. Derek Leith 'Bungie' Reeves seems to have had the same pioneering spirit as his only child. He was an officer in the Navy during the war, then played the stock markets with inherited wealth while working as a solicitor. He married Betty during the war and Mike arrived on 17 October 1943. It was a happy marriage, but periodically overshadowed by Bungie's manic depression, seemingly a legacy from his own father, and extending even further back in the family. This was well known to the wider family, unusual at the time and a sign of its severity. His early death was seen to be an aspect of his troubled aura. Thus Mike had become the centre of Betty's world and could not put a foot wrong. The context for Mike's particularly obnoxious teenage years was therefore set in place from an early age (and the means would be available at 15, when he inherited a considerable amount of family money) – and something of a bolshy and self-centred persona remained with him throughout his life. Mike would introduce Betty to his King's Mead friends as 'Twerpy', much to her feigned annoyance. Betty would soon treat Mike more as a companion, which hastened his early maturity and confidence. He would unwillingly accompany her on an annual cruise – for Mike, always something of a chore – together with a number of cousins and family friends.

'The Seaford Slug' (as the boys called the school train) delivered Reeves to King's Mead in time for an outbreak of German measles and a documentary about Dr Barnardo's Homes for underprivileged children. Mike seems to have kept a low profile for his early years (expected of those lower down the school, at any rate) but soon came to be well liked by all ('a very steady bloke', 'thoroughly good bloke'[5]) and was physically big enough to avoid trouble. Within a few years, he emerged engaging in notable events: he read the lesson at the Carol Service, put in solid work on the cricket pitch ('A good innings by Reeves'; he would open bowling for the Cricket 1st XI), and trod the boards with some distinction – Alfred in *Toad of Toad Hall*, the Centurion in Shaw's *Androcles and the Lion*, and the Frog-Footman in *Alice in Wonderland* ('outstanding performance'). The school play was an all-in event; those not in the cast would paint scenery, prepare costumes and furnish the performance with sound effects. From acting, Mike moved on to write and direct for the Patrol Plays competition (taking second place). The title of the drama could almost be a summation of the plot of *The Sorcerers*, *The Tragical History of Homicide Henry*, except that it was a comedy, and was 'very funny indeed'. Mike's latter-day Faust no doubt murdered accidentally and frequently in a series of set pieces, as would the protagonist of *The Sorcerers*, minus the slapstick.

Two of Barrett's particular passions – boxing (endless matches since Barrett was aware that the pastime was drifting into the realm of the unfashionable) and archaeology – offered little of interest to Mike. Nor was he particularly taken with the religion on offer (mild rather than hellfire), but developed a fondness for the threadbare grandioseness of it all, lifting high Anglo-Catholicisms from the service and inserting them into daily speech, a practice he retained until his death. In the swinging Chelsea of 1968, Mike would typically bid farewell to friends with a mock-serious 'And may God be with you 'til we meet again', accompanied by a papal gesture. However, the ceremonial and collective aspects of the frequent religious services would have left a strong impression. One event rich in ceremony, and drama, was Remembrance Sunday – 'and the Roll of Honour of those from this School who gave their lives for their country is read by an Old Boy': a procession would shuffle its way into the chapel (lit only by candles) from the gym, led by boxer and chorister Euan Houstoun (the hind legs to Reeves's horse in *Toad Hall*), singing 'Once in Royal David's City' (entering the chapel at the end of the first verse, the congregation joining in for the second), to be followed by 'For All the Saints', Psalm 121 and 'O God, Our Help in Ages Past'. Old Boys were present to remember those who were not, the 'horrendously long'[6] roll of honour would be read out, adults with cheeks wet with tears. The war was still close.

During recreation periods, Mike preferred to spend his time with his cherished film magazines (and even film catalogues), studying them with such regularity that he soon came to know the credits by heart.

Peter Barrett remembers Mike well:

> As a pupil – friendly, intelligent, always able to contribute some-thing to whatever was under discussion, certainly bright, certainly always engrossed in the film world (I won't use the word 'obsessed'), perhaps because of that we didn't always take him as seriously as perhaps we should have done, possibly. But he was much liked on the whole. He was academically strong, a goodish games player and he made friends with everyone ... He was never much in trouble or anything like that.[7]

By the time Mike left, Easter 1957, two principal characteristics were fully in place: a determined love of film (apparent to all) and, also noted by Barrett, some evidence for the potential for mental instability – 'His character was probably capable of romancing himself a bit. He would be open to depression, I think.' This gave rise to a slight seriousness and intensity, something that was not seen by most of the other pupils – Reeves was a level-headed fellow – but only by those closer friends. The 'slightly sensitive'[8] nature, the 'slightly frenetic enthusiasm'[9] suggested the existence of areas that were best left unprobed. Mike implicitly agreed; it was a self-imposed embargo that he managed to observe throughout most of his life.

For a sensitive and self-romancing young boy, there was plenty to fire the imagination. Could the bonfire nights have left an impression on Mike that informed the bonfire witch-burning of *Witchfinder General*? The horror of the sequence is more in the amassed onlookers than the pyrotechnics. King's Mead bonfires are remembered by all (the boys, after all, would have built up the pyre over the winter months) and they had a special resonance in Sussex, a part of the world where the bonfire night had been seen in the context of ancient, pagan (or, rather, partisan: anti-papist) rituals and celebrations. It was a 'terrifically exciting'[10] event: first a fireworks display and then the igniting of the dry tinder and the eventual incineration of the Guy on top. After an accident in the mid–1950s (a stray firework doodlebugging into the crowd), the boys were placed in the dormitories to spectate in safety, looking out at the bonfire – such peering faces in the first-floor windows reappear during the *Witchfinder* bonfire too, thrilled by the destructive force of nature, harnessed to implement the murderous intentions of man. The orthodox ceremonies of the church services would also find their place in *Witchfinder*.

This 'consuming interest' in film, 'from an early age', was nurtured in King's Mead. There was a film culture, of sorts, centred around the weekly Saturday evening film slot. The films were shown either in the library or in the main teaching area (with the shutters that divided the space into classrooms drawn back; pupils at their desks and the juniors on a bench at the front). However, the programme consisted almost entirely of whimsical British comedies of the 1950s, Empire exotica and dusty wartime heroics: *San Demetrio, London, Kim, Appointment with Venus, The Wooden Horse, The Overlanders, The Happiest Days of Your Life, Androcles and the Lion, The Happy Family*. The films could be said to be intelligent entertainment of a mature outlook, and were perhaps apt for the school, but were barely dynamic. It was little surprise that Mike would go on to spend almost the majority of his time at Radley College sneaking out to watch American films (now free of King's Mead rule number eight: 'At no time in the term are boys allowed into Cinemas or Theatres'). The excitement in the King's Mead programme of the early 1950s came from Laurel and Hardy in *Way out West*, constant Chaplin, Byron Haskin's garish *Treasure Island, Winchester '73* and, a couple of years later, Clouzot's *The Wages of Fear*.

Clearly, Mike needed to take things into his own hands. He discussed film with Barrett and oversaw the improvement in the 1956 programme. He compiled lists, the films he had identified in his magazines as must-sees, and briefed Barrett accordingly. Barrett was soon to give way, and allowed Mike free reign over the programming. Along with this responsibility, came film projection duties. Mike enlisted a close friend, Tony Shellim, to help and then fired him for his inability to change to reels quickly enough in the darkness: a measure of the gravitas that Mike gave to all things film. Film-watching only increased when the holidays came; Mike would memorise the locations of London cinemas in relation to the Underground map so that the afternoon's programme could be meticulously planned in advance. Tony recalls:

> I remember my mother taking us to see *The Bridge on the River Kwai* on the first day of a school holiday. The film had just come out and was a huge hit. Michael enjoyed it (although he had made a short list of things he thought could have been done better). As we left the cinema my mother asked what we should do next, and Michael suggested seeing another film which was about to start over the road (we didn't). Typical.[11]

A further front of the masterplan was apparent in the Christmas term 1956 issue of the school magazine, the 'Terminal letter' (sent back with the boys at the end of each term, a kind of receipt of goods for waiting parents). It now sported a new section of creative writing and reportage, the 'King's Mead comment', and this included 'The critic' with his 'Film news'. Although The Critic predominantly offered a brief précis of the plots of films seen, his writings show an awareness of the existence of some kind of standard formulation behind the narratives – for *Fangs of the Wild*, 'The solution comes in a fight scene between the crooks and the two dogs at the end of the film'; for *An Alligator Named Daisy*, 'This is a story with a moral ... The film is in three reels and has a U certificate'. It is an indication of the enormity of Mike's approval that for *Sky Bandits* information was withheld ('The climax will be found out only when the film is seen'). This tendency towards plot synopses indicates the interest in recording and being aware of the detailed minutiae of films. It was something that Mike would find classroom fame with at Radley – his ability to reel off names from film credits unaided: 'He had almost an encyclopaedic knowledge about films ... he would challenge one to ask him who acted in what, who directed what.[12] This was the defining characteristic for Reeves; it was more than a party trick – it was who he was. King's Mead terms would start with Mike reciting a list of the innumerable films he had seen during the holidays – so many titles that, for Tony, 'It was hard to believe that the holidays were actually long enough.' He would keep a notebook with the good and bad points about the films he saw, and developed strongly held opinions (Alan Ladd was excellent; Burt Lancaster was only to be endured) and tastes, 'He mentioned once that he was horrified to see the reflection of a member of the film crew in a mirror which appeared in a scene.'[13] Mike's friends appreciated the post-film comments and discussions, the inside information about the production and the chance to voice opinions that would be taken seriously.

FILM NEWS

This week's film: 'Genevieve'.
This film, by now well known to most of the School, is the story of the race from London to Brighton – commonly known as the Old Crocks' Rally. At least it is not meant to be a race, but in the film two rival owners in their respective cars bet each other that they will be the first across Westminster Bridge on the return journey from Brighton. Needless to say, Genevieve (one of the two Old Crocks, by the way) wins – but only just. The other car gets its thin tyres stuck in some tramlines and heads back to Brighton.

FILM NEWS

This week we have the firework display and, in consequence, there are only a few short films before the main attraction of the evening. These films are 'Champs of the Chase,' 'Daredevils in Ice' and a cartoon. This week we are again getting our Sunday films from John King. They are called 'Rhineland to the Cote d'Azur,' a travel film, and 'Conquest,' showing how a blind person overcomes his difficulties.

The Critic rendered one other service too – early warnings for coming features:

Films not to be in detention for:
'Genevieve.'
'Titfield Thunderbolt' (if we have it.)
'An Alligator Named Daisy.'
'Man of Aran.'

And presumably contributed a question to the school quiz – 'What is the longest film ever shown?'

Mike would surreptitiously write up these film notes on Sunday mornings after the church service, during the weekly period allotted for letter writing. In a way, Mike was writing home when writing his film reviews. Initially, films had filled the void left by his father's death – a void that had become more tangible as Mike and his love of film rapidly grew – but soon 'films' and 'father' converged: Mike seems to have put it about that his father 'was in the film business'. Perhaps a friend asked if this was the case, and Mike took to the idea and so did not deny it; Mike already knew so much, talked with such authority on film matters ... only a hint of access to insider knowledge via his industry connections would have been necessary to give him a 'one foot already in the door' aura, to propagate the notion that Mike knew what he would be doing, knew who he was. The next stage, at Radley, would be to actually locate a father figure who fitted such a role; Mike was casting film as his father, allowing film itself to father him. And sometime around the age of 14 or 15, Mike found the person he was looking for when he encountered the work of Don Siegel. The film was most probably *Invasion of the Body Snatchers* – that paranoia-fuelled, full-throttle classic that takes its small town setting apart and, by its closing moments, is ushering in the end of humanity, catching the audience up with its own, unique frenzy. Mike would soon be watching this film on a monthly basis and, years later, was to incorporate a far-removed *hommage* to it in *Witchfinder*.

Much of the appeal of Siegel was in his no-nonsense bluntness (which would reach operatic heights in the opening of *Charley Varrick*: the final word in underplaying), which chimed with Mike's anti-intellectual approach to film and film-making. In this respect, Siegel's cinema represented the antithesis of burgeoning 1960s art film (which was fine with Mike; he also retained a suspicion of 'art' – finding some common ground in this respect with the British and French New Wave cinema). Siegel was without pretension, tough and efficient – a self-styled Hemingway of the cinema. His only scrape with the counter-culture involved a grimacing Clint Eastwood blowing away hippies in *Coogan's Bluff* and *Dirty Harry*. Siegel's camera was fluid but never showy – it moves with the unfolding narrative, unfashionably tracking with the story rather than commenting upon it (which was a major facet of the American films made under the sign of the European New Waves). Siegel believed in set pieces, codes of honour, the figure of a lone man and girls, guns and gangsters. Even a straight-up Siegel work-out, as with *Duel at Silver Creek* (a film for which Siegel had ambivalent feelings), delivered in terms of dynamic and trajectory, shuffling saloon scenes, shoot-outs and love interest with a deft hand.

The Killers was the film that Mike, when at his lowest, would rent and run in 16 mm over and over again. He saw it dozens of times, never tiring of its visceral impact. The film is a lesson in low-budget film-making and, more importantly, embodies the Siegel philosophy, particularly in its opening moments. Two heavies hunt down a double-crossing racing-car driver (he has stolen Ronald Reagan's girl, after all), a stone-cold Lee Marvin in figure-hugging blue suit and his inferiority complex-laden sidekick, in black, both straight-faced, murderous and stylish. The doomed man has been located – now holed up teaching motor mechanics in a school for the blind, a premature retirement from a life of hustling – and the duo storm in, tearing through the building like a hurricane, beating the blind staff who vainly attempt to raise the alarm with a stunning brutality, zigzagging across an upper corridor as they methodically check the empty rooms for their man, the sidekick pausing to smell some flowers. Dutch-tilts and sunglasses, pacing feet and frantic panic, snatches of conversation intercut jarringly with the blasting brass on the overwrought soundtrack as the killers inexorably home in. Siegel, who first uses the blind bit-part players as a stylistic tic, now uses them to hold back the eruption – blind old men getting in the way, a class of children listening to a story. When they find the driver (a down-at-heel John Cassavetes), he is already resigned to his fate, trance-murmuring 'I know them.' He knows too, along with the killers, that his time is up – that you cannot escape the past, that vengeance is a driving force. A storm of gunfire and a death essayed in slow-motion ... yet Siegel crash-cuts to the next scene the second his body hits the floor. In the late 1960s, Mike stumbled across Lee Marvin, nursing a drink in the gloom of The Grenadier, off Hyde Park Corner, hoping to hide from the shooting of *The Dirty Dozen*. They wound up back in Marvin's hotel room around the corner, a hyper Reeves describing this opening in detail, and even re-enacting moments, all to its bemused star.

Siegel stays very close to the action. There are few establishing shots (the film was initially made for a television series planned by Universal, then bumped into cinemas as NBC found the violence to be too much), lots of tight angles, enigmatic close-ups spliced in, and little dialogue, and little need for dialogue. Staying close to the action is a necessity for Siegel, television-framing or not, and he conveys a sense that he can barely keep up with the rampage. The film is a rush. That, for Mike, was cinema.

Mike told him so too. Now film reviews and letter writing could be combined into one and Mike struck up a precocious correspondence with the great man, who became a teacher and father-figure from afar. Siegel's work would come to constitute the foundation on which Mike continued his education, after a brief detour via Jean-Luc Godard since, as for so many of his generation, the road to Damascus also took in *A Bout de Souffle*. Here Mike would have appreciated the gangster movie references, the world that revolves around violence and sex, the demonstration of just how long one sequence could last, the attitude-heavy style. These two figures, Siegel and Godard, can be seen to bracket the happening films of the period that coincided with Mike's formative years, which was also the period of the reinvention of British cinema under the influence of the New Waves (and the 'gentlemen of the New Wave', as Siegel addressed them,[14] also saw in Siegel cinema par excellence). The *cinéphiles* who lounged around the Hampstead Everyman tended to work through Siegel (or, rather, American genre film-making of the type he was associated with) to Godard *et al.* *A Bout de Souffle* was the *cinéphile* equivalent of the Visitation. It imparted a new philosophy of film-making, of what films could do and how they could now be made; there was no returning to an Edenic studio thereafter. But, for Mike, this process was in reverse; beyond the lessons of Godard, he found that Siegel's films remained the ultimate template. These were not only the impressions of a *cinéphile*, but of a potential film-maker.

Siegel was just one of a multitude of directors Mike fired letters off to – usually on technical matters. Often he criticised their films in no uncertain terms, and for these letters he would write under the pseudonym of Douglas P English (the D and P as in 'displaced person'). Exotic envelopes would arrive in return.

By 1956, Mike was preparing to bid a fond farewell to King's Mead. He had done well, had become a patrol leader of his 'troop', the Otters, and achieved a high Common Entrance grade into Radley. He presented a prie-dieu desk for the Chancel of the Chapel as a leaving gift to the School, his mother threw a house party for his King's Mead friends, and he would keep in letter contact with the school, and visit when he could, as did many.

Mike entered Radley as a good creative writer in English classes (not as a 'games man'). Since King's Mead, Mike 'had [had] his own dress code'[15] but now he actively dressed down and sported hair just on the wrong side of long; he was the first boy in Radley to wear drainpipes (a trip to a local tailor to have the trousers of the uniform he loathed converted). He cultivated an appearance of idleness, shirked school duties and Mass, and concentrated his energies into the non-stop film festival of his own making. His record was 212 films in one year (when he was 16), including three performances of *Some Like It Hot* in one week. Another favourite was *Citizen Kane*, then back in fashion, and all B-movies. When he discovered that only those of fifteen and over could join the Film Society, he set up his own 'underground' organisation. The majority of the lower school were members (and were charged a nominal fee to join). Alex Waye, another close friend, possessed copies of the keys to a lecture theatre, which would be used for screenings. After Radley, this co-conspirator would provide the ambience for Mike Roscoe, Ian Ogilvy's hip antiques dealer in *The Sorcerers* (Mike kept it secret, and it remained unknown to Alex for over three decades – 'though Ian Ogilvy, a lousy actor in my opinion, was nothing like me – I was more like a younger version of Dirk Bogarde'[16]). Perhaps the idea occurred to Mike while taking Alex and others on a tour of Soho that wound-up in a strip club, just after leaving Radley.

Once fifteen, Mike muscled in on the senior film club, and did his best to relieve the science and athletics master Kenneth Brookman of film selection duties. *The Wind Cannot Read*, *To Catch a Thief*, *Quo Vadis?*, *The Red Shoes*, *The Happiest Days of Your Life* (again) and *Kind Hearts and Coronets* followed. The Film Society was not popular in the Staff Common Room, but Brookman had the foresight to understand its importance, and kept with it: 'The virtue of the society was that it encouraged boys to discuss films.' As Brookman followed Mike's professional career, he saw a very direct connection between his films and his time at King's Mead and Radley: 'his work was influenced almost entirely by his experiences before becoming a Director. Had he become a subject for research at the age of 40, his views would be affected far more by his work in films. A Director cannot show early potential like a writer or dancer.'[17]

Brookman's observation offers the key to Reeves's abilities as a film-maker. Mike made all his films before the age of 25. Not only had he barely been grazed by adult tribulations, but he hung on to the idea of his childhood. His house in Yeoman's Row was littered with toy cars, and was a place given over entirely to recreation (film watching, a 16 mm projector against the wall in his front room, socialising). If he was hungry, he would walk to the Rib Room in the Carlton Towers Hotel restaurant, where he would be served either steak or smoked salmon (other dishes did not interest him) and drink Coca-Cola; he was such a regular fixture they even held a tie for him, which he would attach awkwardly to his black polo neck. He never settled into any sense of regular hours, preferring to stay awake and active long into the night. Relationships with the opposite sex were as much for the company as anything else and, as to the other adolescent vices, Mike remained a puritan in terms of hallucinogenics and mostly used alcohol as slight self-medication, calming him down to allow for sleep. His imagination remained unfettered by the onset of maturity, his soul was grounded in a juvenile realm, a realm in which all things remained possible. Mike's film-making was founded on such a utopian sensibility. His constant protagonist, the actor Ian Ogilvy, made this connection explicit: he appears in the films Mike directed between the ages of 15 and 25, a presence denoting the direct continuity between Mike's running around in his mother's house with an 8 mm camera and working on location for hard-nosed film companies. But the loss of such an enchanted freedom was all the more bitter in this context. Had the censorship problems surrounding *Witchfinder General* occurred one or two years down the line, Mike might have shrugged and let it go, knowing that life is not perfect. But at 25, in late 1968, it was still the suggestion of compromise that was enough for him to walk out of pre-production on *The Oblong Box*; it was not his from the outset, it was alien to his realm of the possible.

Brookman's observation needs to be considered in the context of the peculiar nature of a British public school education, another realm in which anything is, and remains, possible – expeditions to save endangered tribes, archaeological breakthroughs, experimental music collectives, new movements in art, ground-breaking novels – no goal was too high. The Empire had been built on such youthful audacity of vision. In the novel *The Loom of Youth*, 19-year-old Alec Waugh's exposé of homosexuality and moral degeneration in the Eton of the 1910s, he writes:

> when the boy reaches his Public School he finds himself in a world where actions are regulated not by conscience, but by caprice ... On his surroundings during the time of transition from boyhood to manhood depend to a great extent the influence that man will work in the world. He will do whatever he does on a large scale, and people are bound to look at him. He may stand at the head of the procession of progress; he may dash himself to pieces fighting for a worthless cause, and by the splendour of his contest draw many to him. More likely he will be like Byron, a wonderful, irresponsible creature, who at one time plumbed the depths, and

at another swept the heavens – a creature irresistibly attractive, because he is irresistibly human ... His preparatory master said of him once; 'He will be a great failure or a great success, perhaps both.'[18]

Mike's film-maker imagination had the same unrestrained vigour, his behaviour the same ungoverned whim to caprice. He transposed a juvenile naivety into his work practices. If it was possible to film in a certain way, that would be the way he would film (technical considerations little more than a puzzle at best, a secondary consideration at worse). He retained a child-like fascination with murder and deviance, the intricacies of medieval torture, the realness of a character who, indeed, is simply a manifestation of evil. To the letter of Waugh's metaphor, he even cast himself as Byron – it is one 'Michael Byron' credited with the *Revenge of the Blood Beast* screenplay. Even the all-powerful role of film director could be said to be located in childhood, in the Freudian notion of 'his majesty the child' (where everything remains in subservience to the child), and in Mike's early experiences of film – which were not divorced from a consideration of how the film comes into existence; Ogilvy recalls 'His mother told a story about taking him to see *Ivanhoe* when he was a little boy. After it was over, Mike said, "I want to be the man who played Ivanhoe". His mother told him, "You can't do that, dear. You can't be somebody else". Mike responded, "In that case, I want to be the man who told Ivanhoe what to do".'[19] But there is a price for such a prolonged sojourn; Alec's younger brother Evelyn was to chronicle the rude awakenings from such a juvenile realm in *Brideshead Revisited*, and the fate that befell someone who remained in love with his own childhood. Mike's fate had also been foreseen by the prep school master – both great success and great failure.

Brookman came to be Mike's first creative collaborator as the Film Society also made 8 and 16 mm films. The Film Production Unit started with a cautious practice of film techniques ('a "tracking in" shot') and rapidly moved into short film productions. An early experiment was *Reflections on the 139th Psalm* – 130 shots were used, the verses read out in voice-over. It was during the laborious preparation of this film that Mike would have first encountered the idea of a pastoral landscape transformed via a religious recontextualisation – a Catholic sensibility of an echo of ancient times, manifest in the contemporary. The film was a success, hired and shown by the Women's Institute and the British Legion, and was eventually broadcast on the BBC in late 1958. Brookman wrote a piece for *The Radleian*[20] on the film, much in the manner of Roger Manvell's over-earnest, science-tinged film writing of the time. The Unit expanded, film scripts were invited – £1 to be paid for the most promising. College newsreels began, a sequel to the *139th Psalm* and *Eight Oars to Henley*, which scooped an amateur film prize and was shown on regional ITV. Mike initially assisted Brookman with the editing and sound on *The Ballad of the Battle of New Orleans* (shown to the school as a support feature to *The Happiest Days of Your Life*, against which any film technique would look flash) and soon Brookman found that his grip on the camera equipment being gently, but persuasively, loosened. No sooner had he loaned a camera 'and a few feet of film' to Mike than he himself was being cast in Mike's early forays into filmmaking, financed by the Unit, and with assistance from Alex. Brookman had the ideal appearance for a villain – 'a 5 o'clock shadow and hooked nose'[21] – and in *Down* a number of boys chased him around various locations in the college (underground passageways, the kitchens) and finally up on to the roof of the Mansion House, from where he fell to his death at the conclusion of the film. Possibly in this, or another, he was cast as a mad scientist, found in his lair (the school labs), bubbling test tubes in the foreground, animated via a vacuum cleaner, and all other available equipment crammed into the frame. *Down*, directed by Mike, reached the finals of the National Amateur Film Festival and was shown in the National Film Theatre in April 1959.

This confirmed for Mike the kind of films he should be making. There would be no religious paeans or informed documentary enquiries – it was straight to the action, and with a seriousness in this endeavour equal to the gusto: 'He always took for granted that everyone else would share his enthusiasm when film-making and sometimes got tetchy if other people got it wrong. He always thought out his plots very succinctly and had a very clear vision of what he wanted to achieve – sometimes leaving the Indians bemused.' Already numerous takes were deemed necessary; one cadet's uniform was unacceptably ruined as Mike had him repeatedly scramble through a muddy pond. Next up, a blind bend on nearby train tracks seemed the obvious location for B-movie mayhem. Tomato ketchup was acquired, fake monster hands were bought from a joke shop on the Tottenham Court Road, a student was 'tied' to the tracks and the camera turned over when a distant train was heard approaching. In this case the plot and the getaway were especially carefully planned out in advance. Once the shot was in the can (and the unfortunate train driver recovering from a near heart attack, hands still clasping the emergency brakes), the film-makers took off on their bikes. It did not matter that the film was never developed; it was filming itself that was the *raison d'être*. Likewise, the weekend filming in the laboratory produced no usable footage (the film was loaded incorrectly into the camera) and the 'out of bounds' status rapidly enforced by the masters once they discovered what was going on prohibited the possibility of a reshoot.

Filming was also going on at home, Foxbriar House, during school holidays, and with the same gruesome preoccupations. Betty had given Mike an 8 mm camera, and a room was surrendered as a 'dark room' for camera-related activities. The first attempt at a complete film occurred in 1958, a black and white exercise in violence called *Carrion*. A psychotic attacking a girl in a wheelchair is remembered, a bottle smashed into someone's face, and three escaped Borstal types. The camera was attached to Betty's tea trolley to try out tracking shots. The cast included Ian Ogilvy, who was then at Eton with Michael Gross, a friend of Mike's from King's Mead. He had been acting in school plays and was keen to continue in a professional capacity. An introduction was made, as Mike was in need of an actor, and Ian was soon staying with Mike so as to appear in the film. Other cast members included Mike's Radley friend Tom Baker (also from the same village, Cold Ash, near Newbury; Tom had known Mike from the age of 13, when he had told Tom that from the age of 8 'he already wanted to be a film director'[22]), Diana, also the sound girl, Mike's girlfriend Liz, and

Mike's mother's gardener. Tom was the reluctant mud-caked victim, dragging his 'broken' leg through swampy woods in Cold Ash towards a phone box. A house is broken into and the burglar whacked over the head by the waiting owner. The End. Next was a plan to cast Joyce Grenfell, familiar from the screenings of *The Happiest Days of Your Life*, a friend of the family and located nearby, in a new short film.

The word 'carrion' probably came from an early encounter with Shakespeare. Mark Anthony's words to Caesar's corpse would have been Mike's thing – 'Cry "Havoc," and let slip the dogs of war;/That this found deed shall smell above the earth/With carrion men, groaning for burial'. 'Carrion' would become something of a slight motif in Mike's work. It is alluded to by the priest in the opening sequence of *Witchfinder General* ('and all the birds were filled with their flesh') and remains a remnant of Mike's involvement in *The Oblong Box*, in which Vincent Price exclaims 'Do you think those carrion doctors could put his face together again?'

Once Radley had yielded all it had to offer in terms of film-making opportunities, it was time to make an early departure. Mike announced a roundabout route to university; on his leaver's form, for 'plans for the future', he neatly wrote 'Geneva University, then Trinity College, Dublin. Film Technician'. 'Geneva University' smacks of a ruse; the plan was to clear out of Radley before the bother of A-Levels to pursue the 'film technician' side of the plan through all means possible. The first task was a 16 mm remake of *Carrion*, after the success of *Down*, to be called *Intrusion*. Betty was keen that Mike should attend Trinity (unaware of its reputation as a bolthole for the lazy), but what could Trinity offer him? What would he study, and why, and to what ends? Since the desired destination was the film set, why wait? He would move into the industry directly. A 16 mm camera was hired from Samuelsons and preparations for the shoot began. This time Mike would situate the action (violence and style in the manner of Siegel) within a strong narrative. This would be his showreel, his entrée into the world of film-making proper. It would be 'A Leith Production. Written and directed by Mike Reeves.' 'Leith' was the family middle name.

Preproduction included multiple viewings of *A Bout de Souffle*. Images were noted (messy bedrooms; long-shots of figures running frantically across landscapes, under-lit but so what?; POV driving shots; women unselfconsciously in underwear) and would be redone. The *Carrion* remake could then be graced with an audacious opening title: 'The film is dedicated to Jean-Luc Godard'. It was an *hommage* to an *hommage*: *A Bout de Souffle* opens with 'Ce film est dédié a La Monogram Pictures' (a small Hollywood outfit that turned out the cheap B-movies beloved of the French film critics and makers). Mike would have been thrilled to have seen himself enmeshed in such a nexus of posturing.

For *Intrusion*, Mike cuts between two narratives: escapees, scrambling through the snow towards a house; and inside that house, a woman, having taken leave of her husband, preparing to soak in a bath. Each narrative is in turn overshadowed by the other. The bare branches, heavy sky, deep snow and desperate men contrast with the warm interiors of the house, the deep bubble bath and the disrobing woman. The effect is ominous. Gunning for verve, Mike delays the opening credits. The camera, operated by Tom Baker, takes in the skyline with a very steady pan and then moves down to frame a low shot of a plain of snow in a woodland clearing, deep focus, and two sets of footprints heading towards the vanishing point. We see the men on the run (Mike doubles as one of them) – long-shots, as Godard does with Belmondo once he has shot the policeman and sprints across fields. A car goes by, they dive into a ditch, then run towards and past the camera; title fades in – 'Intrusion' – fade to black, opening credits. The cast consisted of local friends and Ogilvy who, suffering from 'flu, was relegated to the roles of make-up man and 'the Spanish butler'.[23] Paul Vestey, another Radley friend, was the production manager.

We first see the wife flicking through a colour supplement (we catch the words 'modern economy'; irony – the film is a take on primitive justice and old-fashioned theft in the modern age) before bidding goodnight to the fey Spanish butler and heading to her bedroom. There follows a prolonged and relatively explicit striptease, news of the escapees playing on the radio, then into the bath (leg up, sponge applied, *à la* Jayne Mansfield glamour shot). The intruders ring the bell, are let in or break in (either a cutting error or a Godardian jump-cut at a crucial moment – as when Belmondo pulls the trigger to kill the policeman), and the ordeal begins: they toy with her, one fiddles threateningly with a dainty cheese knife, they bicker among themselves, turn out some drawers. In the midst of this, the husband telephones, detects something is amiss in the knife-point answer his wife makes, smokes moodily, then sets off to the house, shakily overtaking cars on the night road. Meanwhile a struggle between one ruffian and the wife has occurred. His cigarettes spill out on to the floor as he lies on top of her, and his knife with them – which she grasps and plunges into his waist. The husband arrives, clocks the body, bursts in on a rape preamble upstairs, beats the ruffian, drags him through to the bathroom and ducks him several times, until he is incapacitated. This is done with reverse angle shots that denote – possibly even unconsciously on the part of Mike – that it is all seen from the point of view of the wife. The couple embrace twice, fade to black. The End.

Intrusion is extraordinarily good – in the light of Mike's subsequent preoccupations, it is a near-revelation. The scratched print, a couple of out-of-order shots and absent soundtrack aside, it represents a debut proper of a born film-maker. Despite being essentially an exercise in putting together an action sequence, the film is so personal that it comes to work as an index for the themes and concerns that are to come; as a professional film-maker, on location in late 1967, with time pressing and a Hollywood star urgently needing to shoot a final sequence, Mike would remake, with a twist, the final moments of *Intrusion* for the climax of *Witchfinder*. Violence in the immediate wake of love-making, if the assumption is made that the film begins after the couple have made love, would also be reprised. Both *Intrusion* and *Witchfinder* begin with twisted branches fracturing the symmetry of the images. *Intrusion* has the same nihilistic violence, seemingly done for kicks, as *The Sorcerers*, and the same young couple dynamic and the drowning as in *Revenge of the Blood Beast*. The themes and tensions that Mike laid down in the winter of 1961, at the age of 18, would be a constant through his filmography.

Yet *Intrusion*, in itself, demonstrates no thought beyond a number of inventive (albeit unshowily so) camera angles and a willingness to let tension mount; it is the equivalent of an aspiring poet experimenting with form, mimicking his betters. To that end, *Intrusion* demonstrates a physical reflex to make a film that is 'right'. The hours spent in a state of heightened scrutiny in cinemas had allowed film to seep into Mike's consciousness, an osmosis of a Hollywood sensibility. By *Intrusion*, Mike is already thinking cinematically and, in particular, along the same lines as the great Hollywood action film stylists of the 1960s. There is even a *Marnie* shot in *Intrusion* – or, rather, a shot that Hitchcock would also use in *Marnie* – the backs of the legs of an undressing woman, the garment tumbling to the ground. The ruffians in the film, in leather jackets, shades, slicked back hair, are given the crooked panache that Welles allowed his out-of-town gang in *Touch of Evil*. Mike initially shoots the bodies only, their backs to the camera, as they ring the doorbell. They storm into the house and to their fate. As one lies dying, Mike keeps his motionless face in the foreground of the screen while the husband dashes upstairs to prevent his wife's rape. It is a Wellesian device, deep focus photography and depth of field, and it is likely that Mike announced it that way too: 'This is the *Kane* shot'. Only the camera equipment would have been in a position to disagree in the face of such confidence.

Notes

1 Richard Campling, interview with author, 18 September 2001. All subsequent remarks are taken from this source.
2 Sir Digby Mackworth, interview with author, 12 October 2001. All subsequent remarks are taken from this source.
3 G. Payn and S. Morley (eds), *The Noël Coward Diaries* (London, Macmillan, 1982), p. 6
4 Miles Huddleston, interview with author, 15 March 2000. All subsequent remarks are taken from this source.
5 Euan Houstoun, interview with author, 10 September 2001. All subsequent remarks are taken from this source.
6 Peter Bowles, interview with author, 30 October 2001. All subsequent remarks are taken from this source.

7 Peter Barrett, interview with author, 18 July 2001. All subsequent remarks are taken from this source.

8 Christopher James, interview with author, 17 October 2001. All subsequent remarks are taken from this source.

9 Bowles, interview with author.

10 Mackworth, interview with author.

11 Tony Shellim, interview with author, 27 September 2001. All subsequent remarks are taken from this source.

12 Mackworth, interview with author.

13 Shellim, interview with author.

14 A. Lovell, *Don Siegel – American Cinema* (London, British Film Institute, 1968), p. 4.

15 Bowles, interview with author.

16 Alex Waye, interview with author, 16 June 1999. All subsequent remarks are taken from this source.

17 Letter from Kenneth Brookman to Tim Hodgson [undated: early 1990s].

18 A. Waugh, *The Loom of Youth* (London, Cassell & Company, Ltd, 1929), pp. 89–90.

19 S. Swires, 'And now the screaming stops', *Fangoria* 112 (May 1992) 15.

20 K. Brookman, *Reflections on the 139th Psalm, The Radleian* (13 October 1957) 258.

21 John Sellers, interview with author, 12 March 2001. All subsequent remarks are taken from this source.

22 Letter to Tim Hodgson from Tom Baker, 31 October 1992. The Tom Baker mentioned here is neither the actor who played Dr Who nor the Warhol associate/actor who appeared in *Hallucination Generation*.

23 Anon, 'Ian Ogilvy', *Films in London*, 2(23) (19 April–2 May 1970) unnumbered.

'This is a Don Siegel shot'

3

And now to infiltrate the film industry. At this point the problem presented itself as the need to secure the requisite union card. Mike had initially tried to do so by marching into the union head-quarters and demanding one, unsurprisingly to no avail. Ambushing minor film company minions with a barrage of pitches and showreel was equally unsuccessful.

> Mike and I were driving through Knightsbridge when 'Follow that car!' was bellowed in my left ear. Did as bid, I gave chase to a very sleek and sporty E-type Jag; despite its best efforts to elude us, I managed to close the gap and eventually smoked to a halt along-side it in the Carlton Tower Hotel driveway. Mike jumped out of my car and accosted the driver, a distinctly ruffled Stanley Baker. Mike's purpose had been to find a way to a union card. Mr Baker could not have been more sympathetic but, pointing to his watch – it was nearly midnight – and with a sidelong glance at his bemused companion, the very glamorous starlet Yvonne de Carlo, suggested that he and Mike get together some other time. An early appoint-ment was arranged – I, of course, wasn't present but I do know that it wasn't long before Mike got what he was after – a union card.[1]

Perhaps inspired by this encounter with Baker, Mike decided that the time was right to directly consult with the maestro himself. He joined his mother flying out to Boston for a trip to visit family. Once there, Mike took a plane to Los Angeles in search of Don Siegel, using the address on the letters he had received from him. In LA, he alerted Don to his impending arrival from a payphone.

Mike later described it as being bored with 'an endless round of Boston tea-parties' and so 'barged into' Siegel's house.[2] The dramatic entrance was mitigated slightly by Don not being at home; Mrs Siegel talked to the charming young man while waiting for Don to return (another version of this story has Siegel answering the door in a vest). When they did finally meet in the flesh, Mike declared that he had come all the way from England to see Don, 'as you are the greatest director in the world'.[3] Don, no doubt substantially taken aback that the prolific writer of letters had actually materialised, was obliged to let him tag along for a day at the studio to watch Don shoot some tests for Paramount (at the time he had been fashioning Elvis Presley vehicles). He gave Mike temporary employment as a dialogue director for the tests and put him up in his guest room. Don would josh with European film critics about their obsessions with the intricacies of commercial American film-making, about which he rarely thought twice. Mike, too, was an example of this new sensibility. Nor was Don adverse to the adulation – he would later iconoclastically reinvent himself as 'the last of the Independents', and 'sign' the opening credits with 'a Siegel film'. His time with Don over, Mike headed back to Boston; they would keep in touch. Mike could use his working with Siegel as a leg-up.

One contact was the producer Irving Allen. He was a vague friend of the Reeves family and the father of a friend from King's Mead, Robert Armstrong, was the trainer of Allen's race horses. Mike had been happy to ingratiate himself accordingly and from the age of 12 he and Robert had been able to watch films being made during the holidays. Mike had made himself known and Allen was aware of Mike's plans from an early age (as anyone who knew him would be). Now back from Boston, Mike called Allen up and described his working with Siegel in detail, embellishing it as he saw fit. On the back of some undoubtedly non-committal promise from Allen of seeing what he could do, Mike took to visiting his office on a daily basis. After a fortnight, a props man took ill and Allen deputised Mike to take his place, with 'Let's see what you can do.'[4]

Throughout the 1950s, Allen had produced a steady stream of films with Cubby Broccoli – mostly modestly budgeted potboilers with few international ambitions. After *The Trials of Oscar Wilde*, Broccoli and Allen split, allegedly over a film about a secret agent, one James Bond. Broccoli went on to make *Dr No* and did not look back. Although he was determined to close the financial chasm that then appeared between them, Allen was stranded somewhere between trying to ape Broccoli's success with Irving Allen Productions (all-star casts and all action in exotic locations) and following David Lean's lead (high 'historical' subjects shot in 70 mm). Thus by the early 1960s, Allen was gearing up for big international co-productions, further financed by Columbia, and had adopted the regulation fat cigar. The first off was *The Long Ships* with Richard Widmark as the Viking and Sidney Poitier as the Moor. A glossy look – 'every dollar up on the screen' – was of primary importance for such a financial proposition and so Allen hired Jack Cardiff to direct. After his extraordinary work as a cinematographer for Hitchcock and Powell and Pressburger in the 1940s, Cardiff had reinvented himself as a classy director for hire. He had also shot *The Vikings* for Richard Fleischer just a few years before and so, for Allen, he was a very sure bet.

Mike was, of course, on hand, and entirely at Irving's disposal. It was summer 1962. Race horses were needed in abundance and, as the film was to be shot in Yugoslavia, no union card was required for Mike. These beginnings were humble enough, but it was professional work. Mike was assigned to the Second Unit, as a personal assistant to Cliff 'Tex' Lyons, who had worked with John Ford and Raoul Walsh. Mike acted as a runner, called actors to the set, relayed messages and, of course, made the tea. As a potential blockbuster, the *Long Ships* shoot involved the construction of elaborate sets and crowds of costumed extras to be marshalled. But as a runner Mike is remembered as a little too thoughtful, and lacking the rough camaraderie of those who populate the lower echelons of film production. Cardiff only recalls the film in terms of problems with Richard Widmark, disputes with Allen, who kept at a distance, and his own attempt to walk off the picture – 'It was a soul-destroying film to work on.'[5]

Mid-point through the shoot, a list arrived: names of those who were to be deported as political undesirables. Mike vanished, along with a fair number of other equally harmless actors and crew members. The reasons remain obscure. It may well have been a periodic reorientation of Tito's antagonistic attitude towards Soviet Russia, in which film had always been utilised as a battleground – at times Yugoslav cinemas were encouraged to flaunt films from the West to demonstrate freedom and distance from Moscow and socialist realism, at other times they were kept strictly in line. More prosaically, Paul Maslansky, also working on the film, recalls Mike's vanishing to be in pursuit of a girl. But, more importantly, on the set Mike had found a mentor to replace Brookman – one of the assistant directors, Derek Cracknell. They did not work together again but Mike would keep in touch, turning to him for advice and contacts, even trying to cast Derek's wife, Julie, in *Witchfinder*. Derek was a useful friend; an insight into the burgeoning world of 1960s mainstream film, and a film with which Mike would be enormously impressed – Kubrick's *2001*. Likewise, when Mike encountered Ogilvy's RADA mentor Jack Lynn, he interrogated him on all things relating to acting. Who did he think were good actors? Why were they good? Mike stated his belief in Hitchcock's maxim of the essential difference between theatre and film – 'there's only one frame there for the whole play'.

The next step was to relocate, permanently, to the capital. London was there for the taking, and Mike had the money to do as he pleased; considerable funds were now at his disposal via his mother and Mike would feed her stories about the headway he was making to justify the expenses. Mike took a flat in Scarsdale Villas in Kensington. Now both Siegel and Allen could be used to prove his expertise and so Mike found employment as an assistant director for television commercials. The work was sporadic, done only to gain further experience, and Mike did not refer to it often once he had a feature film under his belt. It is unlikely that he did little more than hang around during ad shoots.

During this period Mike consolidated the film viewing marathons, a practice which continued uninterrupted throughout the 1960s when Mike was free from film sets. Mike would plan a programme taking in four or five films a day. Friends would join and leave, watch a film or two, stay for a bite to eat, discuss the film and discuss how certain scenes could have been made more effectively, or differently, or better, and then some or all would head off to the next show, prepped by Mike as to what to look out for. By night, Mike would rework the films in his head. The old days of sneaking off for an unaccompanied exeat from King's Mead or Radley to cram as many films as possible in to the space of a Saturday could now be turned into a full-time occupation. In this respect, Mike completed his education himself. And it was an exciting time to be a cinema-goer. The films favoured by King's Mead in the early 1960s had all but vanished from the screens, eclipsed by the European New Waves and greatly refined US action films. Films were challenging, provocative, unapologetically licentious and violent, an arena for expressions of the new classlessness and sexual promiscuity, the medium in which Swinging London began to visualise itself, the focus for writing, the things to be discussed. Unsurprisingly, film remained aligned with the dissenting voices of the 1960s throughout that period.

Meanwhile Mike was making the most of the trust fund. He attended parties with school friends, where he chanced upon a new girlfriend, Liz. She introduced him to the members of the band the Moody Blues and he began to observe the youth explosion that was shaking pop music in a dynamic way. Michael Gross remembers a startling phone call in the early 1960s: would he care to join Mike in 'his' suite in Claridges for a meal? It was hired for the stunt; old school friends trying to out-louche each other. Mike worked on a casual demeanour: jeans, jackets, open-neck shirts, cravats (modelled after Siegel). He furthered his interest in cars, spurred on by Radley friend and now flatmate Paul Vestey, equally wealthy, and his circle of car enthusiast friends – Vestey was then financing his invention of himself as a 'racing-car driver' along the same lines that Mike was financing his invention as a 'film director'. It seemed that anything was possible – cars, music, films ... the young were storming these strongholds and Mike always saw his status as film director in these terms, as evidenced in a press release a few years later:

> At just 24, Michael Reeves must be one of the youngest – if not THE youngest – feature film directors in the Britain. Slim, good-

looking, sincere and completely dedicated, he accepts without surprise the fact that he finds himself, at so early an age, in control of veteran actors like Vincent Price ... 'After all,' he asks, with perfect justification, 'in this age of Youth, when young actors and actresses are coming forward in such great numbers, why not directors too? There is no mystique about making films, just know-how, plus ideas and enthusiasm'.[6]

Mike was more interested in the experience of speed, and the dynamics of car handling, than fetishising the latest model or nuances of engineering. This interest in speed would be amply reflected in *The Sorcerers*. While at Radley, experimenting on some scrub ground with friends, Mike took the door off his mother's Morris Minor on a tree stump (her displeasure is recalled to this day). Now he was able to accompany Vestey to Brands Hatch most weekends – even taking a few turns around the course in his Mini in amateur races. Practice was taken with Michael Gross as they raced up and down the A4 to Heathrow in a yellow Lotus Elan. Mike had a penchant for open-topped sports cars, and eventually bought a 1965 Sunbeam Tiger V8 in which he would tear through central London, for a limited period only; he wrote to Vestey 'By the way, by the time you get back to our fair isle in a jewell-ed sea (or whatever) I may be minus a licence – I nearly killed a cop on a zebra crossing at about 80 in a 30-limit. Whoopee'.[7]

Crashing into the 'jet set' in this way hardly endeared Mike to his wider family, who felt that Betty was allowing him to run wild. He gained a reputation as 'not at all pleasant'[8] but only in that his rebellious phase was then particularly and loudly so – not because he displayed the arrogance of some of those he kept company with, also buoyed by private incomes. When visiting family, people would tend to clear out of the way once Mike arrived – usually only for the shortest period of time: 'He was a pretty obnoxious 18 year old, I remember. We all thought "Christ!" you know, "Let's avoid Mike Reeves!". He was so self-absorbed, so completely full of himself, throwing his money around. He was just sort of objectionable, really. He wasn't exactly rude but he was terribly off-hand.'[9] He had a good line in arrogance and could be abrupt, short-tempered and opinionated. For those family members with time for Mike, he would take them down Sloane Street at 90 mph – seeing how much he could terrify them. Later that year, a moody Mike mostly slept through a European cruise, accompanying his mother and Diana, perking up for a night tour around the 'low dives' of Genoa, awash with prostitutes, soldiers and sailors.

While working on *The Long Ships*, Mike had made friends with a production manager, Paul Maslansky. Maslansky had made a jazz documentary in Paris, financed by his uncle, and was now in Rome, setting up a feature film, to be funded with his own money. He had cooked up the idea of slumming through a very quick black and white horror film, finding and utilising ready-made sets through a thrifty reliance on atmospheric location shooting, and redrafting the script to incorporate whatever other local colour was going cheap. During the *Long Ships* production, while overseeing tank work at Cinecittà, Paul had met Warren Kiefer, a writer aspiring to be a director, then shooting a documentary for Esso in Libya. Both he and Paul were Americans, members of the loose Rome-based ex-pat film community ('runaway productions' – those shooting 'overseas'; Paul was a self-styled 'runaway producer'), both were in their late twenties, and both wanted to make a feature film of sorts so a story was thrashed out. Warren wrote the screenplay as Paul put together a $125–$150,000 'minestrone' fund to cover the budget (that is, money drawn from different European countries, on pre-sales). As Mike's enthusiasm for film and passion for the horror genre had impressed Paul, he invited the keen 'film freak' over to Rome to assist on the production, and 'let him direct Second Unit on the picture'.[10] Although Mike is sometimes also credited with script work, such redrafting would have been slight; Kiefer had spent some time preparing his script. It would seem that the dwarf's role in the finished film owed something to Mike's input at the script stage.

Castle of the Living Dead (*Il Castello dei Morti Vivi*) was shot in roughly twenty-four days in 1963, produced by Maslansky for his Serena Films, and showcasing a turn from Christopher Lee as Count Drago and Donald Sutherland's debuts (he had more than one role in the film). Paul had spotted Sutherland back in London in a Lindsay Anderson Royal Court production of *Spoon River*

Anthology while looking for an English-speaking dwarf. Maslansky pitched the film to Sutherland backstage, offered him $40 a week and the use of Kiefer's couch as somewhere to crash, and bought him a train ticket to Rome. Although the actual director and script-writer was Warren, directorial credit was assigned to a number of pseudonyms (Luciano Ricci, Herbert Wise and Lorenzo Sabatini) on differing prints, entirely for quota and tax reasons. Sutherland wanted an English speaker on set, and so it was suggested that Mike should stick around for the shoot. Maslansky would go on to flog the film to American International Pictures for US distri-bution and to Cineriz for Italian distribution (who promptly went bust before it could be shown), and it appeared in most European countries on the strength of Christopher Lee's presence. The film did not lose money, everyone involved was paid and the investors reimbursed.

The film concerns an ill-fated travelling Commedia del'Arte troupe who hazard across Count Drago, a serial embalmer of animals and humans, busy creating 'my eternal theatre'. One of his victims is Mike – in a few seconds of cameo as an officer. There is a subplot involving bungling police officers, who would reappear in *Revenge of the Blood Beast*, not providing comic relief so much, but more aping the horrors elsewhere. The script is fairly literary, shifting from a variant on Bram Stoker's *Dracula* to a Dr Moreau's Island once inside the Count's castle, and a vein of surrealism runs through the film. It flits through the clichés of the haunted-house movie, the supernatural thriller and, for the more animated chase sequences, elements of the western. The best sequences involve combat between a dwarf and a scythe-wielding coachman, shot in the Parco dei Mostri, a sixteenth-century sculp-ture garden in the Villa Orsini in Bomarzo, outside Viterbo. The huge stone animals, elephants, dragons and gargoyles are used to maximum effect, particularly for a number of dramatic entrances. An orc, an ogre with bulging eyes and a six-foot open mouth, is placed beneath the opening credits of the film.

During post-synch in Phono Roma, a furious Lee discovered that there was no soundtrack at all, and that all the continuity sheets had been mislaid. Fireworks ensued, but Paul won him over and the film was dubbed in its entirety as well as possible. There are sections with characters mouthing words, yet audible only as improvisationary grunts or groans – stretching out the gaps between words. Mel Welles, who oversaw the post-synching, claims the lost continuity sheets was partly a ruse to improve the dialogue.

Some prints of the film do not credit Mike, while the US prints credit him as an assistant director. Mike's role has generally been ascribed to that of Second Unit director. The story goes that his footage was so good that more was used in the final cut than expected, making Mike the ghost auteur of the best parts of the film, or that Kiefer fell ill and Mike took over, making Mike the accidental auteur. Wood cites the dwarf sections as Mike's. Certainly, those sections do have a lightness of touch that make them stand out from the somewhat turgid whole, the occasional stylistic flourish that could be seen to be Reevesian in the light of his subsequent work (although not in the light of *Intrusion*) and, from time to time, a smooth crane or a tracking shot (although often the framing is awkward and displays little evidence of an eye at work). But there was no Second Unit – and the dwarf sequences were shot by Warren Kiefer, who remained in good health throughout, and Frederick Muller (also credited as 'Second Unit' by AIP), without Mike even being present.[11] Those involved simply shot what they could as rapidly as they could. In a film with such a low budget, as much usable footage as possible would make it to the final cut – it is unlikely that an editor weighed up footage qualitatively. Mike oversaw some pick-ups, cutaways and, once principal photography was complete, missing shots. In some circumstances, this would have been considered 'Second Unit' material – but nothing that would ultimately make for any discernable authorial imprint on the film. Lee remembers that '[t]he doomed and clever young Michael Reeves was all the assistants from first to fifth'[12] while Maslansky recalls assigning a number of shots involving the coach in the forest to Mike – those not involving the main actors. For a period immediately afterwards, Mike would, typically, 'talk up' his involvement in the film when useful (after all, he would go on to try to cast Christopher Lee on more than one occasion),[13] but later only occasionally referred to this period as one of 'some rewriting on a script that was being made by a director friend'[14] once he had more palpable experiences of which to speak.

During the shoot, Mike had hatched plans for further films with anyone who cared to participate. The best chance was for a horror, with Peter Cushing or Lee, or, better yet, a childhood idol, Boris Karloff – Mike 'talked incessantly about wanting to make a movie with Boris Karloff'.[15] In this idle speculation were the beginnings of Mike's debut feature film, *Revenge of the Blood Beast*. Paul expressed interest, and he would get back in touch.

Irving Allen called in early 1964: more running, this time in Rome, for *Genghis Khan* (essentially more of the same – this time Omar Sharif as the leader of the Mongol Horde). Mike hung out with the Emperor of China, Robert Morley, whom he had first met when he was playing Oscar Wilde in Allen's biopic six years earlier. Perhaps the work was frustrating. Mike gained a reputation for laziness – more an ambler than a runner, and a late riser too; a runner would have to be sent to get the runner. Yet he had immersed himself in the most commercial and bloated area of film-making – now on track to continue to move from one Allen international spectacular to another, slowly climbing up the totem pole as he went – and so it was hardly surprising that he was unable to make his mark with such a crowd onset and with so many competing financial agendas. Should he not be wielding a 16 mm camera in Hyde Park, calling the shots himself?

This sense of frustration at such a slow progression turned to a sense of urgency after a doctor found a shadow on one of Mike's lungs, an unusual ailment for someone so young. Betty recalled that Mike was 'quite philosophical about it'.[16] The idea of a non-malignant tumour bred a number of possible scenarios for the pensive Mike. If time was limited, or if somehow his future physical abilities would be impaired, it was wise to capitalise on the quality time available here and now. Mike accessed as much hard cash as he could muster, which would constitute the budget for his first proper film, and put his horror film ideas down in script form. He phoned Paul, said he had a £13,000 budget in place, and asked him to produce or – closer to the mark – help him get a film made. Paul scraped together whatever loose change was available and they thrashed out a plan; Mike would direct, it would be shot near Rome and feature a gaggle of the readily available Corman 'alumni' (some flouted the credential, others were just after a break from Roger Corman). Barbara Steele would appear sparingly in it, and it would incorporate a script speed-written in three days by Corman's close associate, Charles B. 'Chuck' Griffith (ostensibly to get his girlfriend over from Los Angeles for a part),[17] melded with Mike's ideas. By the time Mike arrived in Rome with the film's budget in notes in a suitcase, the project was shaping up like Mario Bava's 1960 watershed European horror, the Barbara Steele hit *La Maschera del Demonio* (*Black Sunday*). It had titles too, initially *Il Lago di Satana* ('The Lake of Satan') and then *Vardella* (the name of the female monster), but also had the customary shooting title for budgetary purposes: the archaeological documentary, as documentaries cost a lot less to license than a fiction film, *Ruini Etrusci* ('Etruscan Ruins'). Location filming, specifically, was cheap in Italy at this point; permissions were easily obtainable and, at any rate, not always entirely necessary. For the first time, and not the last, Mike had fallen in with the right people.

In this way, the film is very much a product of the independent film production scene in Italy in the 1960s. Those who were associated with *Revenge of the Blood Beast* were drawn from a fairly tight-knit group working on European productions and hanging out in Rome, Maslansky and a brace of English character actors among them, part of the ex-pat community that constituted 'Hollywood on the Tiber'. Many had been dragged along with the tide of the almighty production of *Cleopatra*, subsequently found ample work dubbing ('The Dubbing Community'[18] – at that point almost all films were dubbed for the English markets), or as extras or technicians, or just general hustling. The Cowboy, Dave's Bar, run by retired British boxer Dave Crowley, and cafés on the Via Veneto were the regular haunts, where stars unselfconsciously rubbed shoulders with those who, elsewhere, could only hope to be onlookers, and Mel Welles, surveying the scene from a pavement café, would decide on the 'Hair of the Night' award. The living was easy and inexpensive. Fellini peppered his gatherings in *La Dolce Vita* with such characters and many remain in Italy, still working, today. Those who left came to determine much of the commercial Hollywood cinema of the 1970s and thereafter, particularly Maslansky.

As well as the Corman alumni, Mike was welcome to do some casting himself. In the manner of *Carrion* and *Intrusion*, Mike turned to friends to tag along, and for moral support. Ogilvy, who had lost touch with Mike since *Intrusion*, was alerted through his agent that he had been offered the male lead. He had since been a stage manager at the Royal Court Theatre (honing his angry young mannerisms) and then to the Royal Academy of Dramatic Art (the finishing school for the Eton actor – thus completing Ogilvy screen persona); this would be his first professional film. Mike's new girlfriend, Annabelle, would be the set dresser and Diana would produce character designs for Vardella to Mike's specifications. Paul Maslansky, who did not yet trust himself to direct and was slightly wary of Mike's inexperience, hired Mel to keep a watchful eye over him – 'he was a kid ... the youngest director I'd ever seen'. In the event, Mike was fine, even as an outsider to the group.

Once on location, F. Amos Powell, an Anglophile member of the Corman group, assisted on the script and doubled up, along with the Chuck and Paul, as hapless policemen (Paul is the one sporting open flies; only spotted after the shoot). Steele worked for a day or two, with Paul ensuring that a day was measured as eighteen hours of work, before returning to Rome with a $1,000 fee for her troubles. It was money well spent; she could stretch languidly across the Italian posters – an invitation for a sensual as well as horrific experience. Surprisingly, the film does deliver on the former with some relatively heavy sequences by the honeymooning protagonists, all initiated by a brazen Veronica (Steele), which unnerved Ogilvy, and with an attempted rape elsewhere to make up any deficit. Steele's use here is consistent with her screen persona and appeal, described by Hogan as '[her ability to express] a tantalizing sort of evil, and a sexual ambivalence that is at once enticing and ghastly'.[19] The Italian release title, *La Sorella di Satana* ('Sister of Satan'), alluded directly to this. Yet for the majority of her screen time, Steele's role – as possessed by Vardella – was played by a colleague of Mel's, the American dancer, actor and leader of the Gospel review *Trumpets of the Lord*, Jay 'Flash' Riley ('he would do any damn thing'[20]), sporting a knotty, plastic face mask. Ogilvy recalls 'During the lunch hour, he would hide in the bushes along-side the main road to Rome, still wearing his hideous Vardella mask and costume. When he saw a car coming, he would leap out and try to hitch a lift. He took great pride in seeing how long the skid marks were.[21]

Chuck Griffith had been involved with AIP since the early days of *It Conquered the World* and *Attack of the Crab Monsters*. His initial script was written as a comedy, 'a low budget farce'[22] in the manner of Corman's *The Little Shop of Horrors* (on which Griffith had also been a Second Unit director). At first, AIP had been unsure what to do with *Little Shop of Horrors*, worried that it would be perceived as anti-Semitic. When they eventually made it the lower half of the heavily hyped release of *Black Sunday* (not mentioning *Little Shop* in the ad campaign), and both proved to be massively popular, the 'horror comedy' genre was suddenly deemed a very bankable new direction. Mike turned up with film magazine clippings about the Chuck Griffith-scripted *A Bucket of Blood* and told a startled Chuck about the cult appeal of *Little Shop*. Chuck and Mel had both been in *Little Shop* and Steele in *Black Sunday* so the hybrid nature of this film was inevitable – the comedy aspect a natural choice and the easiest way to implement 'a quickie picture'. So Chuck's script had been fashioned along these lines – even specifically written for the actors involved, particularly Mel. It was intended to be, and mostly proved to be, a laidback shoot.

When the much-talked-about Mike arrived, he was keenly observed by the ex-pats; for sound editor Lars Bloch, 'He was no turkey. He seemed at least to know what he was doing';[23] surfer and bit-part actor Edward Randolph (the man who brought skate-boarding to Italy) recalls 'Michael, quietly intense, lean, almost gaunt, intelligent looking English face, longish lank hair'.[24] For Chuck, Mike was 'eager, young, opinionated' and a 'film buff picture maker':

> ... we had a big fight about day for night ... Mike had been told by some big name cameraman to shoot day for night with the sun at your back and heavily underexposed.[25] I said 'That's terrible. He's

pulling your leg. Don't ever do it that way. It'll look like shit.' We both shot completely opposite techniques for day for night on that picture and his shots had that quality that newsreel concentration camp shots had. And I shot Hollywood-style day for night which is, of course, directly into the light.[26]

The differing techniques are clear enough to underline which sequences were directed by whom. Certainly Mike's are murkier, while Chuck's come across as almost floodlit. It is unlikely that the elderly but quick cameraman, Gioacchino Gengarelli, was bothered either way.

This 'big fight' was a facet of a wider difference of opinion; Mike's perception of the film was at variance with Chuck's, despite Mike's appreciation of the horror-comedy genre. With Mike, the comedy was sidelined, pushed into the incidentals of throw-away remarks between the young couple. The more knowing jokes that litter the film originated in Mel and Chuck's onset improvisations (the oft-noted sickle, thrown iconoclastically across a hammer once Vardella has used the former to dispatch Mel; and name-checking Joseph Crater from Chuck) went over Mike's head, even during post-production. A farce is a hard place to start for a film-maker with great expectations and a towering role model to live up to: 'Mike was very ambitious. He knew every shot of every picture that Don Siegel had done and he was about to duplicate them.'[27] By this point, Mike's encyclopaedic knowledge of film credits had expanded to an ability to describe sequences, shot by shot – the type of camera movement, the angle, the framing. Nor was this confined to just the obvious sequences from *Citizen Kane* or *Psycho*. Although this sensibility would have been vastly at odds with the project at hand, Mike proceeded anyhow – even declaring at one point during the shoot 'This is a Don Siegel shot.' Chuck, whose *hommages* had only ever extended to once stealing a grue-some moment from his namesake's *Intolerance*, replied 'Who's Don Siegel?' Mike implemented his Siegel shots all the same. As a result, the film's construction recalls, from time to time, standard Hollywood techniques, and the fluidity of the film also owes some-thing to this: Mike steadily tracks with characters as they walk, keeping them centre-frame, or pans with a speeding car, breaking off to frame the hotel against the sky, or frames characters against the sky, as in American westerns. Such things are hardly remarkable in themselves, and jar a little against the watery look of the film, but in this context at the very least indicate overreaching ambitions and, even when redundant, their execution would have schooled Mike in the idea of what, as a director, he felt he should be doing. The others recognised his naivety (Chuck: 'He knew very little about the industry or about the tricks of the industry or about shooting a film or directing a film') but in that he was 'always in a good humour', were happy to help out. According to Ogilvy, Mike's philosophy at the time was 'If we make rubbish, but really well-made rubbish, then our well-made rubbish will make money. If we make money then producers and studios will be interested in us and we will go on and make bigger and better films because we will get bigger and better budgets.'[28]

For a while, an actual title for the film eluded the makers because, even as the film was being made, it was not entirely clear what kind of film was being made. Mike was shooting gore and flashbacks of period villagers lynching Vardella (including himself in a one-second cameo close-up), to be intercut with a young, contemporary couple in modern-day Transylvania, while Chuck's Second Unit busied itself with 'comedy' footage, principally a Keystone Kops-like chase. Mel recalls: 'Paul couldn't make up his mind whether he wanted to do it as a comedy or not,'[29] while Chuck remembers 'They took all the comedy out. It was a comedy and they got cold feet at the last minute. I even shot a great comedy car chase.'[30] The UK release title, *Revenge of the Blood Beast*, was a spur-of-the-moment suggestion made by Mike during a brainstorming session – a joke that stuck (but not an easy title to remember, especially in the multitude of horror films at that time). It must have occurred to Mike, fairly early on during the shoot that their resultant film was best to be taken as so much campery. But the title also suggests a certain reticence in relation to the material as a 'Mike Reeves' film, as does the pseudonym screenplay credit 'Michael Byron' (the surname, apart from the obvious allusions, could also be said to denote the exiled Corman alumni contributors; Byron is Chuck's middle name). Rather than his astonishing debut, the film was more an opportunity for Mike to work out ideas – to test the waters, and to display an archness about the clichés of the horror genre itself. As a result, the film has both a conceptual sophistication and a lightness of touch that keeps it going (almost) to the end; it runs on gusto, *joie de vivre* and panache. The script remains bad, but the film pre-empts judgement by commenting upon this itself: Veronica (Steele) says 'What a strange place – it's all so full of weirdies and werewolves' to which Philip (Ogilvy) replies 'Terrible line, darling. Great alliteration, but terrible line'; 'What's the matter with you? Bath taps running blood or something?'; 'Do you know the Draculas by any chance?'

The film was shot in eighteen days in the summer of 1965, mostly with one camera, a little village outside Rome doubling for Transylvania, *Ruini Etrusci* appearing on the call sheets and clapper boards, and was shot in Cromoscope.[31] Mike prepared a precise shot list before each day's shoot, noting exactly the specifications of each set up required. Every favour was called in by those involved in its making, including borrowing a siege catapult left over from an epic and reinventing it as the ducking stool for the one day they had to shoot the lake sequences. Much of the film was shot in and around a restaurant (the inn, the kitchen, the bedroom and many of the exterior locations). The shooting ratio was closer to 1:1 than 2:1 and the crew numbered about 16. The police van doubled as the production office, and cash was paid to the crew on a daily basis, after shooting, usually at about midnight. Ogilvy was paid so little that he subsisted on cheap spaghetti and oranges in his room in a pensione.

Another friend of Mel's, the first-time film composer Ralph Ferraro (who had set off to Rome for a honeymoon and stayed for eight years), composed and recorded the score with a sizeable orchestra and used a pump organ for added atmosphere. Once the footage was assembled into a rough cut and most of the post-synching completed in Rome, using the same technicians as for *Castle of the Living Dead*, a screening room was hired to show Paul the film. Chuck remembers it as 'a disaster'. The film was half an hour too short, but for Paul seemed to drag so much that his first response was to ask what could be taken out. The 'slapstick' chase sequence which, although it seems to belong to another film altogether with its speeded-up footage and bumbling policemen, was used to pad the film out so as to scrape it in at feature-length. Indeed, time considerations probably informed the making of these sections; Mike would have been spending too much time putting together the opening 'origins of Vardella' sequence, and the couple experiencing the idiosyncratic joys of Cold War-era East Bloc tourism ('Transylvania – Today'); for the Second Unit it was necessary to get stuff in the can if the film was ever to be finished on time and within the budget. The budget did not extend to Mike's original idea for the ending: the couple, reunited and now back home in their London flat, sleep after making love, Philip wakes, turns to look at his new bride in the moonlight, and sees the hideous face of Vardella staring back at him. In the event, driving off at the end of the film, this twist was done with Veronica's verdict on the holiday: 'I will return.'

Miracle Films bought the UK rights and, after some trimming at the hands of the British censor, the film played in Kilburn in late 1966. Even after *Witchfinder*, Mike would make a point of calling into the Miracle office and checking the rental profits. For his *Films and Filming* review Ray Durgnat found that 'the film has quite a vein of daffy humour ... the makers have clearly set out to make a rather jolly and soothing horror film'; as to the horror: 'One or two macabre notes are tinkled rather than sounded'.[32] Hardy refers to the resultant film as 'untidy'[33] – which could apply to the film on a number of levels, and the scrappy unconnectedness of the comedy and horror strains. Mike would later be even more dismissive: 'quite possibly the worst film ever made'.[34] But it was passable enough for Paul to sell the film to AIP, who opened it in the US as *The She-Beast* in 1966 for a drive-in 'This is Terror!!!' double-bill.[35] For AIP, *The She-Beast* was 'Deadlier than Dracula! Wilder than the Werewolf! More frightening than Frankenstein!' and, upon its US release, made 'not a ripple'.[36] In Italy it was a hit, and a *Sorella di Satana* comic was issued. It was only in the late 1990s, with a renewed interest in Reeves's work following on from partly restored releases of *Witchfinder General* that copies from old, ragged 16 mm prints of *Blood Beast* began to re-emerge.[37]

Until then, the film was only really noted, with disappointment, by diehard Barbara Steele enthusiasts, more used to classier fare.

If anything carries the film, it is Reeves's certainty and his ability to ground the film in an understanding of its genre. The characters are drawn with broad strokes, and function in generic ways. The couple, like the lost holidaymakers in *Mark of the Vampire* (a typical horror device), work hard to remain unruffled – Philip in shades, open-neck shirt and neckerchief, Veronica in pure art-school get-up, trim, at ease, and effortlessly sexy – and the caricatures, Welles' peeping-Tom inn owner and a rough, Spaghetti extra-esque truck driver, do not jar in this context. John Karlsen is given plenty of room for English character acting eccentricities as a contemporary Van Helsing, gotten up like George Bernard Shaw. His sluiced 'ex-Lordship', living in a cave (old books, cigars, tea chests, skull) now that the government has confiscated his castle, is entirely fun, as are the odd camera angles and use of 'classic cars'. The playing off of the 'tensions' between the old and the new, the everyday and the supernatural, history and the contemporary, a socialist republic and deposed aristocracy, the teaming of the young Philip and old Van Helsing fill the scenes; the film virtually makes itself. It is the threadbare nature of the film that has endeared it to others: it is intimate, the humour so evidently off the cuff with at times a near-anarchic disregard for the norms of 'good' film-making. After Warhol's film work, such elements were perceived as intelligent film-making rather than lacklustre film execution.

The opening sequence, however, is as uniformly good as anything else Mike went on to shoot; Wood tentatively draws a comparison with the imagery of Hieronymus Bosch.[38] Count Van Helsing introduces the legend of the witch Vardella after a night on Transylvanian vodka. Mike opens the accompanying flashback with a petrified child running across the landscape, church bell tolling and wind in the trees, bursting in on a peasant funeral in a church. The villagers form a lynch mob, grab improvised weapons and flaming torches, *Frankenstein*-like, and set out to avenge the death of the boy's brother. Outside Vardella's cave, the lynching is shot in close-ups, some hand-held, and is frenetic, confusing and with a waking-nightmare quality.[39] Vardella, a hideously disfigured but superhuman crone, is dragged down to the lake, skewered to a ducking stool with a red-hot stake driven through her chest, and drowned. Our sympathies remain with her against the anonymous and brutal villagers, who look on impassively. There is an elemental aspect to the sequence: fire, wind, water, blood; peasants and an intoning priest. Cutaways to a distant onlooker, Count Van Helsing's ancestor, confirms that the sequence works as a dry-run for the near-identical opening of *Witchfinder* (where villagers and cleric again engage in a lynching). Other such parallels are apparent: sex and violence are intimately linked when Philip breaks off love-making to beat the voyeuristic inn keeper and the structuring device of separating the central couple early on, leaving the male to risk his life to protect the female (as in *Intrusion*), determines *Witchfinder* and, to a lesser extent, *The Sorcerers*. Likewise, as Pirie notes, the explicit connection between evil and the everyday is already in evidence;[40] particularly in the child who sets off the lynching. The sequence ends with a slow zoom away from the action, to close off the past from the present, safe in the knowledge that time is about to be put out of joint.

Ralph Ferraro's ominous, Morricone-tinged soundscapes (wind, bells, tympani, mournful strings) remain throughout, but once the policemen start grappling with Vardella later on in the film, or she is propped up on the backseat of a car, the mystique and dignity of the monster is eroded for the sake of misplaced comedy.

But what of that? Mike had directed a film, intermittently showing in the UK and the rest of Europe, the US, and who knows where else. It was a 'Mike Reeves' film and, as sure as Vardella, he would return.

Notes

1 Michael Gross, interview with author, 22 January 2002. All subsequent remarks are taken from this source.

2 Anon., 'Programme Notes 17 January 1970', *National Film Theatre* (held by the British Film Institute), unnumbered.

3 Ian Ogilvy, interviewed by BOUM Productions, 1999. This and all subsequent

BOUM interviewees were interviewed for the 1999 documentary *Blood Beast: The Films of Michael Reeves* directed by Pete Tombs and Andy Starke for BOUM Productions, broadcast on Channel 4 (UK), 1999 and 2001.

4 Sarah Sesti, interview with author, 14 April 2002.

5 J. Cardiff, *Magic Hour: The Life of a Cameraman* (London, Faber & Faber, 1996), p. 241.

6 Anon., *Programme Notes*, unnumbered.

7 Huddleston, interview by author.

8 Huddleston, interview by author.

9 Murray, *Remarkable Michael Reeves*, p. 72.

10 Paul Maslansky, interviewed by BOUM Productions, 1999.

11 Frederick Muller, interview with author, 26 March 2002. All subsequent remarks are taken from this source.

12 C. Lee, *Tall, Dark and Gruesome: An Autobiography* (London, Mayflower/Granada Publishing, 1978), p. 236.

13 Ironically, Lee would end up in the Price role, this time as Lord George Jeffreys, in Jess Franco's version of *Witchfinder, Bloody Judge*. Lee cannot recall the *Castle of the Living Dead* shoot as any different from innumerable others during this period; Christopher Lee, interview with author, 17 December 1999.

14 Anon., *Programme Notes*, unnumbered.

15 Welles, interview by author.

16 Anon., 'Film director's drug death was accident', *Chelsea Post* (21 February 1969) 1.

17 For further on Griffith's script writing, see 'Charles B. Griffith: not of this earth', in P. McGilligan (ed.), *Backstory 3: Interviews with Screenwriters of the 60s* (Los Angeles and London, University of California Press, Berkeley, 1997), pp. 157–73.

18 Nick Alexander, interview with author, 11 May 2002. All subsequent remarks are taken from this source.

19 D. J. Hogan, *Dark Romance: Sex and Death in the Horror Film* (Northamptonshire, Equation, Thorsons Publishing Group, 1988), p. 164.

20 Lars Bloch, interview with author, 12 May 2002.

21 Swires, 'And now the screaming stops', p. 16.

22 Chuck Griffith, interview with author, 1 April 2002. All subsequent remarks are taken from this source.

23 Lars Bloch, interview with author, 12 May 2002. All subsequent remarks are taken from this source.

24 Edward Randolph, interview with author, 9 May 2002. All subsequent remarks are taken from this source.

25 This would have been Aldo Tonti, who had shot sequences in *Castle of the Living Dead* in such a way – a 'big name cameraman' presumably for his work with Visconti, Rossellini and Fellini.

26 M. T. McGee, *Faster and Furiouser: The Revised and Fattened Fable of American International Pictures* (London, McFarland and Company, Inc., 1996), pp. 274–5.

27 McGee, *Faster and Furiouser*, p. 274.

28 Ogilvy, BOUM interview.

29 T. Weaver, *Interviews with B-Science Fiction and Horror Movie Makers* (North Carolina, McFarland and Co., 1988), p. 391.

30 McGee, *Faster and Furiouser*, p. 275.

31 Only cropped duplicates now circulate; the 2.35:1 Cromoscope ratio is lost until the negative is rescued from storage (it has passed through a number of companies during bankruptcy sales) and a hefty storage bill settled. The film is the only Reeves film composed in 'scope and the awkward framing indicates how much the 'panned and scanned' versions have subsequently lost.

32 R. Durgnat, 'Revenge of the Blood Beast', *Films and Filming* (November 1966) 18.

33 P. Hardy (ed.), *The Aurum Film Encyclopedia: Horror* (London, Aurum Press, 1996), p. 174.

34 Anon., 'Shows – horror clicks', p. 12.

35 The other half of the double-bill was another Italian horror, the unremarkable *The Embalmer* (*Il Mostro di Venezia*).

36 Griffith, interview with author.

37 It previously had a limited video release in the US in the early 1980s, and had been available on the grey market since. In the UK, Channel 4 screened the film in 1999 and 2001.

38 Wood, 'In memoriam Michael Reeves', p. 4.

39 Mike seems to have studied Tony Richardson's New Wave techniques for this, particularly the cutting in *The Loneliness of the Long Distance Runner*, and Lean's *Great Expectations* for the running child.

40 Pirie, *Heritage of Horror*, p. 148.

The Sorcerers happening

4

I'd like to say what I believe about outer/inner space, psyche/ physiodelics, etc... The nature of the world is miraculous. The only way to accurately recognise the nature of the world is by wonderment. Wonderment is man's only function. Bereft of it he becomes absurd and meaningless ... The really revealing thing about the teenage drug thing, in the first place, is that deep down young people don't care any more whether they live or die. The future has just stopped being a real thing and without wonderment there isn't any other means to a sense of one's own meaning. Drugs have, therefore, become a modern city-dweller's only access to wonderment, because they break down the utilitarian identity of things. They are the painful recapturing of a *natural way of seeing*. (Jeff Nuttall, letter to *The International Times*, 1967)[1]

Mike, now a semi-proven quantity, arrived back in London in early 1966 with the sole intention of netting an established production company for the next film. Like *Intrusion*, it would be a 'Leith Production'. He enlisted his Radley friend and *Intrusion* cameraman, Tom Baker, as a generic 'assistant director' and drove him out to Kilburn to see *Revenge of the Blood Beast* for which Mike provided a running commentary. This was a common occurrence whenever Mike spotted the film playing. Tom, graduated from Trinity and working on shorts with Iain Sinclair, had been keeping an eye on Mike's progress and was keen to join in the fun. After *Carrion*, Tom had written a fanciful script for him, much in the manner of the European art cinema of the time; females as ciphers for aspects of the male protagonist, embodiments of different philosophies towards life. Here an artist ditches his 'straight' girlfriend for an older, bohemian woman and they elope with straight girlfriend in pursuit; soul-searching, romantic ennui and canal-bank walks follow. But even then Mike was only interested in refining his abilities as an action director; some sequences were shot but *Tale of an Artist* remained unfinished.

Emboldened, Mike now forcibly introduced himself to a number of London film types and, so looking for trouble, encountered Michael Klinger of the Compton Group. Klinger already had a couple of ultra-cheap horror films under his belt, and from his vantage point on film-making, Mike would have been seen as a 'do-er' in a field, low-budget horror exploitation, that was eminently do-able. There was very little to lose, so Klinger made a token investment by packing Mike off to Rome, with Tom in tow, to develop their next film. The intention was that it would star Christopher Lee, utilising Mike's Maslansky connection. Offices were hired, a script of sorts was pieced together, 'research' into seventeenth-century costumes was underway, locations were scouted and a palace was examined. There would be a shot seen from across the palace gardens; Lee looming out from a window and glowering into the night. But things were slow. Mike would disappear off to see his girlfriend, who had a temporary position as a PA to Raquel Welch, then filming in Spain. Raquel's future husband, Patrick Curtis, was living in Rome and fell in with Mike and his friends at the Cowboy, a hamburger and rib joint part-owned by Patrick. Klinger arrived for a few days to see how things were progressing. By mid-1966, Mike had little more than talk, pitches, a useful trust fund to keep the spaghetti and Peroni flowing and a track record as film director consisting of *Revenge of the Blood Beast*. Lee passed and everyone decamped back to London.

Mike took up residence in a cottage in Knightsbridge, 23 Yeoman's Row. He stuck Hopper prints on the walls, placed a display hash pipe on the mantelpiece in the same way that, at the start of the decade, a prized copy of the Penguin *Lady Chatterley's Lover* would be deployed and installed a 16 mm projector in the untidy living room. He hired prints to watch with friends, read the film trade papers, read books that might make good films, prepared pitches and scripts (*Manic Mind, The Crooked Cross, Blood Moon,* retitled *Flame in the Blood*), all under the aegis of Leith Productions; despite the blow, Mike was determined to keep Leith Productions active. A strong script was needed rather than just persuasive talk. The opportunity arose when Mike chanced upon the writer Alfred Shaughnessy at a party. Shaughnessy had previously directed a number of potboilers and was now turning out film and television scripts to order ('Some writers call this "whoring"...'[2]). For Mike, Alfred was someone who could bring his extensive film production experience to scripting Mike's ideas, as well as providing advice and contacts, assist with the casting, and lend a professionalism to any proposed project. Mike hit him with the Siegel story, Alfred approved and liked Mike. His talent – 'he could think in images'[3] – was apparent even if, at present, there was little of quality to show for it. The idea was psychological horror: a villa in the south of France, twin brothers, one a brilliant musician but quite insane, and a monstrous, Hitchcockian mother. It was called *Appassionata* and was to be a film under the sign of Roman Polanski, whose new film *Repulsion* showed just what could be done. Mike and Alfred thrashed out the *Appassionata* script over lunches (after one, Mike surprised Alfred with a print of his 1960 film *The Impersonator*). It would be pitched straight to Compton using the Klinger connection – and Compton had made *Repulsion*. The film was constructed along modest lines, designed to be manageable within the confines of a low budget. The cast would include Christopher Lee, Flora Robson and Susan Hampshire. Compton made positive noises, but the film was not to happen in this form.

At any rate, subtle psychological horror may have been Polanski's forte, but it was not at all Mike's beat nor, Polanski aside, was it really Compton's thing either. *Appassionata* was the second dead-end.

Patrick Curtis was a frequent guest at Yeoman's Row and someone that Mike had now cast as a producer for an anticipated Leith Production. Patrick was an American film type (an actor and producer) then between Rome and London with Welch, the other half of his Curtwel Productions Inc., and was happy to join the gang for loud Monopoly games back at Mike's place when in London. Patrick found Mike 'effervescent about film'[4] and so was keen to oversee the next film, which could even be ideal for Raquel, although the nature of the production would clearly be a few cuts below the type they were getting used to.

Robin Dalton, the literary agent, then making headway into London's artistic and aristocratic circles, introduced Mike to John Burke. John had been European Story Editor for Twentieth-Century Fox, earning money on the side by 'novelisations' of film and TV scripts. At the point when the latter became more profitable than the former, John went freelance and so the meeting with Mike was timely. He had sold an option on his 1965 treatment for *Terror for Kicks*[5] which had since lapsed, and so the treatment was rapidly bought up by Leith Productions Limited of St Helier, Jersey, most probably with Mike's own money. John recalls that '[Mike wanted] a film produced fast because of some deal he was setting up'.[6] It may have been an impulse buy as Mike seems to have soon gone cold on the idea – perhaps a horror action film featuring a young Mod mechanic seemed limited. Such details in the outline belong firmly to the identity-crisis interzone of British mid–1960s film production – northern realism out, and the swinging London wave yet to occur. The resultant films often sported proles in the context of 'intelligent' entertainment (Reisz's *Night Must Fall*, for example). But John also had a treatment for a more intriguing proposition, *The Devil's Discord*, and an option was taken out on 18 August 1966 and *Terror for Kicks* shelved. John began work on *The Devil's Discord*, expanding it to feature-length and adjusting the characters so that the film could accommodate Raquel, and a substantial role that would be offered to Christopher Lee.

The Devil's Discord was a solid haunted-house story. Havoc ensues when a lost piece of music, Sanducci's 'Satan's Sonata', is discovered. The locals are suspicious, experts are called in, a bloody history is seen in flashback:

> Sanducci must have been working on some extraordinary harmonic theory. In writing the music the way he did, he must have been aware of special resonances that can't be shown on paper. You know ... a lot of the hysteria produced by so-called magic spells

could be due to the musical content of the incantations. When witches and sorcerers claimed to call up devils, it wasn't the words that counted – most of them were gibberish anyway. What cast the spell – on the audience, if nobody else – was the musical rhythm and melody. That's *why* so many of the words were nonsense: it's the overall sound that counts ...[7]

The music raises the dead lover of the protagonist's eighteenth-century ancestor, Sanducci. There is unfinished business; she was executed over an affair with Sanducci and is now 'a creature from some cold hell'. It draws from the same mainstay of horror films that *Blood Beast* also tapped, with the breaking of the past–present dichotomy. Had it been shot, the film might even have made *Blood Beast* seem like a dry-run. The final screenplay was complete by early October, but when 'casting complications' arose, Tigon decided to pass; this was the third dead-end. Classy horror featuring Christopher Lee was not working.

Something altogether different was needed, something with few ambitions, and perhaps the answer came when Mike saw Compton's new film, *The Projected Man*: straight-up sci-fi horror, idea unashamedly ripped off from *The Fly*; scientists bark mumbo-jumbo at each other, experiment goes wrong, one of their number – a murderous mutant afizz with electricity – sets off on a killing spree around London by night. The film gingerly pushes the envelope in terms of nudity and innuendo. It was flat and formulaic, across a limited number of locations; the script seemed to have written itself. It opened in a handful of small cinemas and few people cared less. This is what Compton could and did do – Mike had been wrong to worry about a strong script; what was needed was an outline intrinsically suited to a Compton film. He contacted John and requested rewrites on *Terror for Kicks*; the first thing that needed changing was the protagonist's profession and social class. Beyond that, the film must represent a framework for a highly contemporary London setting. And Polanski, who had unintentionally sent out the wrong signal with the success of *Repulsion*, was now about to unintentionally facilitate an opportunity for such a Compton-style project to get a green light; it was Polanski's scrambling, first out of Poland, then out of London, that allowed Mike to slip in.

Polanski's calling card was *Knife in the Water*. He had then attempted, unsuccessfully, to court Hammer with the script *If Katelbach Comes*. But Compton were prepared to bankroll his intentions for an English-language film, which was then to be called *Loveli Head*. While Mike was in Rome, Polanski arrived in London at the invite of Compton, hoping he could replace the drab Lodz soundstages with at least some of the fabled trappings of western wealth. Polanski recalls:

> 'The Compton Group' rejoiced in a high-sounding name, an elaborate letterhead, and a board of directors that included the Earl of Kimberley. Everything seemed to suggest that it was a major entertainment and communications conglomerate. Actually it owed its existence and main revenue to a small, seedy Soho establishment called the Compton Cinema Club, which showed what currently passed in London for porno movies ... The Compton Group had been making so much money out of this operation that it was anxious to change its image ...[8]

Low-rent, new and ambitious directors were ideal for such an image change; they need not be remunerated too highly and enthusiasm short-circuits questions of overtime.

The Compton Group was run by Klinger and Tony Tenser. Both were streetwise and hardnosed, from the East End Jewish milieu. Klinger was then perceived to be (and feared as) a criminal, a man with underworld connections, supposedly on good terms with the Krays, and with extensive business interests in strip clubs. He was an embodiment of that 1960s intersection of glitz and trash; in a rough cut of *Witchfinder*, during the witch-burning sequence in Lavenham, the executioner turns to his assistant and shouts 'Klinger – fetch the rope!' Such an in-joke could only be made once Tenser and Klinger had parted ways. Klinger first came across Tenser in 1960, when Tenser phoned him to hire strippers for a publicity stunt. It was a meeting of minds; Compton-Cameo Films was soon formed and an underground flesh empire was founded: 'The godfathers of British sexploitation, Klinger and Tenser were connected in some way with virtually every sex film maker in the business ... Klinger managed London's famous Nell Gwynn strip club, and Tenser was the head of publicity for Miracle

Films (he was the first to label Brigitte Bardot the "sex kitten".) In 1960 the pair went into business together to open the Compton Cinema Club.'[9]

It was a small step from projecting smut to producing smut and in 1961 Tenser and Klinger presented *Naked As Nature Intended*, directed by Harrison Marks. It was a time when the Soho flesh trade was still fairly discreet (a necessity during those years of solid Conservative rule), but would soon come to reap the benefits of the lurid revelations that fired much of the coverage of the Profumo affair. The Establishment's mistresses more often than not graduated from the Soho school, sometimes leaving damaging 8 mm films, or persistent rumours of such films, behind them.

Those who worked with Klinger and Tenser were unable to tell if, ultimately, they were more interested in making films or making money. Soon the company had three London cinemas and produced and distributed Marks's subsequent 'naturist' skin flicks, and the less innocent Arnold Louis Miller and Stanley Long productions. Long and Miller were partners from the heart of the early 1960s Soho film business – strip shows, photographs (such as the 'views' bought from under-counter photograph albums in seedy newsagents – a ritual that Michael Powell inserted into the then-contemporary *Peeping Tom*), then to 8 mm 'glamour films' and on to breathless exposés, shot on borrowed equipment, such as *London in the Raw* and *Primitive London* ('The jungle behind the bright lights ...').[10] They formed Stag Films and claim to have dispatched one thousand prints a day at the height of business. They split in 1965, but both would come to work with Mike, and Tenser, Klinger and Long were all behind Polanski's *Loveli Head* – now called *Repulsion*. *Repulsion* and Polanski's next, *Cul-de-Sac*, embody something of this time and place; they straddle the art–exploitation divide, capitalising on the new permissiveness with explosive vulgarity. Perhaps Compton was, indeed, the only company that could back and market them at this point. Thus Polanski and Compton had given the film-going public the first (aural) female orgasm in a feature film. Tenser: 'I signed him up, signed Polanski up – because I'd read reports on *Knife in the Water* –

another new director. I'd met the man. I thought he had possibilities. The script that we had was quite horrifying in its own way, but mentally so. The visuals were not horrifying but mentally so – makes you think a lot. It would scare you. He got away with quite a bit that normally wouldn't be shown because of the intensity of the film.'[11]

Repulsion charted a psychological odyssey through the flipside of pre-summer of love London with a supremely cool and modern sheen: isolation, madness, twisted compositions, rotting meat and a nightmare of rape, extreme close-ups, the wall that sprouts writhing arms, jazz and the fetishisation of the young Catherine Deneuve. It was soon doing the rounds of European film festivals and picked up the Silver Bear in Berlin. Klinger hung on to the statuette; it signified Compton's successful transformation from Soho sleaze merchants to a fashionable international film outfit. For those in the know, 'Michael Klinger and Tony Tenser present ...' and such lofty critical acclaim was incongruous to the point of hilarity. After all, it was only the impulse to have a 'respectable' wing of operations on the cheap (*Repulsion* cost a mere £95,000, all in) in case of problems with the police over their less salubrious films that had brought Polanski into Compton's orbit in the first place.

Delighted with the *Repulsion* statuette, Klinger financed Polanski's experimental, Pinter-influenced script *If Katelbach Comes* which, as *Cul-de-Sac*, took the Golden Bear in Berlin in 1966. Both *Repulsion* and *Cul-de-Sac* received international releases and hit the American markets hard (albeit with mixed success) – and Polanski followed in their wake after the Hammer spoof *The Fearless Vampire Killers*, a score settled with the company who had initially turned him down. Klinger, now with a taste for international film production, split with the more provincial Tenser, amicably and informally, after *Cul-de-Sac*, in 1967. Tenser was finishing off *Mini Weekend* and it was at this point that he picked up Reeves, as the replacement Polanski, for *The Sorcerers*. This was to be for Tenser's post-Klinger company, Tigon British Film Productions Ltd. Like Compton, Tigon, from its Wardour Street office, would produce and distribute. To this end, Tenser had bought a stake in a small number of West End cinema clubs, including the right to empty the slot machines of their day's takings. One of the first films Tenser released in the UK was the unsettling American B-feature *Carnival of Souls*. Thereafter, he also released American International Pictures exploitation films, establishing a business relationship with the California company that would form the basis for the next Reeves picture, *Witchfinder General*. Tigon, able to move quicker than the bigger distributors, could provide an eclectic variety of films; who else would present Godard's *Une Femme Mariée* with *Take Your Clothes Off and Live* (directed by Miller) as a support feature?[12]

Even when mostly out of the 'nudie' business, Tenser retained the streamlined producing skills honed during this period. He was known by his 'don't fucking worry about it' approach to pre-production, for better or worse. Yet despite this, Tenser in person was warm, concerned and jovial; he had been the approachable half of Compton. For Mike, *Revenge of the Blood Beast* showing in Kilburn was a far cry from the international distribution and acclaim that Polanski gained with Compton, so working with Tenser was a palpable opportunity.

Mike also appreciated the fast and shady Soho company. He took to hanging around the Soho offices and studios associated with Tenser, making cutting suggestions as he watched hacks slap 16 mm porn together. Mike liked to be about the business of film and would have soaked up the milieu and the bustle even if he had no actual need to be in the vicinity. His auteur status can be partly attributed to this – simply, a great interest in all the aspects of the film-making process.

By mid–1967 Mike was 23 and beginning to establish his haunts and habits. He had an amicable girlfriend in Annabelle, 'an archetypical sixties girlfriend. Slim. The shortest shirts from Biba. Serious too',[13] also on the fringes of the film industry. His school contemporaries were on the bottom rungs of their professions, their time organised for them, and Mike wanted a demonstrable working life too, within reason, to confirm what he did. He was able to allude to his movements in the seemingly slightly dangerous Soho underworld; when King's Mead or Radley

Old Boys asked him what he was up to, he would shoot back with 'Editing the balls out of blue movies'.[14] He would invite his friends and their friends to Yeoman's Row to watch 16 mm films and chat about forthcoming films projects; 'food and drink flowed in his house – he loved having people around'.[15] These prolonged socials became known as Mike's '"chewing-the-fat" sessions'[16] and soon substantial crowds would be a constant. They continued in Esmeralda's Bar in Belgravia and for pub crawls down the Fulham Road. Mike enjoyed being the centre of attention; he is remembered as funny, kind and a touch mercurial, hyper and highly strung. He worked at being enigmatic, and made himself difficult to get to know – part bolshyness, and part a genuine restlessness. Philip Waddilove, who first met Mike in 1967, recalls 'He was very much the ex-public school boy – very well mannered and extremely articulate – he certainly wasn't part of the London swinging scene of the sixties.'

Mike would switch crowds often, leave parties on a whim to lose himself in the anonymity of the streets. He would catch a late-night film, stroll and take in the night air, stop for a hamburger, walk some more, return home and read film magazines. This habit would be directly transposed into *The Sorcerers*, as was his interest in cars and speed. The protagonist, the Mike alter-ego Ian Ogilvy (with the barely concealed name 'Mike Roscoe' – which Mike had altered from the original 'Mike Moore')[17] would pound the paving stones at night too, abandoning a group of friends for no given reason, oscillating between the company of others and his own. Mike had found himself centrally placed to explore the rapidly changing London scene during his night-time strolls. Yeoman's Row in 1967 was within walking distance of the epi-centre of the birth of the chemical-fuelled psychedelic under-ground, 'the "Swinging London" Babylon of hucksters, fixers and double-agents'[18] – all of which held a fascination for Mike. After long nights, he would head back to Yeoman's Row, have a shot of whisky and go to bed with an F. Scott Fitzgerald short story as dawn was breaking, or would sit up fielding expected calls from America about his possible film projects.

Mike would discuss film with the earnest young *Films and*

Filming critic David Austen – particularly in relation to the *Cahiers du Cinéma* auteur approach to jobbing American film-makers; long, long conversations about the *artistry* of Howard Hawks and John Ford are recalled. Shelves and tables held piles of film books. Perhaps 'jobbing' was the notion that warmed Mike to the idea of *Terror for Kicks* after it had initially been shelved. Patrick took heart at the idea of the freedoms of a film made on the cheap; he decided that *Terror for Kicks* would be 'underground film-making with a bit of style',[19] completely unfettered by studio restrictions, and the two of them put together a modest package for Tenser. Patrick and Tenser had previously done business and, post-Polanski, Tenser was available, interested and waiting. John's 1966 *Terror for Kick* screenplay, written in November and December, was talked up as having strong exploitation potential and squarely aimed at the lower end of the market. The deal around it would consist of a name actor, and whatever cash Patrick and Mike could muster. This would make for as good a chance as they would get.

John, Patrick, Mike and even Annabelle had brainstormed their way through the script for a number of sessions, shaping it into the modest and doable film proposition they needed. The script was the blueprint, from Tenser's point of view, for an effective remake of *The Projected Man* – but also provided a sub-lime idea: the notion of film as voyeurism was worked back into the story, reimagining the violence and sex (the 'kicks') as a critique of the nature of this kind of film in itself. In the context of 1966 Soho, this is a very potent premise; foremost in Mike's mind would have been the desire to avoid making a film anything like those that Tigon then produced. What must have clicked when Mike read John's script was that it included within its narrative a thematic device that offered the possibility of distance for Mike and his film from the sensibility of the Soho film world; the film could be both of it, and defiantly against it. This sentiment would find its way into the film's opening; Karloff's character's advertisement is placed on a newsagent's board along with those of prostitutes.[20] In this way, the characteristics of *Terror for Kicks*, as *The Sorcerers*, are founded as much on its company of origin as was *Repulsion* – and in both these instances, this mix makes for unique film-making and films. Mike would also capitalise on the distance in terms of the wider scene; the critique would extend to swinging London – and a fair amount of John's film script was equally dismissive of the phenomenon (Mike Moore, surveying the basement club, says 'Five years from now ... There'll be a new shop, a new name – a new rave. A new generation, even. And this little lot will probably all be married and settled down by then'[21]). Wary of the rapidly changing times, John had placed invites throughout the script for improvised contemporaneity in terms of music and fashions ('We see in through the window of a with-it dress shop – whatever is the rave at the time the picture is made' for example[22]) in placing the action in the heart of London. One final connection is apparent: John's Mike was now drawn from the same mould as Mike Reeves himself; a Chelsea-based, restless young man of means, half-in, half-out of the environs in which he finds himself, studiously detached from the vagaries of fashion:

> [Shot] 10 Int. Basement Club – Two Shot Mike and Penny Night
>
> MIKE is bored. Not ostentatiously yawning but remotely, cosmically bored. We should realise as we go on that he had practised a pose of non-involvement for so long that he had lost the ability to relax.[23]

Even the protagonist's hip profession had been lent by the antiques dealer and Radley friend Alex Waye – drawing on the Christopher Gibbs school of London cool (and Roscoe, like Withnail, exudes the feeling that the party is somehow happening without him). Mike's friend Iain Sinclair, upon seeing the film, would see in the protagonist 'a sympathetic caricature' of Mike, via Ogilvy, now 'more than ever the director's alter ego'.[24] The final screenplay has Roscoe describe himself at one point as 'Mercurial Mike, man of many moods'.[25]

The Leith Productions 'chewing the fat' sessions retained their informality, even now that they had been converted into full-throttle film development. Mike was preparing to make a 'proper' film – no longer a 'Mike Reeves' film, but a 'Michael Reeves film'. John: 'We got along very well indeed in all the preliminary stages, though other work kept me from attending any of the shooting. I found him sociable yet sometimes distrait, if one can put it that way. He was quite impulsive, and would suddenly ring up and suggest a meeting, largely from a desire to chat rather than for any specific reason.'

Since going for broke seemed to be working, Mike saw no reason to temper his vision of the kind of film he intended to make, so it only seemed logical that Karloff should be the 'name' in the film. Mike caught up with him accordingly in Madrid, where he was guest-starring in *I Spy*. Karloff was coherent, but very old and ailing rapidly. He had contracted pneumonia in Rome while working on Bava's estimable *Black Sabbath* in 1963, was suffering from acute emphysema and beginning to glide downhill. For *The Sorcerers* he sported a metal leg brace on one arthritic leg, which had to be oiled so that the squeaking would not find its way on to the soundtrack, but was more comfortable in a wheelchair, as he also suffered from an arthritic back. Mike would have to shoot around the brace and so kept Karloff as immobile as possible (the brace is still slightly visible in some scenes). Curtis could not secure insurance for Karloff on the film. The wheelchair itself was included in his few scenes in his next film, the diabolical *Curse of the Crimson Altar* ('a strange concoction of cod-H. P. Lovecraft and M. R. James, dressed up in psychedelic clothes'[26]) – uncomfortable scenes of Karloff being wheeled around the grounds of Grimsdyke House in the cold night air. For the few performances after that, Karloff came with oxygen tank too and, by most accounts, could barely talk. Karloff died on 2 February 1969.

Mike pitched the film, offered the £11,000 Karloff wanted (which, for the bedraggled gravitas alone, was a bargain) and readily agreed to accommodate Karloff's wish for script alterations. Karloff needed his character, Marcus Mesmer, a retired variety act 'mind reader', to come good in the end. This could be achieved through an eleventh-hour gesture of self-sacrifice on Mesmer's part, without Mike having to dilute the relentlessly downward spiral of the film. Tom recalls: 'In the original … the old folks use the transmission of sensation from the Ian Ogilvy character purely for their own gratification. No holds barred. But Karloff wouldn't buy that. He said his character had to have redeeming characteristics, or he would not do it. So we turned the ending round – he putting the brakes on his wife and ultimately sacrificing himself. To save the world.'

In some ways it is surprising that Boris cared at this point, after recent appearances in films like *Bikini Beach*, *Die, Monster, Die!* and *Ghost in the Invisible Bikini*, but maybe he sensed that his time was near and had an urge for a swansong. In the event, he dished one out to Mike and then one to another young upstart – playing himself for Peter Bogdanovich's debut, *Targets*. Why did he accept? Fee aside, the production conditions were hardly agreeable. Maybe Mike reminded him of another Englishman abroad, also film-mad and slightly depressive – the long-gone James Whale. In the days of *The Bride of Frankenstein*, Karloff had to wear leg braces to deliberately degrade his ability to walk; things were coming full circle. Mike would have known Karloff's films well, would have talked incessantly about them ... had some experience on the pitch as a bowler, and public schoolboys, of whatever epoch, speak the same language. The Uppinghamian would have delivered his party piece to the Radleian by way of accepting: 'My leg in a steel brace – operating with only half a lung – why it's a public scandal that I'm still around! But as long as people want me, I feel an obligation to keep on performing. After all, every time I act I provide employment for a fleet of doubles! ... I am never really alive unless I am at work, merely recharging for the next spell. To know that I was never to work again would be something akin to the death sentence for me.'[27] The latter sentiments were true for Mike too; another circle of sorts. For Boris, it was a chance to render a human portrait; the man whose name had become so synonymous with monster performances that Graham Greene had referred to 'the Karloff' as a type of character and acting,[28] could now bow out on a note of humanity and redemption. Once the producers had made their way to Madrid to thrash out the contract fine print, Karloff was fully onboard. On-set he was impeccably professional. Even Tenser felt a frisson of respect for the old school: 'I can't say enough good things about Boris Karloff. He was a wonderful man, and a brilliant actor. He was nearly 80 then, but he remembered his lines and spoke them clearly. He interpreted his part absolutely correctly and uniquely, as only he could. He was the most unassuming man you could ever wish to meet. He couldn't even understand why people would want his autograph.'[29]

The package seemed good – Curtis and Tenser struck a deal and a state of rapid pre-production was declared. There was precious little time to implement the changes Karloff needed – they would have to be made on the hoof. Curtis had been able to offer Tenser Mike, the script, half the budget already in place, agreements from Karloff and Catherine Lacey for the leading mature roles (Lacey suggested by Shaughnessy, who had just worked with her for a BBC production) and Ogilvy, of course, to play the young protagonist (who by now had something of a name on the back of a TV series, *The Liars*), and Ogilvy's RADA colleague, the actor Victor Henry. Pouty Elizabeth Ercy, who Mike was parti-cularly keen on, would fulfil the lost 'French bird' role, in the manner of Deneuve in *Repulsion* or Jacqueline Sassard in *Accident*. From Tenser, Curtis needed the other half of the budget, and help with UK and 'worldwide' marketing. It would be cheap enough all in, a total budget of £25–£26,000 (including Karloff's fee) – Tenser could pick up his half of the bill with ease,[30] mostly on pre-sales of the film, and cast a gaggle of his aspiring actresses in bit parts. Tenser's only request was that Mike pep it up a bit, make it a bit more, as *Time* magazine had it, 'London – the Swinging City' – give it some flashy footage that could then be used in the trailer. The shoot would begin almost straight away, mid-January 1967, as a 'Tigon-Curtwel Global Production released through Tigon Pictures'. Karloff had clinched the deal for Tenser: 'Boris Karloff was one of the idols of my youth. I had followed his career ever since I saw *Frankenstein*, and had always been in awe of him. I had heard of Michael, and knew that he had directed an earlier low budget horror film which was successful. From the way he spoke, he seemed to have great talent. After I met with Pat a couple more times, I knew I could trust him.'[31] Just as Mike had schmoozed Karloff, so Tenser did too, with one eye on further films. There was flattering talk of establishing a Karloff Theatre.[32]

The next obstacle was a meeting with John Trevelyan of the

British Board of Film Censors (BBFC). Mike was mindful of the kind of reaction names like Miller and Long would provoke, and so met with Trevelyan, a distant cousin of his, under the aegis of 'Vardella Film Productions Limited' to discuss the script. Mike played the Karloff card to illustrate his seriousness. Trevelyan understood that the film would be squarely aimed at the 'X' category, and the two discussed the horror film per se.

Script approval was an arduous process whereby a draft script of the proposed film would be submitted to the BBFC for its blessing and advice. Trevelyan was first and foremost a diplomat, described by Peter Evans as having 'a face like a 1933 walnut case radio set: comfortable, reliable, emitting the Home Service sounds of English commonsense and autumnal bronchitis'.[33] He relished his position at the BBFC, socialising with the likes of Ken Russell, Polanski, Andy Warhol and Paul Morrissey, pipe clamped between his teeth and glass of red clamped in his hand. He had been with the BBFC since 1951 and by the late 1960s was easing his way to retirement, his policy of liberalisation, in 1967 at least, seemingly a quiet success. He kept a supply of whisky and Benson and Hedges in his office and would often wile away afternoons discussing the ins and outs of all kinds of things he had seen fit to cut. He once even institutionalised this; a censorship symposium at the Royal Festival Hall, in which he showed the material he had cut from films and chatted about it at length. But he was forward looking in terms of his appreciation of films, and held the art in high regard; by the late 1960s, his ideal films were those that combined an intellectual approach and challenging material – particularly those of Joseph Losey, Stanley Kubrick and John Schlesinger – and so understood censorship in utilitarian terms (he cut the Compton Cinema Club slack as he knew the money from their sex films was 'used to enable an outstanding film-maker, Roman Polanski, to make his first two feature films ...'[34]). Trevelyan saw himself more as an enabler than censor. He even acted as unofficial agent for Tenser at times, sending aspiring film-makers in his direction. His engagement with *Witchfinder* was far from satisfactory but, in some ways, he acted to protect the film, and shielded Tenser from the wrath expressed behind closed doors at the BBFC.

In a letter to Mike, from 3 January 1967, Trevelyan wrote: 'our general policy with regard to horror films is that there are two areas which from time to time cause us concern. These are (a) horror laced with sex, and (b) horror which goes over the edge into disgust.' In terms of his latter point, he advised Mike to shoot tamer alternative takes, particularly for the close of the film, and to be careful with Estelle's (Lacey) 'sadism'. For Roscoe's murder of Laura, Trevelyan noted: 'Great care should be taken with these scenes. As I explained, we are advised that strangling scenes can be stimulating to certain mentally unbalanced people, so I always advise keeping such scenes short, and if possible, without close shots. Perhaps you might even consider omitting, wholly or partly, the strangling, and leave it at stabbing.'[35] Tenser also had ideas about horror, and the kind of horror that Tigon wanted:

> How have we [come] to understand [the term] 'horror film'? The experts were Hammer Films, as they make quite a lot of them. And they were really great films: a style of horror ... We thought we could make similar films. We did make a few films, not with Michael Reeves, but with steady directors who had made these sort of films before. You know, we watched it carefully. We made sure that all of our money was spent on the screen, and not chauffeuring people about and what have you. Unnecessary expenses – which could be very high. These were the days when money was limited, and British films were not attractive worldwide.

Once Tenser had his team in place, he was happy to leave Patrick Curtis to watch over the West London Studios set (he would remain 'about' on the set from time to time). The crew meshed well, with everyone happy to lug the heavy equipment around between set-ups. Arnold Miller occasionally showed in his capacity as executive producer and the film would be shot by his former Stag Films partner, Stanley Long.

Long might have spent many hours shooting Soho interiors, but he was no amateur – when *Repulsion* ran over schedule, Tenser brought Long in to shoot the final third (including many of the main set-pieces).[36] Long was able to replicate Gilbert Taylor's style – the man Kubrick had used to shoot *Dr Strangelove* and whom Polanski had insisted on as the one non-negotiable 'luxury' for the *Repulsion* shoot, despite Gilbert being 'one of the most expensive cameramen in the business'.[37] But for Polanski the film had to look expensive if nothing else; another facet of the world of *Repulsion* in which surface appearances are always deceptive. Long also simultaneously ran a film equipment rental company, an aviation company, and held a commercial pilot's licence. Yet even Long, who had seen more than most in the world of exploitation film, was startled by Reeves's set decoration – he would 'go berserk on the set sometimes',[38] drenching it in 'Kensington Gore':

> He was flinging blood about on the set like it was going out of fashion, I mean gallons of it. I used to constantly be checking him. He had this obsessive thing about throwing it up the walls, and when Susan George [as Audrey] was stabbed with a pair of scissors, it was going all over the cameras and all over the crew and everybody's clothes, and I said, 'Really, you know, come off it.' But he loved it. He seemed to revel in it. He definitely had a kink about blood.[39]

For this sequence, Mike had devised a 'special effect': 'The knife comes into the shot again, bloody, the scene whirls as she falls. Blood spatters over the lens. A gurgle O.S ...'.[40] But, as Trevelyan feared, such a wildly over-the-top sequence was unacceptable and the majority of Audrey's murder did not make it to the final cut. It also left Tenser's Biba-clad young actress more than a little traumatised. Mike's unorthodox set-dressing technique, like an Impressionist squeezing paint straight from the tube on to the canvas, was something he would use during the *Witchfinder* shoot too: 'Mike used to walk about with a viewfinder and a blood squirter; he'd just come up and squirt it over you. He had it with him all the time ... He'd also come at you with scissors and cut your clothes so that there were proper bullet holes in them.'[41]

Tenser's need for some marketable contemporaneity, Karloff's requested script changes, and Mike's tendency to map his own personality on to the incidentals of his films meant that the screenplay, although technically finished, remained something of a work in progress. Mike was immersed in pre-production, scouting for locations, and was not particularly interested in the Karloff idea of 'redemption' anyhow, and so asked John to implement Karloff's requests in late November – could bouts of bad consciousness be put in, could the telepathy be reconfigured as a potential 'benefit to mankind' rather than just a device of heightened voyeurism, could Mesmer save the day?

> Mike rang me to tell me about this, and asked for a short rewrite to accommodate Karloff's wishes, which he was entitled to do before I was paid the final small portion of my fee. I didn't much care for this distortion of the original, and as I was very busy at the time collaborating with Bill Fairchild on a TV series, I suggested he should adjust the scenes himself and I would waive my final instalment. He rang a little while later to say that he had done this, but I would still get top credit.

Mike had brought Tom Baker in to make the alterations. This involved stripping down John's script, reordering some scenes, ejecting a third sorcerer and much of the character development (and a sequence seen from Roscoe's point of view, while under control, in which the tatty reality of a Soho knocking shop becomes wildly erotic), and a substantial car chase, which ends the film, was inserted, along with the actual streets for most of the location shots. The title was now *The Sorcerers*. For Karloff, the relatively straightforward evil-minded grotesque went and in its place came the battle of wills between (as he was now called) Professor Marcus Monserrat and his wife Estelle, and his former profession upped to a 'medical hypnotist'. He was now more akin to a fallen cousin of Professor Bernard Quatermass. After this process, Tom got a generously large credit for his work, and John was disappointed to find that he had been unfairly reduced to the status of 'mere supplier of an idea', despite the promise of top credit.

Whereas in John's script the Monserrats had just utilised telepathy and a series of potions to gain control of Roscoe, the redrafting wedged in a scene of psychedelic brainwashing to meet Tenser's request for flashy footage. John's script had originally left space for new trends, but patterned the telepathy on Mike's addiction to the daily potions that the sorcerers give him. This addiction would have suggested drug use to Mike and Tom and, by the time the film was in production, the logical step was to link this reading with the emergent dope and LSD-fuelled scene; in the small space between John's original script (outline 1965; script mid-1966) and the production (early 1967), everything had changed. It is no surprise that, riffing off the changing times, the brainwashing sequence came to parallel the experiences of the emerging underground London scene, and recontextualises the film accordingly. Mike's nocturnal explorations were paying off – a liquid light show, coupled with what John later referred to as the 'tinpot B-movie gadgetry' was introduced; Mike had stumbled across the Pink Floyd and the Spontaneous Underground, that occurred in the Marquee Club in Soho on dates throughout 1966. The Soho underground was both pornographic and psychedelic.

The Pink Floyd had emerged at the point when acid eclipsed hashish as the drug of choice, at the turn of 1966, and provided the soundtrack to the new consciousness, then concentrated specifically in Mike's London stomping grounds. By the end of 1966, with a gig in the Roundhouse and a stay at the Tottenham Court Road UFO Club (both 'Unidentified Flying Object' and 'Underground Freak-Out'), the Pink Floyd were an obligatory event, finding themselves forging their own mythology, culminating in the 14 Hour Technicolour Dream in Alexandra Palace in April 1967. LSD fired the cutting-edge music/media events which had to be experienced, *Astronomy Domine* and the 'Blob Show', 'the Giant Mystery Happening', or the Sensual Laboratory at the UFO Club in collaboration with The Soft Machine.

Mike's fascination with the evolving scene would have been amply rewarded. In the jam-packed basement, a sweltering art school and hippie crowd, kitted out in the boutique fashions of Granny Takes A Trip, would get stoned or drop acid and give themselves up to the spooky sounds of the psychedelic space jams, turning their minds over to the hypnotic strobes and liquid wheel light shows. The music did not interest Mike as much as the sonics and the event itself – something which Michael Horovitz referred to as 'the new solar sound-systems of beat caverns, pop charts, and psychedelic "trips"'.[42] Despite the psychedelic pretensions to visualise an under-the-influence 'experience', the events were, as Kubrick, Siegel, Michelangelo Antonioni, Peter Whitehead and others also noted, eminently cinematic. Allowing psychedelia to infiltrate *The Sorcerers*, particularly after opening club scenes that grate with their unhipness, would lend an authenticity to the world of the film, would dally with the subversive in a way that few horror films could have accommodated before:

> Psychedelia depended primarily on visual disturbances, anamorphoses and what could be called the perspectives of narcosis. The debt to a certain satanic English Romanticism of the early nineteenth century, evident in contemporary dandyism and revivals of the occult, could entail a condition which de Quinc[e]y had recognized, in visual experience: 'Space swelled and was amplified' [in *Confessions of an English Opium Eater*].[43]

Casting the psychedelic experience as the telepathy-brainwashing element in the film aligned the film to the subjective sensibility of the psychedelic happening, only months after the scene first emerged (it was so close that Mike had to explain to the film's editor what 'psychedelia' was). *The Sorcerers* does not grind to a halt before the surface of the London scene, diligently recording the fashions, the sounds and the locations of choice, as so many films were to, but works the sensibility into the film so as to attempt to penetrate the scene and gauge what lies behind. Mike squirts psychedelia over the film at close range, much as he had done with the Kensington gore. In this respect, and in terms of Roscoe's hidden psychopathic identity, the population of *The Sorcerers* is not unlike that of the invite for a Pink Floyd gig at the Spontaneous Underground in February 1966: 'Who will be there? Poets, pop singers, hoods, Americans, homosexuals (because they make up 10 per cent of the population), 20 clowns, jazz musicians, one murderer, sculptors, politicians and some girls who defy description, are among those invited.'[44]

In the pseudo-religious ceremony that the Floyd's Syd Barrett presided over, all the activity merged into one oceanic pulse – black mass and psychedelic be-in, the new sound and the new consciousness: the happening. This is what Mike needed to recreate. He located Joe Gannon, then taking his light show from club to club. Gannon had worked with the Floyd in the early days of the Spontaneous Underground and had been the driving force behind the use of film, projected on to the wall behind the band, to supplement the coloured slides. Much of his equipment was plucked from the rubbish tips of closing West End theatre shows, rewired and set up on his rig. Mike arranged for Joe to bring his equipment into a studio in Barnes to shoot the sequence. This was to be horror with no worrying about stage blood, costumes, skewerings ... this time it could be music, lights, zooming, wires, dials, and Karloff as Syd Barrett, or like some demented DJ, would preside over the psychedelic chaos; 1960s meets 1930s, the swinging mad scientist, the swelling and amplification of space. There is a kind of logic to it; for the Beatles and their 'Turn off your mind, relax and float downstream' Karloff offers 'Relax, clear your mind, empty your mind of all thoughts' as he starts up the psyche-delic brainwashing machine, its sound mimicking the Pink Floyd wall of sound of prolonged UFO jams.

Mike expressed a keen awareness of this contemporaneity, even acknowledging the limitations of an immersion in such a close reality, via Austen, in *Films and Filming*, where *The Sorcerers* was described as 'The film's surface appearance will date quickly, for it is so securely anchored at this particular crossroads of space and time. But anyone in the future seeking an accurate reference to the quintessence and mores of the "now" generation will find it here far more so that in some other recent films ostensibly con-cerned with this.'[45] Mike even puts a reminder *in* the film of the distance between it and that which had previously passed as youth films; in Nicole's flat, Cliff Richard's *In the Country* warbles from a Dansette record player. But memories of *The Young Ones* and *Summer Holiday* are soon banished once Roscoe beds her.[46] She pulls Roscoe down on top of her, into the foreground, as the camera pans down; a dissolve later and she's found in a pose of studied post-coital nonchalance, much like Steele. It would seem that Mike was even honing his film director's eye in the bedroom.

In *The Sorcerers*, psychedelia is contextualised in terms of the darker currents in underground culture and its antecedents. Professor Monserrat's quasi-scientific interest in hypnosis, the seance-like table across which the Monserrats exert psychic con-trol of Roscoe, and his wife's witch-like qualities, denote the way in which 'witchcraft ... [had] become an eccentric adjunct to sixties pop culture'.[47] Mike is a believer in the psychedelic ethos, and so warns against it from that vantage point – he is a summer of love heretic rather than atheist. This rejection of the fledgling philosophy of swinging London places *The Sorcerers* a considerable distance from those films gearing up to exploit the myth or revelling in it, as Austen would note in the review. For Mike, the set of *Performance*, for example, with its art school bohemians, high pretensions (an unchecked exploration of 'the transforming quality of hallucinogenics on the collective consciousness ...'[48]) and Cecil Beaton snapping away, would have been of little interest. The psychedelic sequences in *The Sorcerers* still indicate the ways in which the liquid light shows were 'attempted analogues for narcotic experiences ...'[49] but here, rather than opening up the mind, they work to shut it down – control rather than freedom, blackouts rather than hallucinations; a trap, not a trip. The brainwashing also pushes the film into science fiction territory, with the same 'it could be happening now' vision of the future that Siegel offered in *Invasion of the Body Snatchers*. As British science fiction, *The Sorcerers* is also vastly at odds with the general trends, as outlined by Hunter.[50]

Consciously or otherwise, the film rebuts the notion, then in the air, of the dawning of a new, cosmic consciousness and the recommended 'giving in to strange forces' – seeing in the age of Aquarius not the summer of love, but the civil unrest of 1968, Altamont, the Manson murders and the shattering of the mantras of peace, love and harmony. Mike would engage again with this theme in *Witchfinder*, fashioning an equally circumnavigational reaction to the times.

In person, Mike only expressed distaste for the hippies, their drugs and happenings – they represented a degree of liberation that Mike perceived to be self-centredness disguised as revolutionism. Tom recalls 'Mike and I had a long recurring argument about selfishness. He maintained that all human action was at base selfish. I held that altruism was possible. I think I came of my opinion as much from hope as experience. But I could never shift him from his position. It wasn't something that depressed him. It was just something he could see, he would say, even if others were not prepared to face it.' Mike would have felt a measure of distance from the UFO crowd, through this and through his reticence about acid use and entering into the spirit of such an event; 'open yourself up' for someone slightly intense and depressive would have sounded more like bad advice – Mike's karma was in short supply at the best of times. He had sufficient cynicism to see through the revolutionary posturing, but the experience could not have made anything other than a substantial impact, and demanded some kind of response. This was, after all, his generation, even if Mike preferred American music (of course),[51] did not wear the gear, and was a confirmed puritan about any drug use. For Mike, all the talk of changing the world was slightly ridiculous, paisley power just another fad, 'legalise pot' neither here nor there. More to the point, as the hippies got stoned, the war in South East Asia intensified, unimpeded by the 'professed apolitical stance of the average flower child'.[52] Mike would attempt to grasp this contradiction in psychological rather that ideological terms, attempt to understand and pin down a collective mindset. It was easy to see who constituted the psychedelic underground, and why, from the vantage point of Yeoman's Row, but to understand the dovetailing of two seemingly mutually contradictory narratives in early 1967 (peace, love and harmony, and better dead than red) was a pressing, more engaged task. This interest in the place of violence in society had informed Mike's attraction to film in the first place, was evident in *Intrusion*, and would now be readdressed. To draw such a film from the London scene was to find the murder in the psychedelia, and the psychedelia in the murder. Such connections were tentatively being made in other areas, with Internationalism as the bridge that connected the war zone to the peace zone, and this sensibility would flourish in 1968. But Internationalism, even in the unification of dissent against imperialist slaughter, functioned to locate the problems outside the collective consciousness – they remained something 'over there'. Mike would attempt to draw the problem into the heart of the London scene.

Monserrat's experiments are presented as both operating and experiencing a psychedelic light show, and Roscoe is complicit in his own reconfiguring. The sequence reproduces the ambiguity that Mike experienced in the UFO Club; Roscoe's underground freak-out controlled by Monserrat's white-interior Unidentified Flying Object-like lab, referred to as 'The Psychedelic Room' in the final shooting script:

59. ON MIKE VERY CLOSE

As the beam hits him. The lights moving over his face now are a constantly shifting hallucination. The sound, reverberating through the headphones into his eardrums, is a shattering mixture of discords that modulate terrifying into one another without ceasing – and all the time getting stronger and more piercing.[53]

Here, LSD and film are both reduced to their common denominator: false experience for those hungry for experience. And Roscoe, who cuts a dapper figure in the new London in a variety of turtlenecks, his time his own, women there for the taking, the nightclub offering a vista of possible pleasures, becomes a victim of the psychedelic body snatchers. Despite the proofs of freedom all around him, his mind is no longer his own.

John was horrified when he saw these unwieldy sci-fi happenings wedged into his polished script in favour of other, more important parts, now missing – mostly the development of the dramatic trajectory whereby the Monserrats become addicted to the compulsion to experience more and more, and the 'gradually cumulative menace, which Mike vulgarises over and over again'. It was apparent in the 'brilliance of the direction and editing' that the film could have been restrained and made for a complete realisation of the script and its central concept, but it would seem that Mike had seen, in John's script, something that was not there to begin with, and had run with that impulse during production. *Terror for Kicks* had been 'used ... as a vehicle for a sequence of gimmicks – some quite brilliant, apart from his Schoolboy's Own Electricity Kit'. The revised script, done by Mike and Tom, was indulgent and lacked John's polish and precision, but represented a challenge, the kind of thing Mike could rise to and use to explore spur-of-the-moment ideas, rather than John's script, which represented a good film that would simply need to be well made.

The rapidity with which the film moved into production caused immediate problems. The crew lacked sufficient experience to work under the limitations of such a low budget (so small as to be unrealistic from the outset) in a high-pressure environment. Yet Mike would make no concessions in terms of how scenes were to be shot, and he planned an impossible shooting schedule to give the film the kind of scope he wanted; 'endless locations were drawn up' all over London, lengthy night shoots planned, weeks' worth of set-ups crammed into days. Even shuttling the crew from one location to another could not be done in the time Mike had allotted for it. Perhaps because of the easy-going nature of the Maslansky films, where hard slog and collective long days were all that was needed to overcome production shortcomings, Mike remained unaware of the factory-line nature of exploitation film shoots. It was a naivety that was crippling and for Long, who had ample experience, Mike was 'a very inexperienced director, out of his depth'. This was apparent in his lack of understanding of the technical aspects of film-making (although working in such circumstances would have been a baptism in fire for even the most able), which soon rendered Mike highly insecure on the set and unable to see that his expectations and demands for perfection were going to be the film's undoing. All of Long's practical suggestions – handheld shots rather than dollies, conversations in one shot rather than reverse angle shots – were unequivocally rejected as compromises Mike was unwilling to take. It became Mike's defining characteristic as the director: 'Mike Reeves was a person who would not compromise.' This extended to the cast as well; while shooting Karloff crawling across the floor, then lifting himself up to look directly into the camera (for the sequence in which he looks impotently on as Estelle smashes up the laboratory equipment with his walking stick – 'I'll stop you if it's the last thing I do'), Mike demanded one take too many. The ancient actor crawled across the floor as required for the umpteenth time, looked into the camera and asked 'How much fucking longer?'.[54]

Long could see that Tenser believed in Mike's abilities, but the situation had conspired to place Mike in an impossible position. And Mike, who felt he had made every compromise in order to get the film made in the first place, and had hatched the plan long before Tenser and crew were invited onboard, found that the film that he had set out to make was now deemed to be a film that could not be made. One week into the projected four-week (maximum) shoot, an emergency meeting was called in the Park Lane Hilton for Tenser, Patrick Curtis, Mike and Long. Mike's schedule for the following week was impossible – a 'totally ridiculous task' – and could not be implemented; not even Long, a highly proficient lighting cameraman used to working at speed, could work *that* fast. At best, the film would fall behind schedule and go massively overbudget; at worse, the film would not be completed at all. Mike, still unable to accept possible compromise, objected to the suggestion of scaling back the production; since it was necessary to get the key scenes in the can, why not just shoot them outdoors as he intended to? Why use any old alleyway for the nightclub murder when he had found an ideal one elsewhere? Long, unhappy to find himself cast in opposition to the idealists on the set, pointed out the insurmountable technical problems with Mike's unrealistic schedules in relation to the budget and the size of the crew. His expectations were way out of kilter; there were only so many hours of darkness each night; forty set-ups in six locations across two nights was impossible. Mike, initially insecure and upset, was now in tears. Tenser was very fond of Mike and rather paternal toward him, and Mike found that he was able to handle Tenser and respected him. For Tenser, Mike was quiet and unassuming – 'the last word in a dictionary that he would understand was "ego"'.[55] So the film would be made; a new schedule was drawn up for a much truncated version of the film as originally planned. This reduced the action in the final screenplay to less complicated sequences but also whittled down the wordiness of the Baker/Reeves rewrite, which contained an abundance of expositional dialogue. Long would assist in the implementation and Tenser, who had been known to truncate film productions by tearing random pages from their shooting scripts, was firm in his backing of Mike's revised vision.

However, not even this scaling back salvaged the film's production from the fundamental budgetary problems, resulting in a film costing twice as much as originally planned, mostly because of a vast shooting ratio. Despite Mike's stylistic perfectionism, in terms of its aesthetic, the film looks like its budget – particularly the interiors (other than those in the Monserrat flat), which are often blasted with unsympathetic light. Many critics expressed dismay at the execution when seeking out and viewing *The Sorcerers* after first seeing *Witchfinder* (for Wood, *The Sorcerers* is 'at once the finest of his films in conception and the worse in execution'[56]). The night location shots work well though; uncluttered, neon against the inky, starless sky, and a selection of dank back alleys which provide Roscoe with an apt Jack the Ripper setting.

From the second week onwards, the shoot moved with extra speed. As with *Revenge of the Blood Beast*, Mike worked hard on those sequences that he knew could be outstanding, and gave way on the filler. The formal procedures of location work were the last thing on anyone's mind and so most non-studio sequences were made without any permissions whatsoever. Where permissions were applied for and denied (the Dolphin Square Hotel swimming pool, for example), bribes were freely used (£20 in this case, to a night guard). The opening scene (in the South Kensington nightclub, Blaises) was shot as rapidly as possible because of the cost of mini-skirted extras. Once the scene was ready, and the band playing (the short-lived R & B group Lee Grant and the Capitols, lip-synch-fronted by Mike's friend and sometime lodger, the actress Dani Sheridan), all hands were on deck, the crew snatching whatever glimpses of flesh they could (and you could guarantee that Long's crew would be doing so). Even Patrick found himself lying on the floor of the nightclub, filming upwards as the extras gyrated (until he caught sight of his wife's face looming into the camera viewfinder). Street shots were filmed from an old taxi that Tenser had bought for the shoot (and sold for a profit after it), while the chase sequences used Patrick's Rolls Royce Convertible, *sans* top. For the motorcycle scenes, shot without permission on the A4, Mike placed himself in the boot of the speeding car, beneath the camera, yelling directions to Ogilvy to 'come closer'. In was only a matter of time before the police caught up with the production – and fortunately this did not occur until the very end of the shoot. The scene was the final moment of the film; Roscoe perishes as his car crashes and bursts into flames. An old bomb site in Notting

Hill was located and the effects man told on the sly to pack as much petrol into the car's tank as possible, Mike noting that 'if 10 gallons are good, 50 will be even better'.[57] The car was ignited and the resultant explosion so big that it blew out house windows all around. In a scene anticipated on the railway tracks during Radley film-making days as Mike and friends scarpered on their bicycles, the entire crew, now temporarily without hearing, scrambled to pack up the equipment and clear out in the knowledge that police cars, ambulances and fire engines had already been dispatched. By the time they arrived, Mike had long gone, but those who been unable to get away found that their names were taken.

Tenser allotted little more than a week for post-production, a strategy for ensuring that his aspiring auteurs do not have the time to indulge in perfectionism. Mike oversaw the cutting with Ralph Sheldon, whom Patrick had called in after he had worked in Rome on the Welch film *The Biggest Bundle of Them All*. Time was so tight that Ralph and Mike had to cut reel by reel – sending individual reels away as they were done so that the negative could be cut and returned and work started on the dubbing, overseen by Ralph's assistant David Woodward. They were unable to see a fine cut right through. Ralph, nervous of what the finished product might therefore look like, was happy to leave for another commitment, handing over to Woodward, and to allow others to take the screen credit for the editing. When Tenser asked why, he replied 'You wouldn't expect Rembrandt to sign an unfinished piece.'[58] When the first cut was ready, a Wardour Street preview cinema was hired for the screening, with Tenser and Trevelyan present. From a running time of 90–95 minutes, Tenser asked for 10 to be cut (no reason was offered), and so beginnings and ends of scenes were trimmed – no sequences were removed entirely.

Stealing shots, location shooting and cutting loose from both the studio setting and the script made for the elements in the film that push against the more conventional aspects of *The Sorcerers*. The film seems a dialectical struggle between the thrills and freedoms drawn from Mike's guerrilla film-making, and the excellence of the realisation of the conventional trajectory of the script, each element periodically threatening to overwhelm the other.

The film's resultant freshness and ability to surprise, in spite of the datedness of so many of the settings, can be attributed to this, and the continual juxtapositioning of the two narratives through the intercutting (most dramatic in terms of the sound), keeps the film on edge. The only scenes that drag are those in the basement nightclub; bad dancing, groping extras (sexless in that way unique to British cinema), 'clever' repartee. Unfortunately, the nightclub becomes the regular meeting place for the protagonists, just as the film regroups itself by retreating back there too on several occasions. Roscoe's friends, Alan (Henry) and Nicole (Ercy), also inhabit this milieu and are equally uninteresting – she two-dimensional, little more than a model peeled off the pages of the *Nova* magazine that Roscoe leafs through in her flat, and he kitted out in tweed jacket, seemingly and inexplicably like Dylan Thomas during his lost London years. Once Roscoe has taken off on his killing spree, the Monserrats in tow, and before the police procedural strain of the narrative kicks in, these two wander around commiserating with each other and continually represent little more than dead air.

The Monserrats are a latter-day Adam and Eve. He still broods over the yellowed clippings of a tabloid exposé that saw him hounded out of business many years before, and has the air of the persecuted Wilhelm Reich in exile, or a benign Aleister Crowley in his dying years. She has endured years of humble living in their dingy flat as a result. So the Garden of Eden that the telepathy machine represents offers a new beginning – a chance to relive youth, to sample the newfound freedoms of the 1960s. Despite their age, they are now no longer locked into the logic of Larkin's dour perspective on things in *Annus Mirabilis* and can plunge headlong into the world of pills, porn, sex and violence that the film constructs. Even Alan's garage foreman (Mike's regular stuntman Alf Joint, whom he had met during *The Long Ships*) feels that he has missed the boat in terms of the new, youth-orientated world, commenting 'wish I was your age' over Alan's plans to meet up with Nicole. However, this being 1967 BBFC rather than 1967 AD, the film cannot make good on such a promise; Estelle initially uses Roscoe as a personal shopper (whereas in John's version he heads straight for a prostitute) and they both enjoy the sensations of some innocent swimming. The obvious sensual kick – sex – only occurs when Roscoe is tuned out. But the violence is there; Estelle alternating between whimpering and commanding Roscoe on, their gestures mirrored and deftly cut together. The experience revitalises her – a caterpillar-to-butterfly performance, sparkling eyes greedy for further sensation. What goads her on? Female empowerment as she spars with her psychologically weaker husband?; material gain, initially (middle-class aspirations?), then drunkenness by the close of the film (middle-class comeuppance); a lust for those sensations denied to her generation, to be 'Someone young [like] all these children out on the streets at night, taking pills to keep themselves awake' – a return of the repressed?; original sin revisited, albeit with the genteel elderly replacing Golding's youths of *Lord of the Flies*? All these possible readings gather under the Reevesian preoccupation of the potential for man to find within the propensity for violence.

The temptation is to read the Monserrats as personifications of Roscoe's already-present psychotic tendencies, 'these moods of his' as Alan calls them, the 'bloody artistic temperament'; the Monserrats as the witches to Roscoe's Macbeth, capitalising on the existential angst that indicates a volatile and possibly violent character from the outset. Roscoe's behaviour under hypnosis is in keeping with his prior traits – ditching Nicole for no reason, antagonising Alan for little gain. Hutchings notes this,[59] and Sinclair configures his reading of the film around it, so that 'The interest is in the vivid demonstration of the Reeves thesis: how Ogilvy ... is pushed from ennui towards unmotivated acts of violence; how there is no redemption, no way of sidestepping fate.'[60] Pirie expands upon such a reading too: 'For the other characters, including Mike's girlfriend, the film is about psychopathy ... And on yet another level it could be regarded as a study of schizophrenia (the old couple are Mike's parents or superego "inside his head").'[61] This had also been present in John's screenplay; schizophrenia is mentioned as Mike's friends look at his corpse (after plunging into a fire on a building site), confessing that they cannot understand his behaviour, and Alan dismisses Mike's talk of others controlling him as 'phantoms of his imagination'.[62]

In terms of the film itself, however, the reverse seems truer in citing one of the narratives as a metaphoric subtext accounting for the other; the film tilts in the Monserrats' favour in terms of realism. They live alone in their lived-in flat, a setting worthy of any of the realist movements of British post-war film, while it is Roscoe alone who engages in fantastical experience sprees, coded in the manner of the tabloid imaginings of today's youth – pills and sex, nightclubs and hedonism, and the lack of moral shame that is the price of the recent onset of classlessness (and, classlessly, Roscoe even drops common inflections into an otherwise pristine accent). After all, the film pointedly strips Karloff of his make-up, grand entrances and star status – opening with the self-effacing Karloff as Karloff in ridiculously drab surroundings; Greene would have approved. Since the Monserrats anchor the film in the realm of realism, Roscoe is left as a better candidate for that of metaphor. This 'cipher' status is then thematically looped back into the film since, despite the ambiguity of a metaphor-as-characterisation, the film itself is constructed around Ogilvy's young protagonist. As the questions of Roscoe's role in the film (that is, the determining forces that make up the actual character) remain unanswered, something constantly voiced by Nicole and Alan, this 'metaphoric' ambiguity defaults to a thematic ambiguity, and the result is Roscoe's blankness and boredom, his 'blackouts', his unengagedness with the world around – he remains an uncertainly animated vessel for the desires of others. Even his vestiges of personality seem more drawn from ideas of who he thinks he should be rather than who he actually is. This then makes sense of his near-immediate willingness to follow Professor Monserrat back to his flat, even at the point when the talk of 'complete abandonment with no thought of remorse ... intoxication with no hangover, ecstasy with no consequence' seems entirely concerned with the liberalisations of the 1967 Sexual Offences Act – *despite* Roscoe's sexism and machismo, here indications of an aggressive heterosexuality. In this way, Roscoe is both a blank canvas and the centre of the world of the film by dint of his freedom, youth and attractiveness, and the way that the characters, and the camera, choose to follow him. The character comes to resonate with a sense of Mike's gut-reaction critique of the generation who too willingly embrace a code of the annihilation of the self, as also manifest in the hippie philosophy, buying into the 'multicoloured miracles' and 'dazzling, indescribable experiences' without a second thought, shirking a responsibility to take control of their own destinies (an idea dramatised in the film with Roscoe's literal loss of physical and mental control). He is both everyman and, in the manner of Eliot, hollow man.

The cutting together of the Roscoe and Monserrat narratives recalls a similar parallel in *Revenge of the Blood Beast*. Mike cuts between Vardella (as she attacks Van Helsing) and the innkeeper watching television, both grotesque and laughing hideously, the juxtaposition suggesting an association between the characters of the she-beast and the innkeeper. She attacks Van Helsing and he will shortly attempt rape. It is another form of possession, the 'dark side' in ascendence – akin to the idea of Vardella as the flip-side of Veronica. Like a variation on the original ending for *Blood Beast*, now back in London, Roscoe turns into a monster, dragging the singer Laura (Sheridan) out of the nightclub, down a dark alleyway, and strangling her, and slaughtering Audrey. As Estelle gains the upper hand in the telepathic battle between the Monserrats, a new parallel for Roscoe emerges; both he and Marcus lose autonomy and are reduced to puppets of Estelle's will. The precedents then become apparent; they both feel cut off from the world around them, share the same restlessness and so pace the streets at night, they both reside in similar environments – Roscoe's antiques shop packed with the same dusty bric-a-brac as the Monserrats' flat – and, iconically, both are stars in the Mike Reeves horror firmament. It is from this vantage point that Marcus realises that he must utilise his understanding of this parallel to defeat Estelle; he notices the stigmata facet of the tele-pathic communication, the cuts on the Monserrats' hands, shared with Roscoe – and that therefore physical sensations can be physically manifest too in a reciprocal telepathic connection. Roscoe's 'awakening' seconds before his death, as Marcus exerts his mental control, and then Roscoe's final scream as the car crashes (expressions of his last-minute regaining of his ability to act independently) denotes a small measure of cooperation in the 'ultimate sacrifice' death pact he strikes with Marcus to destroy the common enemy.

There is little question that the real monster in this film is woman, now given the power to act independently, outside the historically assigned roles; the Eve who first tempts with illicit delights and then destroys essentially decent males. Hutchings assembles a reading of the film along such lines, typical of analyses of horror films; 'one can place alongside these representations of a troubled heterosexual masculinity the presence of several independent women'[63] and that 'it is the prospect of a woman actively desiring rather than being the desired object that it [the film] finds alternatively so appalling and so enthralling ...'.[64] In this way, the destructive force in the film is the return or revenge of a primal femininity, a she-beast, where female autonomy is codified in sexual terms and gestures (Hutchings notes the reference to the contraceptive pill in relation to generically liberated French girl Nicole and a telling cut to barren Estelle in the context of this allusion to potential reproductive capacity[65]) – sexually wanton, or just wanton in terms of destruction (the '*King Kong* syndrome'). When Estelle fails to find any connection to the female victims of Roscoe's rampages, this 'depoliticises'[66] the film along the lines of such a gender reading. Thus, the notion of a monstrous female is demonstrable in terms of the unconscious constructions and prejudices of the film, making the film another apt candidate for 'the standard critique of horror as straightforward sadistic misogyny'.[67]

The conscious 'meaning' of the film, on the other hand, is one that so blatantly suggests itself that all subsequent critics have taken up the invitation to elaborate on it: that the modus operandi of the sorcery is, in fact, little more than the heightened experience of cinema itself. Pirie, for example, concludes that 'the last shot of The Sorcerers is logically the burning of the cinema where the film is being shown'.[68] It is a reading that originates with Mike himself (via Austen in the *Films and Filming* review):

> The real weight comes from the extent to which [the telepathy] is analogous to cinematic sublimation ... They entice a young man to

be their guinea-pig, explaining that he will be mesmerised 'with the aid of light and the use of sound' and that he will be able to feel 'intoxication without a hangover, and ecstasy with no consequence.' That sounds awfully like the cinema, and the questions that the film triggers off about vicarious experiences soon trap one in a mirror maze of identification.[69]

These questions, as noted by Wood,[70] are ones that imply that the film audience is guilty by proxy – cheering on the destruction from the safety of their seats, which may be film-fantasy destruction, but supposedly taps into that real hidden reserve of 'perverted and sadistic desires' that is personified in Estelle. All drafts of the screenplay call for 'subliminal' shots of Estelle beckoning Roscoe on, aligning her desires with the effect that such shots would mimic. In this respect, the film is almost a dramatisation of BBFC policy towards the dangers of horror, '... stimulating to certain mentally unbalanced people'. However, mapping the invited reading on to the unconscious one produces a provocative synthesis: that cinema itself is a feminine-like entity since it entices with the promise of illicit thrills, and – in another stereotypical female behavioural trait – then refuses to let go, dragging everything down towards destruction. The addictive and terminal vicarious identifications suggests that the danger is not that of (as advertised) 'no consequence' but quite the reverse – one of true 'vicarious experiences'; the experience of gaining secondary pleasure by primarily pleasuring a loved female. Certainly, much of the texture of the interactions of film work in this fashion; Roscoe keeps Estelle on the point of orgasm-like quivering and whimpering for a fair part of the film's duration. The final crash is an orgasmic release, the climax of the vicarious thrill-seeking, the severing of the connection and a shared *petite mort* for all those concerned, and the film itself ('The End'). Thus the fear of women as intrinsically destructive is displaced on to an ambiguous view of cinephilia; cinema first entices with a promise of quick satisfaction, and then reveals itself to be a true object of love once the spell has been cast – and the consequences will follow in the void of a loss of control for those who step in. In this respect, cinephilia seems as suspect as the psychedelia that the film rounds on; both are false gods since both dupe reality, opiates that render 'space swelled and ... amplified' and false, that deny a perspective on the real world.

In ways already noted, the film invites a biographical reading too. For Mike to situate film itself as the heart of *The Sorcerers*, just as film was the centre of his world and the thing that defined him, and then to track the destruction and chaos that follows, seems to express a fear of the completeness of his own identification with film. He seems to cite himself inadvertently as also open to the dangers that he sees in those, less exacting, who follow the hippie philosophies. Mike's doom-laden alter-ego is, and not for the last time, psychically destroyed by the close of this process. Mike had placed himself in *The Sorcerers* and allowed the film to access himself. Like a dream recounted for the purpose of psycho-analysis, the film had found and expressed things that Mike himself had not yet realised or articulated; the film had controlled and lived vicariously through him, drawing on his experiences to make it real, determining his emotions and actions, as would the next film, as would the lack of film-making, and in this void, Mike feared that a price would be exacted. There was no going back. The only defence would be to sever the childhood connection between Mike and film, to leave behind the juvenile realm and weaken the sorcery of film over him, to move into the next period of film-making where Mike may still get his fingers burnt, but not be totally engulfed by flames. Mike had recognised himself as an innocent, prone to a powerful form of sorcery.

Boris was overjoyed when *The Sorcerers* opened in the West End in June 1967. It was the first Karloff film to have done so in many years. To Tenser's delight, it was selected as the British entry for the Sixth International Festival of Science Fiction in Trieste, where it picked up the Golden Asteroid in June 1968; a Silver Asteroid went to Catherine Lacey (despite her strong dislike for the film and her part), and a specially created award went to Boris. It also took the Grand Prix at the San Sebastian Science Fiction Film Festival and picked up tidy notices in the US trade press, under Patrick's astute marketing. It was sold to Allied Artists and opened in the US in January 1968. In Germany, it opened as *Im Banne des Dr Monserrat* ('The Spell of Dr Monserrat' – shades of the venerable Drs Caligari and Mabuse), in Spain as *Los Brujos* (a direct translation), in Italy as *Il Killer di Satana* and in France as *La Créature Invisible* ('*L'Ultime Création de Boris Karloff*').

When some British reviewers failed to rave, Mike marshalled Austen to pen a polemical appreciation of *The Sorcerers* for the October 1967 edition of the middlebrow UK film magazine *Films and Filming*. It would also be a UK heads-up for the precocious emerging talent, then shooting *Witchfinder*. The piece sounds as if it was cooked up in Mike's front room, Mike's role changing from that of feeding Austen production facts to overseeing a part-defence of the film, part-press release for it:

> It makes me heartily sick to continually hear of complaints about the dearth of young talent in this country and the poor quality of British produced films (the few that there are nowadays) and then to witness the reception accorded this picture. To be fair, a handful of 'daily' reviewers highly commended it but the remaining majority of film journalists either ignored it or wrote it off in a brusque paragraph. The facts in the case of *The Sorcerers* are that it was made (a) by a young Englishman, 23-year-old Michael Reeves, and (b) produced by a new British company for the remarkably realistic budget (one of the few that there are nowadays) of £40,000. For these facts alone the film deserves sympathetic attention and constructive criticism. These remarks are in no way intended as special pleading, for this pictures needs no apologists.
>
> Michael Reeves, the director of *The Sorcerers*, is certainly no apprentice. His background includes time spent in Hollywood, assisting in the production of some well-known mini-epics, script-writing, and his own promising first feature ... I understand that the independently produced *Sorcerers* is getting bookings from both major circuits, which is an encouragement and, I hope, a spur to further films from smaller companies willing to give young talent a chance to prove itself.[71]

The review goes on to praise the performances and the construction of the film (especially the cross-cutting).

Curtis used the profits to develop further pictures, including Welch as a Mata Hari in *Mademoiselle Docteur*, and *The Devil's Discord* was dusted off and put back into development. But Tony Tenser had other, and immediate, plans for Mike.

Notes

1 J. Nuttall, 'seedy jeff', *The International Times* (13–26 March 1967) 2. Emphasis in the original.

2 A. Shaughnessy, *A Confession in Writing* (Cornwall, TABB House, 1997), p. 46.

3 Alfred Shaughnessy, interview with author, 2 April 2002. All subsequent remarks are taken from this source.

4 Patrick Curtis, interviewed by BOUM Productions, 1999. All subsequent remarks are taken from this source.

5 J. Burke, 'Terror for kicks' (unpublished outline, F. H. C. Productions Ltd, 1965).

6 John Burke, interviews with author across 2001–2. All subsequent remarks are taken from this source.

7 J. Burke, 'The devil's discord' (unpublished screenplay, 'original story and screenplay by John Burke'), pp. 32–3.

8 R. Polanski, *Roman* (London, Pan Books, 1985), p. 206.

9 D. McGillivray, *Doing Rude Things: The History of The British Sex Film, 1957–1981* (London, Sun Tavern Fields, 1992), p. 54.

10 Their careers are outlined in detail in 'The legends' in McGillivray, *Doing Rude Things*, pp. 27–49.

11 Tony Tenser, interview with author, 2 June 1999. All subsequent remarks are taken from this source.

12 McGillivray, *Doing Rude Things*, p. 51.

13 Tom Baker, interview with author, 1 November 1998. All subsequent remarks are taken from this source.

14 Richard Poore, interview with author, 2 November 2001. All subsequent remarks are taken from this source.

15 Shaughnessy, interview with author.

16 Gross, interview with author.

17 Ogilvy remains ambivalent about his former status as the Reeves alter-ego, but seems to have been subsequently persuaded.

18 M. Horovitz (ed.), *Children of Albion: Poetry of the 'Underground' in Britain* (London, Penguin, 1971), p. 371.

19 Curtis, interview with author.

20 The number given is that of Tenser's Wardour Street office.

21 J. Burke, 'Terror for kicks' (unpublished screenplay, 1966), shot 13, pp. 4–5.

22 Burke, 'Terror for kicks', shot 4, p. 1.

23 Burke, 'Terror for kicks', Shot 10, p. 2.

24 I. Sinclair, *Lights Out For The Territory: 9 Excursions in the Secret History of London* (London, Granta Books, 1997), p. 292.

25 J. Burke, M. Reeves and T. Baker, 'The sorcerers' (unpublished screenplay, Tony Tenser-Curtwel Productions Inc., Vardella Film Productions Ltd, 1967), shot 98, p. 41. All three authors are afforded equal screenplay credit.

26 A. Boot (ed.), *Fragments of Fear: An Illustrated History of British Horror Films* (London, Creation Books, 1996), p. 184.

27 J. Brosnan, *The Horror People* (London, Macdonald and Jane's, 1976) p. 55.

28 D. Parkinson (ed.), *Mornings in the Dark: The Graham Greene Film Reader* (London, Penguin Books, 1995), pp. 29, 403.

29 S. Swires, 'When the movies got tenser', *Fangoria* 128 (November 1993) 18.

30 Yet the recorded book value of the film is just under £54,000 (some sources have £52,000). The film went substantially overbudget, possibly to the tune of £15,000. Speculation on the nature of the remaining discrepancy is beyond the scope of this book.

31 Swires, 'When the movies got tenser', p. 18.

32 P. Underwood, *Horror Man: The Life of Boris Karloff* (London, Leslie Frewin Publishers Ltd, 1972), p. 1.

33 D. Bailey and P. Evans, *Goodbye Baby and Amen: A Saraband for the Sixties* (London, Condé Nast Publications Ltd, 1969), p. 127.

34 J. Trevelyan, *What the Censor Saw* (London, Michael Joseph, 1973), p. 122.

35 Letter from John Trevelyan to Michael Reeves, 3 January 1967. Held in the BBFC archives.

36 McGillivray, *Doing Rude Things*, p. 35.

37 Polanski, *Roman*, p. 210.

38 Stanley Long, interview with the author, 4 April 2002. All subsequent remarks are taken from this source.

39 McGillivray, *Doing Rude Things*, p. 37.

40 Burke, Reeves and Baker, 'The Sorcerers', shot 274, p. 90.

41 Nicky Henson, quoted in J. Rigby, *English Gothic: A Century of Horror Cinema* (London, Reynolds and Hearn, 2002), p. 148.

42 Horovitz, *Children of Albion*, p. 327.

43 D. A. Mellor and L. Gervereau (eds), *The Sixties: Britain and France, 1962–1973 – The Utopian Years* (London, Philip Wilson, 1997), p. 25

44 M. Watkinson and P. Anderson, *Crazy Diamond: Syd Barrett and the Dawn of Pink Floyd* (London, Omnibus Press, 2001), p. 40.

45 D. Austen, '*The Sorcerers*', *Films and Filming* (October 1967), 25–6.

46 Tom, Paul Ferris and Iain Sinclair would go on to prepare an unmade sci-fi script for the group the Shadows.

47 Lachman, *Turn off Your Mind*, p. 232.

48 Christopher Gibbs describing *Performance* in J. Savage, 'Turning into wonders', *Sight & Sound* (September 1995) 25.

49 Mellor and Gervereau, *The Sixties*, p. 21.

50 I. Q. Hunter (ed.), *British Science Fiction Cinema* (London and New York, Routledge, 1999), pp. 5–6.

51 During the *Witchfinder* post-production, mornings began with the ritual of Mike playing Otis Redding's *Sitting on the Dock of the Bay* on his portable record player; a moment of calm before the storm and assistance with the keeping of cool.

52 J. Green, *All Dressed Up: The Sixties and the Counterculture* (London, Pimlico, 1999), p. 180.

53 Burke, Reeves and Baker, 'The sorcerers', shot 59, p. 28. In this final draft, as Mike initially enters the room, he exclaims 'Strewth! Where d'you keep the Daleks then'.; Burke, Reeves and Baker, 'The sorcerers', shot 37, p. 23.

54 Long, interview with author.

55 Tony Tenser, interviewed by BOUM Productions, 1999.

56 Wood, 'In memoriam Michael Reeves', p. 5.

57 Curtis, BOUM interview.

58 Ralph Sheldon, interview with author, 2 July 2002. All subsequent remarks are taken from this source.

59 Hutchings, *Hammer and Beyond*, p. 140.

60 Sinclair, *Lights Out For the Territory*, p. 239.

61 Pirie, *Heritage of Horror*, p. 149.

62 Burke, 'Terror for kicks', shot 224, p. 92.

63 Hutchings, *Hammer and Beyond*, p. 142.

64 Hutchings, *Hammer and Beyond*, p. 143.

65 Hutchings, *Hammer and Beyond*, p. 143.

66 Hutchings, *Hammer and Beyond*, p. 144.

67 C. J. Clover, *Men, Women and Chainsaws: Gender in the Modern Horror Film* (London: British Film Institute, 1992), p. 19.

68 Pirie, *Heritage of Horror*, p. 150.

69 Austen, 'The Sorcerers', p. 25.

70 Wood, 'In memoriam Michael Reeves', p. 5.

71 Austen, 'The Sorcerers', pp. 25–6.

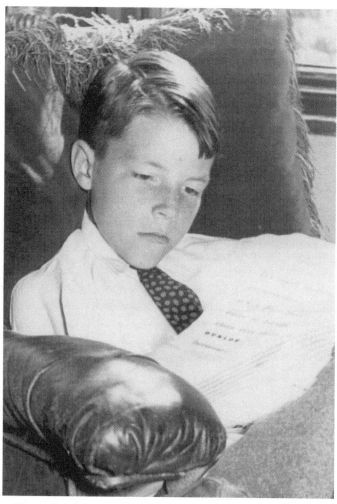

1 Mike reading about cars, early 1950s

2 The annual cruise, Mike with his mother, panama and 8mm camera

3 King's Mead School, Seaford. 'Such an atmosphere would allow Reeves (no longer "Mike") to reconfigure himself in the wake of his father's death'

4 King's Mead *Goonery*: Mike sports two watches for the 1956 King's Mead school photo

5 On the set of *The Sorcerers*: Boris Karloff (Professor Marcus Monserrat) and Mike. '[He] could now bow out on a note of humanity and redemption'

6 On location for *Witchfinder General*, 1967. 'Mike always knew where his camera was going to be, and how he was going to shoot everything …'

7 Improvising a tracking shot in the time-honoured manner

8 Mike prepares Ian Ogilvy (Richard Marshall) and other Roundheads for the boisterous campfire scene

9 Sandwich, cigarette and a chat with Rupert Davies (John Lowes)

10 Between set-ups: Hilary Dwyer (Sara), Rupert and Mike

11 Script consultation: Robert Russell (John Stearne), Mike and Vincent Price (Matthew Hopkins)

12 Preparing to shoot interiors in Lavenham

13 Tracking with the village mob for the pre-credit hanging. 'The sequence recalls the opening lynching of *Revenge of the Blood Beast*'

14 John Coquillon executes a handheld camera shot

15 Mike prepares the witch-drowning sequence. 'Flashes of a kind of violence more associated with the latter half of the twentieth century'

16 Mike and Vincent. 'Like married royals, barely able to conceal their loathing for each other…'

17 An encounter with Cromwell: producer Philip Waddilove stood in at the last minute as one of Cromwell's officers (third from the left), Mike (left) surveys the scene

18 Mike and stuntwoman and actress Gillian Aldam. 'He was gentle, he was understanding, and he got out of me everything he wanted'

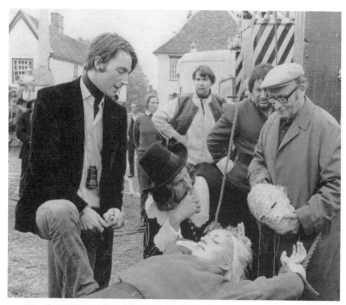

19 Mike (with Paul Maslansky's viewfinder), Vincent and Gillian. A props man holds Gillian's protective mask

20 Gillian is hoisted into position for the Lavenham witch-burning

21 Gillian is lowered into the pyre as Mike looks on from the cherry-picker. 'One-take wisdom informed this all-or-nothing approach...'

22 'Cut!' – and the pyre is rapidly extinguished

23 Recording the Paul Ferris score in Olympic Sound Studios, early 1968: Mike, Philip and Keith Grant

24 Portrait, early 1968

'This is England, Vincent'

5

> He rose himself to his full height, six foot three – with his clothing he looked even taller – and he looked down upon his small, young, boyish director, and said:
> 'Young man, I have made 34 films. How many have you made?'
> And he looked up and said:
> 'Two good ones.'
> Vincent Price laughed more than anybody else. (Tony Tenser)[1]

An associate of Tenser's, who worked for the publishing house Herbert Jenkins Ltd, had sent him the galley proofs of Ronald Bassett's 1966 paperback *Witchfinder General*. Tenser liked the title and bought the film rights on impulse.[2] The book was tedious low-brow popular history but the potential for some English Civil War gore was not lost on Tenser – '[it] had some scope, had some breadth to it; there was a canvas for a film'.[3] Mike wrote an outline, Tenser approved and requested a full film script while he pieced together the funding; at £100,000 this was to be the biggest production for Tigon yet. Optimistic, Tenser set Mike to work at great speed, and Mike drafted Tom in. The overriding factor was to go into production by September to avoid weather problems.

Matthew Hopkins, the historical Witchfinder General, was a psychotic murderer whose sadism was institutionalised and lent a divine justification during the English Civil War. For Mike and Tom, Donald Pleasence was the actor to portray him. Pleasence's face was so open and his eyes so wide that he could only be up to no good, and an extraordinary capacity for stillness communicated a searing sincerity to his performances. His turn as William Hare, procurer of fresh corpses for Peter Cushing in *The Flesh and the Fiends* in 1959 began to remould his screen image, away from the mild-mannered everyman, and his startling transvestite break-down in Polanski's *Cul-de-Sac* proved a willingness to embrace experimentation (as did his role in the original production of Pinter's *The Caretaker*) – and to take direction. For Mike and Tom, Pleasence's Hopkins was to be part ridiculous authority figure (perhaps in the manner of the hapless Hitler of Chaplin's *The Great Dictator*; perhaps drawing on Pleasence's own experiences when interned in a POW camp in 1944–45) and part Franken-stein's monster; humanity eclipsed. This Matthew Hopkins was to be ineffective and inadequate, bitter and ugly; a scene was en-visaged in which he would attempt to mount his horse only to fall straight off, to the amusement of onlooking villagers. Pleasence's period 'acting up' was all a defensive surface of twitches and mugging, ideal for such a portrait, yet his almost abstract charac-terisations, shorn up by a sublime screen charisma, never unravel. Something about Pleasence in a film conveys intensity, and the joy of the surrender on the part of the audience to the make-believe on the screen – no matter how ludicrous the film, and no matter how at odds with such a nondescript figure. Pleasence accepted the role and Mike and Tom constructed their adaptation with him in mind from June 1967 onwards, building the film around the idea of Pleasence's screen persona. He was to have been the dead centre of the film, the eye of the storm. He was to have presided over the bloodbath of an England in upheaval, a vicious circle of violence, but perhaps only half-knowingly, distractedly, and then to be drawn inexorably in – another doomed Mike Roscoe, both complicit in and caught up by events beyond his ken. His Conradian hollowness would have hinted at notions of the illusory nature of fascism, tyranny, of the banality of evil – and of the texture of history.

With such ideas in place, the required script called more for outright invention than adaptation. Bassett's book, like much of populist 1960s British culture, was partly didactic, constructed to dramatise history for the young readership. As in the early *Dr Who* episodes of these years, there was perceived to be room for both thrills and hard facts in the suspect area of 'popular entertainment'; a Reithian impulse. The central contribution of Bassett was the title: *Witchfinder General* was something like *Ben-Hur* – a loud statement of intent for the film to follow. Mike and Tom extracted Bassett's principal characters and some sequences (such as the ending, for the first draft of the screenplay) but otherwise only looked to the general ideas, like that of a love story subplot, and then they themselves filled in the rest. Historicity was a concern, including research into details of the tortures then visited on suspects. Hopkins was, in fact, a lawyer, from Manningtree in Essex, as was his companion John Stearne. They both went on to publish accounts of their roles in the witch hunts; Hopkins's explanation of his actions and methods was in the form of answers to accusations later made against him – *The Discovery of Witches*.[4] The real John Lowes was the Vicar of Brandeston for nearly fifty years until 1646. His torture under Matthew Hopkins involved four days of sleep deprivation and being run around; he must have been close to 70 at the time. The moat at Framlingham was used to 'test' him, and he was hung with seventeen other 'witches' in Bury St Edmunds after a ceremony that involved him reading out his own burial service. In all, Hopkins and Stearne executed approximately 200 people. Hopkins died either from consumption or, as rumour at the time had it, after being lynched and interrogated himself by a makeshift rabble.

The first draft of the script seems to have been near-unfilmable by 1967 standards. We see the woman in the pre-credit lynching in death spasms at the end of the noose, the sniper's victim somersaulting through the air and slamming into a tree, Lowes is jabbed fifteen times with a steel spike, Hopkins is seen 'savagely' kissing Sara's 'well shaped' breasts (whereas Stearne later 'pushes his great bearded face down into her bosom'), Stearne pours beer down the cleavage of a wench, Hopkins and Sara are seemingly seen actually making love, he 'sweating obscenely', she revulsed (Richard later screams at Hopkins – 'Because *you* touched Sara! Made her a common whore!'), Stearne rapes Sara twice ('Come on, girl, you've had me once and you enjoyed it more than with your pal Matthew, I'll be bound'), a soldier's head is 'hacked off' during the Battle of Naseby, those tied up and dunked from the bridge are filmed drowning underwater and Stearne attempts to rape a gypsy girl (she digs her nails into his eyes, half blinding him). This occurs during the original ending, of which no trace appears in the actual film; Stearne falls in with some gypsies and is staked to death after the attempted rape. Margery (the original name for Ogilvy's Richard Marshall) arrives soon after and persuades them to help him ambush Hopkins, who is then mercilessly beaten by Margery as he makes *him* confess as to his ways. Margery half drowns him (thumbs tied to his feet) then hangs him (this ending is mostly from Bassett). Nor would these outright depictions of brutality overshadow any opportunities for suggested brutality; an opening scene was envisaged in which soldiers ride past a ditch without looking twice at the corpses rotting in it. The whole is wildly unrealistic, but a measure of the seriousness of the intent with which Mike and Tom wanted to present a savage, brutal, animalistic world. The way in which Sara, the one pure element, has intercourse repeatedly with Margery, Hopkins and Stearne is an indication of the assault visited on the innocent in this context. The catalogue of atrocities would be locked into a form akin to the western; an eminently cinematic sweep across the countryside. Of the intentions for the script, Tom recalls:

> from the start we wanted movement across the landscape and across the country to be a strong theme. I don't know if it works all that well. There are rather a lot of stops and starts. Hellos and goodbyes. It takes a lot of money to bring that kind of story telling to coherence on the screen. Looks pretty easy when a Sam Peckinpah group of horsemen mount up and head for the horizon. And convincing. On an English afternoon it can look different.

This underlying structure was realised to the degree that the marketing campaign for the film, centred on its supposed horror status, would prove to be a surprise to Mike. The collision of the elements of the western structure, the horror iconography and the biopic-like narrative, in an utterly outlandish rural England context, gives rise to a tension at the heart of the film, as with *The Sorcerers*. Just as the film was envisaged as attaining an element of the western, at the same time distance would be found from the iconographic significance of (in the event) Vincent Price as Hopkins. Price brought with him a sulphurous whiff of the grand horrors of the 1930s Universal variety, but films constructed around hammy leading men and a rattle-bag of voodoo dolls, creaking doors and the living dead, would not resonate in *Witchfinder General*. Mike and Tom would seek to banish as many elements of the horror genre as possible, capitalising on the way in which, as Pirie notes, the British horror in the mid–1960s offered both the chance for a film-maker to work 'within a tentative cultural tradition', and that the tradition itself 'had lost some of its original rigidity and was beginning to hunt for new talent and new ideas'.[5]

Tenser would have goaded the boys by telling them that Polanski and his writer dashed off the *Repulsion* script in seventeen days. As the script took shape, Mike persuaded Tenser to employ Philip Waddilove (then the co-owner of Locations TV and Films Ltd) to undertake a location hunt. Philip had first met Mike during the *Sorcerers* post-production and his wife, Susi Field, had known Mike since his days in Rome. Both would end up in the film: Philip as one of Cromwell's young officers (the intended bit-part actor had failed to show – Mike grabbed him and instructed him 'Into make-up!')[6] and Susi as one of the unfortunate women of Lavenham in the pigpen (when Mike's girlfriend, after a minor traffic accident, was unable to cameo). Philip had both military and media experience and would come to be the key figure in the production of the film. He recced East Anglia with the Bassett book and Reeves outline in hand and returned with a slew of photographs, nailing 95 per cent of the actual locations used. He then rapidly moved to hiring the crew, became the locations manager and, finally, producer.[7] Philip: 'I persuaded Tony and Michael that, to cut down costs, we wouldn't use a conventional studio but shoot the entire film on location in East Anglia. I rented three World War II aircraft hangers at a disused airfield outside Bury St Edmunds as "weather cover" ... This was the first time this was ever done in the industry – before the Beatles used an aircraft hangar as a studio on *Magical Mystery Tour*.' Then, while waiting for the money to fall into place, Philip and Susi retired to their villa on Spain's Costa del Sol for a vacation, only to be cabled in early August with the news that American International Pictures (AIP) were putting up half the total budget and the film was now in pre-production. 'Michael met Susi and I immediately upon our return and I said to Michael: "Who is actually producing the movie?" Michael replied: "You are!" So, Tony Tenser gave me an office at Tigon and told me to "get on with it."'

For their half of the budget, AIP would call the shots for *Witchfinder*. They needed a star, not Pleasence, and their own Vincent Price was made a condition of the deal. For AIP, Tigon was an ideal company – a stepping stone that could be used to help them continue their breaking into British film production. By 1970, AIP had dropped Tigon but kept a fair few members of the regular casts and crew to make their own British productions, such as the period horror *Cry of the Banshee* (a flat remake, of sorts, of *Witchfinder*, again with Price) and *Wuthering Heights*. Louis M. 'Deke' Heyward was AIP's newly appointed director of overseas productions, and had set up his stall in the AIP London office just months before, in June 1967. *Witchfinder* was an ideal project in all respects. Deke's take on things was very straightforward: '[Reeves] had a script called *Witchfinder General*, which was in some sort of condition but not completely correct; and he had some good locations scouted. What he *didn't* have was the full amount of money for total production, and he didn't have a star. We had a contract with Vincent Price, so what we did was make a trade: We gave 'em Vincent Price and a few dollars, and in exchange we got western hemisphere distribution rights.'[8] By AIP's 1967 standards, a £100,000 film was nothing much, little more than a tax write-off. AIP's half, paid by Sam Arkoff, covered Price's expenses and fee (announced as £30,000, but in fact £12,000) and left £20,000 cash for production costs. For this, AIP took American (North, Central and South), Canadian, Japanese and Philippines rights. Philip Waddilove was pressured into contributing £5,000 to the Tigon half (to secure his associate producer credit, under the guidelines of the Association of Cinematography, Television and Allied Technicians; but, under his profit share, was reimbursed during the first twelve months of the film's release) and when the film went slightly overbudget, Tenser had been happy to cover the expenses and not exercise his contractual right to request half the excess from Arkoff. To ensure that the film sat easily in the AIP fold, it was to be retitled for the US release as another film in their Edgar Allan Poe cycle (and as a useful way of exercising their copyright on Poe's poems). The cycle had nearly run its course by this point and so if one more could be quickly dashed off before everything went to biker films, blaxsploitation and flower children, so much the better.[9] With Poe and Price, this was to be another of those films that McGee refers to as the 'Heyward-Price pictures' in his study of AIP.[10] Arkoff:

> By this time Jim Nicholson and I were fairly expert on Poe, so we looked at the poems and found one called *Conqueror Worm*, which fit pretty well in a way – although I guess a title like that could've fit a hell of lot of things [laughs]![11]

> We weren't actually sure what it meant, but it was pure Poe and seemed to fit with *The Witchfinder General*'s storyline.[12]

Thus *Witchfinder General*, as *The Conqueror Worm* or even Edgar Allan Poe's *The Conqueror Worm*, gained a prologue and epilogue for the US markets – Price reading the first and last stanzas of Poe's poem of the same name in voice-over, much to Mike's annoyance.[13]

From Mel and Chuck and the US releases of the Maslansky films, Mike was aware of the nature of AIP's operations. The authority of the name American International Pictures belied the nature of the product. AIP began as American Releasing Corporation (ARC) in the mid-1950s, making and distributing action pictures such as *The Fast and the Furious*. Corman first worked as a producer on *Monster from the Ocean Floor* in 1954 before directing his debut, *Five Guns West* in 1955. Corman was a maverick and a hustler who once shot a scriptless, feature-length B-picture over a weekend rather than waste the sets and the three contract days left after completing his previous film ahead of schedule. His contribution to American cinema is difficult to overestimate. ARC was founded and run by James H. Nicholson (the PR man, amicable, who would arrive on-set in a white car) and Samuel Z. 'No bullshit' Arkoff (who drove a black car and fired people). Aptly enough, Arkoff began his film career, and perhaps the company, via an association with the legendary Ed Wood.[14] Arkoff's business sensibility and legal background was the sure foundation of AIP's pioneering enterprise spirit; his motto – 'Everything in our whole American economy is exploitation!'.[15] Arkoff could reputedly stand between projection rooms and watch two films simultaneously, giving notes for each to get them up to AIP standards.

ARC became AIP in 1956 and marked the occasion with a double bill of releases: *The She-Creature* and *It Conquered the World.* The titles anticipate the US titles they slapped on Mike's films, *The She-Beast* and *The Conqueror Worm*. Pulpy armageddons and *mâché* monsters, threatening femininity and imminent attack and domination are the motifs of AIP's exploitation oeuvre. They worked the flea-pits (which they termed 'passion pits' – and worked hard to fan the flames; the Hays Office was alerted early and began firing off diktats about 'excessive' cleavage) and the drive-in market, their producers remained as undiscerning of their products as they assumed their youthful viewers were. The early films were often made on half the proposed *Witchfinder* budget and shot in ten days or less, then shipped straight out to the cinemas, frequently as double bills. The exhibitors were glad to take cheap AIP products over the high exhibition charges that were being levelled by the major studios.[16] Reruns of 1930s horrors on TV at this time in the *Shock Theater* series, which rapidly amassed a cult following, meant that the American horror film was suddenly a very viable product and AIP were in the prime position to pick up and dust off yesteryear's cast lists at bargain basement prices: Vincent Price, Basil Rathbone, Peter Lorre, Lon Chaney, Jr and Karloff were back with a vengeance. AIP's threadbare horrors became a staple ingredient in the pop culture diet of American youths in the 1950s and early 1960s – the kind of gothic wackiness so fondly remembered by Frank Zappa as colouring his West Coast childhood in the song 'Cheepnis'.

Price was delighted to be on the AIP payroll. He was a class act, his soft voice could seep into the bones and the bombast of his performance alone would flesh out the cheap sets in a suitably fun manner. He possessed a dignity and pride that would never allow him to seem ridiculous, even in the ridiculous circumstances of many of AIP's films. Prawer describes Price's performances for Corman as 'neurasthenia and a dandified sadism that are clearly *acted*, with occasional signals that seem to say: "don't be frightened, it's only me!".'[17] Deke Heyward recalls Vincent's telling reaction upon reading a particularly grinding piece of AIP-style dialogue: he joked 'Deke – dear, sweet Deke – you are screwing my career into the ground!'.[18]

Together, Price and Corman plundered the works of Poe for fodder for their lurid Technicolor classics such as *The Masque of the Red Death* and *The Tomb of Ligeria*. The films struck a chord (and the box office) and so, even in the case of non-Poe adaptations, an excuse would be found to place Poe's name prominently in the advertisements, usually as a quote from a poem – as in the case of the H. P. Lovecraft adaptation, *The Haunted Palace*.

Poe fell out of favour once AIP found themselves able to cash in on the upheavals in society in the late 1960s and the new-found permissiveness allowable in film. For AIP, 1960s liberalism was translated straight into sex, drugs, nuclear holocausts and violence: *The Trip, Wild in the Streets, Riot on Sunset Strip, Psych-Out* and *Gas-s-s-s ... or, It May Become Necessary to Destroy the World in Order to Save It*. To make these films, AIP accidentally assembled the architects of the New Hollywood: Martin Scorsese, Jack Nicholson, Bogdanovich, Brian de Palma, László Kovács, Dennis Hopper, John Milius, Francis Ford Coppola, Jonathan Demme, Monte Hellman and Peter Fonda. The Movie Brats, given the freedom to act as auteurs, found themselves reinventing American cinema in the wake of the inability of the major studios to understand and entertain their audiences. Heyward: 'At AIP, it was the same with directors as with actors. If you were a young director, AIP was giving you a chance; if you were an old director, your career was on its way down when we inherited you. You were usually afraid to fight because it would influence the next picture'.[19]

The exploitation boom crossed geographic boundaries too. When Bava's heady brew of sadism and eroticism, *Black Sunday*, outgrossed Corman's *The House of Usher*, Bava's star, Barbara Steele, was shipped over to the USA to star in Corman's next picture, *The Pit and the Pendulum*. European cinema was more exotic, baroque, decadent (a by-product of, as Gordon Hessler recalled, 'all the backlots that were full of wonderful sets that we could "steal" for our pictures, plus the very talented art directors and cameramen and the classical actors ...'),[20] and therein was a strong selling point; AIP took *La Dolce Vita* across the USA in 1965 as 'The Film That Shocked Liberal Europe'. Since European productions were cheaper, and were less prone to Union-related problems, AIP set up offices in Rome and London and located some 'facilitators' to get the films made. The US/UK exchange rate meant that UK-based productions were extremely agreeable; AIP relocated their London offices to Upper Grosvenor Street, close to the American Embassy. The location and offices themselves could not have been more prestigious. Visitors encountered a Georgian frontage and porticos and, once inside, candelabra in the front hall and a vast staircase. Unfortunately, all this was located in a building that was only to be used for living accommodation – strictly flats and apartments – and once a year inspectors would arrive to ensure just that. Prior to the inspection, a crack team of props men would be pulled from whatever AIP production was then up and running and would fit out the offices to look like private accommodation, taking out the desks and filing cabinets and putting in a four-poster bed, dressing the bathrooms with toiletries, and providing a 'lived-in' ambience. Arkoff once arrived from the USA, unaware of the need for the one-day transformation, to find that his own office was now a bedroom and no one was in. Once the inspection had occurred, the living quarters would be dismantled and returned back to AIP offices within hours.

Much of AIP's activity necessarily centred around the producer's-girlfriend school of casting, and the beauty of an AIP London base of operations was that it afforded the opportunities for the AIP brass to take wife-breaks in the guise of business trips, and also to go on gambling sprees (then illegal in LA). The AIP casting couch was (gossip had it) an actual bedroom above the London office. One of the very occasional times that Deke visited the *Witchfinder* set in Lavenham, for a half-day, was to oversee the filming of the main sex scene, before then disappearing off to the racing at Newmarket. (Deke arranged an 'Additional Scenes' credit – an entirely fictitious claim.)[21] 'My God, they entertained!' is the enduring impression of the American film people in London at this time.[22] It was a party that lasted until the early 1970s.

Deke was happy to deal with Tenser – they were both of the same mindset – and Deke was impressed with Tenser's 'discovery' of Polanski (describing Tenser to Vincent as having 'turned out a little picture that did all right, *Repulsion*'). Deke drafted a letter to Price to sell him the *Witchfinder* idea, embellishing freely:

> Dear Vince-Baby ... We work together again ... and I must confess, I think this will be the happiest experience we have had together so far ... [Reeves] is a young British talent, very much like Jeremy S[u]mmers [who had just directed Price in *House of a Thousand Dolls*], only far his superior as a picture maker and personality ... I believe you will find young Michael Reeves one of the most inspiring things that's happened to you as an actor in a long time. He is not only bright, imaginative, and well-organized, but he has the [*sic*] cujones to force a crew through to doing things the way he wants to ... He wafted off in a faerylike cloud of ecstasy when he heard we were casting you in the lead .... [23]

Despite the near-immediate start, Vincent was keen on the proposition. He had attended the University of London as a young man, spending his time immersed in the worlds of art and theatre; he was familiar with *le malaise anglais* in all its shades of grey. And, hoping for a quick tryst with a young public school type, found himself at Heathrow airport in mid-September. But it was Philip, not Mike, waiting to welcome him. Vincent was unabashed:

> My first site of Vincent was as he majestically descended the escalator into the arrivals lounge having arrived on the 'red-eye' special from LA. After I introduced myself to him and excused Michael's non-appearance, Vincent's first words to me were something along the lines of: 'Well, Mr Waddilove, take me to your goddamn young genius!'... As Vincent and I were being driven in

the limo' from Heathrow to Central London, I spent most of the drive continuing to explain away Mike's absence ('still busy working on the script').

After a 'brief but heated discussion with Mike', Philip, in his then capacity as associate producer, had reluctantly agreed to stand in for Mike at Heathrow. However, unknown to Philip, Mike's inexcusable absence was a deliberate snub, calculated to offend both Price and AIP. Mike had been told to drop Pleasence, and that *Witchfinder* would only be made with Price as Hopkins, no matter the relative merits of the actors; Price's name on the poster was needed by AIP. No Price would mean no film. Mike talked about walking off the picture to anyone who would listen ('I'm saddled with Vincent by American International!'[24]) but he soon agreed to accept Price, since it was sink or swim. Mike's reluctant acceptance of Price would manifest itself in other ways too during a difficult shoot. Mike's temperament was easily swayed and he would turn on his star, chastising him for being Vincent Price – all tics, eye-rolling and Grand Guignol; he wanted acting, not camping; the film needed a 'hard performance' not the kind of grandstanding Price usually passed off for AIP, where he seemed to both act the part and act out caricatured audience responses to the horrors. Price, the 'Merchant of Menace', had once observed: 'In horror films the odds are always heavily against me ... But then I'm always evil in a keen, clean way'.[25] Mike would have felt that this was what he was up against. Price would grow a beard, wear a hat and cloak – it was as if Mike was trying to blot out his presence on the screen. After all the work on the script, Mike felt railroaded, and in Price he saw AIP personified. He felt besieged – the only one who believed in the film, in film itself. Once *Witchfinder* was made, and while battling with a censorious John Trevelyan, Mike wrote, of the film's violent climax: 'its present ending, I feel, is [sic] salutory, moral, highly depressing (it may even cause the film to lose money, and knowing this, and allowing me to keep it, is one of the reasons I admire Tony; AIP I never consulted, so [sic] thats their hard luck – in fact, feeling as I do about that bunch of ponces (and I mean that almost literally) I hope devoutly that it *will* in the States!'[26] Sure enough, Price soon got wind of Mike's attitude, which was anything but the 'faerylike cloud of ecstasy' of Deke's letter: 'When I went on location to meet [Reeves] for the first time', recalled Price at the 1990 *Fangoria Weekend of Horrors* in Los Angeles, 'he said, "I didn't want you and I *still* don't want you, but I'm stuck with you!" That's the way to gain confidence!'[27]

It was the usual clash of sensibilities. For Mike, *Witchfinder* was an emotional investment and the opportunity to present a full Michael Reeves films, to correct the parts of *The Sorcerers* that were lacking. For AIP, it was just another production line flick, so why would anyone take it seriously? Yet Price's presence soon galvanised Mike; he rose to the challenge. It was to become important to make the film so that Price could be marginalised, could be 'dealt with' in a professional manner by a demonstrably professional film-maker; use Price like a star – wheel him in, shoot the scene, and send him back to his trailer. Mike was 'nervous of actors'[28] at any rate, and so took on Siegel's maxim about casting types and thus working from an established point. So Mike would show AIP, and show every producer to come, that he could handle a star as a star and make an estimable film at the same time. Again, the model was Siegel and classic American cinema. Don had managed Elvis Presley in *Flaming Star*, coaxed a decent performance out of him. Likewise, for Mike, Burt Lancaster might have been an overly studious actor, delivering a tedious performance in Aldrich's *Apache*, but Aldrich had provided vast, glossy, glowing landscapes – a sense of place, of home and heartland, the wilderness. Here was the formula.

This strategy presented something of a double bind for Mike since the other protagonists – the lewd side-kick torturer, the ripe love interest, the upright officer – were already functionally configured along one-note lines, in the manner of Siegel. All the characters had already been stripped down to their bare essentials in relation to their roles in the script. So, what was left if this could not be a character-centred drama? The uncertain, unscripted, as yet unimagined morass of the rest of the film – blood and death, the skies, the countryside, the villages, the hysteria, the executions. This was the material that Mike would concentrate on once behind the camera. And it would work somehow and seep into the dry bones of the rest of the film. The autumnal ambience would rob Price of his cleanness, the sharp Suffolk light of a cold October morning would show him in a new way: harsh, old, set – a death mask for a face. The opening itself would be the index to this: anonymous figures, 'a scene' taking importance – and Price off-camera, off-soundtrack, watching, merely a presence, to be positioned and adjusted as if a shop dummy. The more interesting stuff – a Leone-style camera flourish around a primed noose, a chill wind, a priest thundering holy vengeance to the skies, gasping women in the last seconds of their lives ... that would be the stuff of the film. The sublime subject, that beyond the Price–Hopkins dynamic, is suffering, in the context of religion. It would all also ensure, from the outset, that the film would not be mistaken for period drama with its pleasant pastoral scenes or a literary adaptation (in the year when the BBC's *The Forsyte Saga* was emptying pubs in the evenings). And as the violence increased, he could efface Price – send a message back to the folks at home with their safe matinée horror star now lost and drowning in gore. It was the same patricidal delight that Bertolucci would utilise a few years later, with Marlon Brando in *Last Tango in Paris*.

Another advantage of stripping down the characters to their basic functions was that it avoided the typically British tendency towards 'performance' films; casting character actors and giving them plenty to do banished the opportunities for wordiness, diminished the need for talking heads. The directness meant that characters acted as their role dictated: motivations are on the surface. But this chimed with Mike's understanding of film in relation to Siegel's movies – the interest and depth of the film was to be found in the action, in the wider aesthetic considerations, rather than the evolving psychological dimensions. Such thoughts would have occupied Mike during the waking hours when he took leave of Tom during the scripting process.

The first draft of the script arrived at the BBFC on 4 August 1967, and a report was written that day:

In the last week I have seen two films submitted by Tenser from his [sic] Tygon Company: *How Much Loving Does a Normal Couple Need?* and *Bloody Pit of Horror*. The former a classic sex-ploitation (nastier in some ways than [Russ Meyer's] *Lorna*) and the latter a gem for collectors of horror-comics. Now I get this perfectly beastly script from the same stable. We recommended that both films should be banned. I would like to invite Tenser to re-write this first draft script after he has read our comments ... This ape Tenser will continue to be a time-wasting nuisance until the board puts him in his place. If we do not ask for a new script then I think that we should be very much more severe in our script letter than [D] is in his notes. For example pp 119–121. Good Heavens![29]

A senior examiner, a former military officer and judge in the Indian Civil Service and now filling in his last few years before retirement, was equally aghast at the script ('beastly', 'ghoulish') and he concluded, in his confidential report 'Personally I should not grieve if this script dropped dead in its tracks.' Elsewhere, no doubt fulfilling some other, obscure, BBFC agenda, he noted of the love scene: 'No Lesbianism here!', before going on at length to criticise the historical accuracy of soldiers' titles. Since Trevelyan was on holiday the same examiner returned the script to Tenser, within days of it being received, accompanied with a letter – a formal attempt to 'put him in his place':

> We have now read your script *Witchfinder General* and are greatly disturbed by it. It could fairly be described as a study in sadism in which every detail of cruelty and suffering is lovingly dwelt on. I do not think there is any point in my going through the episodes separately, repeating each time that a film which followed the script at all closely would run into endless censorship trouble. There are few pages on which some helpless human being is not shown being hanged, burned, drowned, raped, beaten-up, dragged about or otherwise bullied and threatened. One of the victims is a helpless young woman and the others are elderly and equally defenceless men and women. Even in the battle scenes there is excessive emphasis on decapitation and other sensational shots. The only relief from this violence is found in sex and nudity which seems rather out of place in a story about Puritans and an innocent girl in the 17th Century.

With this general criticism in mind and your knowledge of our standards I think you will know what changes to make if you want to send in a revised screenplay.

The 'ape' replied immediately, noting that the screenplay was based on Bassett's book (itself based on 'historical fact') and promising a copy of a watered-down script ('as soon as it is received from the printers') which would now be characterised by 'more emphasis on "mood", more attention to historical detail, and allows a much broader panorama for camera work ... I am quite sure that you will be pleased ...' He signs off with mock obsequiousness:

> Young Michael Reeves, who will be directing the film, and who was also responsible for the script of *The Sorcerers*, you probably know is fully aware of his responsibilities with regard to film-making and the censorship that it entails.
>
> Obviously, there will be some verbal dialogue between us after the script has been read, so that Michael Reeves and myself can be well guided by Mr Trevelyan's and your own very valid, sensible and highly instructive opinion.

Elsewhere Tenser notes 'and naturally I would always act upon your advice in the making of a British film', indicating that the more explicit footage for the 'continental' versions would be shot anyhow. The senior censor was aware of this possibility to begin with, noting as much in his report, and had also picked up on the supposed historical basis as something that could be played to justify the depiction of atrocities. Both he and Tenser were equally wily in anticipating the other's moves.

The second draft of the screenplay was quickly submitted (by now Hopkins is only run through with a pike and then incinerated as the dungeon turns into an inferno: 'a holocaust of flames'). An internal note from 20 August 1967 (that is, only eleven days after the original draft was returned to Tigon) raises suspicion about the rapidity of script drafts from Tigon: 'We used, at one time, to have a lot of trouble with Hammer who are now, I gather, about the most reasonable of our customers. The sooner Tenser stops trying it on, the better. The final draft of this script must have been in the pipe-line when we were subject to the first one. This sort of behaviour does waste so much of our time. Tenser knows to within a couple of frames what we will pass.' Likewise, the BBFC refused to be duped by the 'historical' idea as a way of justifying the brutality; Sara's sexuality, in particular, is criticised in terms of being 'more like the 20th century than the 17th'. The script was returned with comments appended to a list of still problematic scenes (that is, all scenes involving brutality or sex):

> Discretion should be used with these scenes. We would not want undue brutality to the old woman ... We would not want too much made of scenes of passion, and I think you should avoid any obvious stroking of Sara's breasts ... We do not want suggestive shots of Sara in what is described an 'an almost-transparent nightgown'; I see that we are to have a silhouette shot, and care should be taken with this also ... you should keep the screams out as far as possible ... These are singularly unpleasant scenes and I hope that they will be treated with great discretion ... We would not want any really nasty shots of hanging bodies ... We never like knee-kicks in the groin, or other foul fighting of this kind ... This is really nasty, sadistic stuff, and I wish you could get rid of it entirely ... We would not want any nastiness here ...I return your script herewith.

The exhaustive list of suggestions, by this stage, seems more a device for the BBFC to cover themselves later should extensive cuts to the finished film be required.

Trevelyan invited Tenser and Mike to arrange an appointment if they wished to talk further. They met on 29 August 1967 to discuss the advice for the amended script submitted by Tenser. Mike agreed to shoot the more problematic sequences of the film in such a way as to allow for BBFC cutting, should it be deemed necessary, without the loss of continuity, and Trevelyan was to view a rough cut of the film during the early days of post-production for further guidance. Another draft of the shooting script was to be prepared, accommodating the majority of the BBFC advise. The brilliance of Trevelyan's diplomatic skills is much in evidence in this process. He managed to get his way, the implementation of the recommendations in relation to the revised script, even those of his most outraged and reactionary examiners (for example, notes on witch-burning scene: 'This whole episode is disgusting and designed only for the pleasure of sadists and should be left out or drastically altered'), yet he shielded Tenser from this outrage. Tenser only has the fondest of memories of Trevelyan (as does Polanski, despite problems with *Rosemary's Baby*, also released in 1968). However, the finished and certificated film still seems to locate the visceral territory of freeform violence identified by the BBFC as unacceptable at the very early stages – so Mike, to an extent, was also to have his way.

The final draft was substantially toned down. With a couple of 'sex' films lined up – *Monique* and *Love In Our Time* – Tenser would have wanted to be as obedient to the BBFC as possible. At this point, Tenser seems to have taken advantage of the BBFC process to his own ends and had the boys exercise both the Battle of Naseby sequence and the gypsies. Tenser had initially been wary of the scope of the projected battle (Tenser's intentions had been 'We'll do it with six extras and lots of smoke'[30]) and reluctant to employ a new group of extras needed as the gypsies. In narrative terms, the gypsies only exist to be incensed by Stearne's third rape and so assist in the capture of Hopkins – they would have been ripe for removal.

The final draft is extremely good. Tom and Mike, keen to impress, understood the first and last rule of film scripts: they exist to conjure up pictures in the jaded minds of unexcitable producers. The script titillated accordingly; rich and descriptive, punctuated with hints of the sex and violence to come. It indicated the speed and the action that would steer the film well away from any period drama tedium and was largely free of camera directions; vague enough to allow plenty of room for Mike's inventions on set. The script would have assured AIP.

66. Ext. River Bank. Day.

SARA wanders along the bank by the overhanging trees, a faraway smile on her face. She stops, gazing out over the water with the swans gliding serenely about. Then, with a little involuntary laugh, sits herself down on the grass bank. She lies back, letting the sun come dappling down through the branches on to her face. CAMERA MOVES in to TIGHT C.U. as she closes her eyes.[31]

302. Int. Castle Dungeon. Day.

A large room below ground level, again with no windows and lit only by torches. Sweating stone walls, along one side a variety of pikes, swords and lances. In the centre a long table, perhaps used for primitive surgical operations during the heat of the battle, perhaps for more sinister purposes. There is one barred door at one end of the room, bolts drawn across, against which WEBB stands, watching grimly, his bovine face expressionless. Against the wall by the table, SARA is held, her hands bound to a roof-beam, her back to her tormentors. STEARNE has got her shirt partially ripped down the back, and is standing waiting for HOPKINS' signal, the metal pin he previously used to exhort a 'confession' from Lowes, in his beefy paw. At the other end of the room, MARGERY too is bound by his thumbs to a roof-beam, but turned to face towards his wife. HOPKINS stands near to him, a satisfied smirk on his face. CAMERA STARTS on HOPKINS, PULLING BACK to take in the ensuing scene.[32]

Mike had asked Stanley Long to shoot *Witchfinder* but Stanley, convinced the film would be another underbudgeted headache, declined. Shaughnessy recommended the Canadian documentary cameraman Johnny Coquillon, who had moved from working as a Pinewood clapper boy in the 1950s to shooting wildlife documentaries across Africa: speeding cameras and savage nature (or so Mike would have hoped). This was a time of documentary cameramen and their lightweight Arriflexes hooking up with filmmakers – most notably Raoul Coutard and his crew of Indochina vets with François Truffaut, Godard and Tony Richardson. Arriving back in the UK in the mid-1960s, Coquillon set up a company to sell generic African wildlife footage. *Witchfinder* was his first full feature film as a lighting cameraman (another device to save on overheads). His eye for the wild and the speed of violence would need to remain in, to be a facet of the style of the film – and Mike and Johnny talked for some time about the look of the film. The question of style itself could be satisfied with almost any coherent visual answer; Mike would have been a little dismayed at the underlit images of *The Sorcerers*, the clotting greys that dissolved the corners of rooms. Perhaps Coquillon could bring some of the burn and liveliness to the images that Gioacchino Gengarelli had brought to *Revenge of the Blood Beast*, where blood was a regal red and grass realistically moist and green. Johnny seemed to be thinking along not dissimilar lines. He immediately stripped the film of its expected surface gloss – striking a completely different note to the previous AIP–Poe films that had served up clear glowing purples and velvety blacks, such as the Colorscope *The Tomb of Ligeia*: 'We wanted the film to look as if it had been hidden away for 300 years.'[33] Degrading the film in this way would create an aesthetic context in which the gore would register, denoting palpable violence rather than stage blood.

Johnny was able to bring speed and the ability to use as much natural light as possible – judiciously placing just a few reflectors and the occasional 'brute' to bolster the light levels, at times highlighting more than lighting scenes. He seemed able to eke out whatever light was left, sometimes beyond the magic hour, and so more often than not wrote his images in shadows (for example, the shot of John Lowes' motionless body hung from a tree). Johnny was another who benefited from Mike's opportunity; Peckinpah and Fuest found the same essential qualities in Johnny's work and used him accordingly; Fuest's hallucinatory Yorkshire moors for his *Wuthering Heights* and, in a series of increasingly blitzed Peckinpah war films, shooting carnage in Cornwall, Yugoslavia, Mexico and LA.

As the typed-up copies of the script arrived, it was practically time to begin; pre-production was nearing its chaotic end. Vincent was booked for costume-fitting on 11 September. This was doubly disconcerting for Philip who, when checking with Tenser that a full unit would be ready for the eight-week shoot (then due to start in twelve days' time with the opening lynching sequence) was reassured with: 'You're always fucking worrying, Philip! Why are you always worrying?' Over the remaining days the small crew was assembled from union unemployment registers (many were freshly unemployed since Columbia Pictures had fortuitously just cancelled a production) with most working above their grades on 'abysmal' pay (not that the cast fared any better). The average age of the crew was about 60 – almost as old as cinema itself at that point. Mike turned 24 during the shoot, making Orson Welles' debut seem tardy. So, despite the shortage of units and crew in the UK in 1967, Tenser's maxim was borne out after all.

As day one neared, Philip deputised Euan Pearson to find the remaining minor locations, arrange permissions and draw up directions for the unit. Euan, an aspiring feature film director himself, tore into the task with relish. He had spent time in Paris in the early 1960s, where he had absorbed *La Nouvelle Vague* and attended Henri Agel's *Art et Cinéma* course at the Musée des Arts Décoratifs. Back in the UK he had worked in documentaries and television and was keen to up the stakes and move into feature films: 'Philip, an ex-Army man, simply supplied me with a series of Ordinance Survey grid references, which I had to translate into "Turn left at the Green Man"-type instructions for the average prop driver.'

It was a cold autumn. Mike, who usually presented himself as casually dressed in blacks and browns (mostly blacks), would sport a jacket over his customary plain jumper or polo neck. His thinness meant that he felt the cold – and the constant working in rain (a practice with which he unwittingly led the crew) necessitated layers of insulation. The hair was inching over the collar – just about enough to carefully tarnish a somewhat clean-cut image, to offer a second opinion to his accent. Mike felt the need to be able to present himself to the crew without inviting too much diffidence. Gaffer Laurie Shane recalls 'He wasn't a very smart man. I wouldn't say scruffy – a bit unruly dressed and not worried about his appearance. Obviously public school – by his manners and demeanour he was well public school. He always wore a jacket, trousers, proper shirt. He wasn't scruffy as Americans are scruffy – he was public school scruffy; casual scruffy, smart-casual. But good clothes.'[34]

On the morning of Monday 18 September, a construction van arrived at the location for the pre-credit hanging sequence (on her way to the gallows, the 'witch' is dragged past author Hammond Innes's house). It transpired that the van was empty. Euan had to procure timber for the gallows at a local yard, then hire a furniture removal van to take it to the set. The sky was overcast and, with precious hours already burned, there was no time to wait for the sun. This set the tone for the film in which master shots were taken in sunshine, close-ups and reverses in shadow. It was not an auspicious start. The film would be shot almost entirely on location, raising a whole slew of potential difficulties and problems. At least *The Sorcerers* had been located in London, rather than the middle of nowhere. Within a few days, the quiet erotic revelry of the riverbank scene became, for Hilary Dwyer, 'Take after take! The scene when I was on the other side of a river bank – all afternoon, trudging along this river bank. All afternoon!'.[35] Prior to each take, and shooting in general, Mike would say 'Gentlemen – let's make love'.

The photos Philip took on the shoot show Mike with viewfinder (a gift from Maslansky on the first day of the *Blood Beast* shoot), the ever-present cigarette, and bangle (his name inscribed, probably from his mother). He looks alternatively distracted or concentrating – the casual professionalism of his appearance does not disguise a seriousness. Hilary, playing Sara, remembers:

> an intense, driven young man. He was completely single-minded. He burnt the candle at both ends in that he was working most of the night on the script. He would stay up late with the cast for dinner, and then work, and then be up early in the morning.

Laurie Shane:

> He was very quiet, quite reserved, but very pleasant, affable. He knew what he wanted to do, he knew exactly what he wanted. He was restricted in some ways by the production, money-wise, so he had to curtail a lot of his stuff ... we needed more extras, but we couldn't afford to have them.

Alf Joint:

> He had a knack of putting his finger on what he wanted, on what was right and what was wrong. A lot of people would be scratching their heads but he had an answer for everything. He was brilliant.[36]

Stuntwoman and actress Gillian Aldam:

> He was a little bit of an enigma on the film because he kept very much to himself ... He seemed to be very quiet, very pleasant, very

polite; no shouting or screaming, I never saw him throw a tantrum, just a nice persosn. We worked quite closely together on the film for long hours, he never appeared miserable. He was gentle, he was understanding and he got out of me everything that he wanted.[37]

Actor William Maxwell, playing Gifford:

> The only problems we all knew about were with the production office who kept wanting him to change things. This I was aware of when we were having lunch from the chuck wagon where for the first and only time, I was chatting to him on an off-shoot personal basis. His girlfriend was there and the three of us were in the same van. Michael asked me about myself in a genuinely friendly way and then how was I enjoying the film. It was only when he mentioned the production office when talking to his girlfriend that the quiet anger appeared and he visibly tensed up. Instead of venting his anger he bottled it up and I noticed her concerned look as he suddenly went into himself.[38]

Euan:

> Mike's response to the enormous pressure he was under was, as I recall, to become quiet and rather uncommunicative. I don't remember him ever shouting or even complaining. He simply grew more aloof. He came over as a very genuine, rather intense young man, single-minded and sure of what he wanted. He was also gentle and friendly – at least until the pressure began to build. If I have a reservation, it is that he spent too much time on the Special Effects.[39]

Ogilvy:

> Mike always knew where his camera was going to be, and how he was going to shoot everything ... He never had to have a conference about getting the geometry of the shots right. His mastery of the technical aspects was absolute. However, Mike never directed the actors. He always said he didn't know anything about acting, and preferred to leave it up to us, but he wouldn't know how to make it better. The only direction he ever gave was, 'A bit quicker,' or 'A bit slower.' If he trusted you, he left you alone.[40]

Philip:

> A couple of weeks after principal photography was completed, when Michael was shooting the opening sequence where the

horses are being ridden through the wooded clearing – just after the credits – it started to pour with rain. Michael wouldn't let the actors put coats on over their costumes. I said 'Michael, you know, some of these people could get pneumonia!' He replied 'I don't give a shit – we can't hold up shooting!' He wasn't very considerate of his actors. However, I saw him working with Rupert Davies, coaching him and others – so I don't believe that Michael was bad with actors.

As with all Tigon productions, costs were cut wherever and whenever possible. A philosophy of things being 'on the cheap' once out in the countryside was predominant – and was applied to everything from buying props to running up accounts with local businesses. Certainly the rustic settings did mean that less needed to be disguised – television aerials presenting the biggest problem (one or two remain in the background for the over-observant). Some of the more senior members of the company only had experience in Tigon's softcore film-making. The construction crew members were rapidly laid off and replaced with 'local' labour – more able that the ancient union crew, but many seemingly drawn from the Suffolk underworld. It transpired that the props van (while still loaded with hired period swords and firearms) had been used for an attempted bank robbery during one evening towards the end of the shoot. The colourful crew remained in a permanent state of macho one-upmanship. Euan:

> Sid Davis, the Props man, could hardly walk, but he was a lovely old boy. We had a pair of horses on set, and they shat everywhere. The first time, Ian Goddard, the First Assistant, called out 'Props!' No-one moved. He called out a second time, 'Props!' No response. The third time he called out 'Sid, move that horse shit!' Little Sid cleared his throat:
> 'How long have you been in this game, son?'
> 'All my life'
> 'Then don't you know that as long as it's in the air it's Props's. Once it hits the ground it's Stagehands's'
> After that Ian called out 'Stagehands!'

Despite their hard work, the labourers still had enough energy to earn themselves an ejection from the Trust House Forte hotel in

Bury St Edmunds early on in the shoot (thereafter dossing in the set caravans). The low pay and unorthodox crew situation soon led to a strike in early October, sparked off by disputes over bad-weather payments to the all-day extras, and the concern that unexploded artillery and tank gun shells on the Stanford Battle Camp and Training Area, near Thetford, which Philip had arranged to use via his army connections (it came complete with a unit of the Royal Signal Corps for communication), were potentially hazardous for the crew. The shoot was already several days behind. Dictating notes to his wife, Philip brokered the strike as rapidly and equitably as possible, with Euan as a go-between. Tigon immediately met the demands from the ACTT and NATKE unions, having reviewed payroll, and ensured that pay cheques would begin arriving on time.

The staid Suffolk countryside did not offer much in the way of entertainment for the restless crew. Somehow one evening's pub crawl through the quiet boozers of the immediate vicinity wound up with an agreement with the residents of the local nurses' home to bring along television star Rupert Davies (playing John Lowes) the following evening in exchange for promised sexual favours. Rupert was known to be fairly 'gone' in the bar of his hotel by mid-evening (after spending the majority of the day with his new portable black and white TV, hooked up to the battery of his new American car) and by 10 p.m. he would be oblivious to goings-on ('Rupert doesn't mind where he sleeps'). The crew piled him into a props van and set off, leaving a wary Euan:

> Sometime in the early hours I got a 'phone call. The unmistakable voice apologised for waking me. 'I seem to be in some sort of hospital, old boy. Can you send a unit car to pick me up?' It took me a little time to rouse the unit driver and get him on the road. I was about to go back to bed when the prop van drew up outside. Out pitched our star, flanked by a beaming crowd of technicians. 'I've just sent the unit car for you,' I told Rupert. 'Ah well, you see, these kind boys suddenly turned up and offered me a lift.'

Mike was mostly unaware of such things. Despite the cost-cutting, he had more autonomy than on the previous shoot, and was fully immersed in putting his ideas into action. For Rupert Davies's torture, Mike had filled the dungeon with pungent water and smeared the walls with blood. Rupert was to be chained to a wall. As the shot was lined up, Rupert overheard Mike commanding 'Right – put the rats in': 'Nobody had told me anything about rats! They had a rat fancier and he put in three rats. They started crawling up me. Mike was saying "Don't move, Rupert. Don't move. Wait till that one starts nibbling your jaw, then you might move your head a little." I said, "I might, yeah!" The continuity girl who was sitting there with her knees through the bars ... shrieked and flew out.'[41]

Despite the lofty intentions, *Witchfinder* was still an exploitation film, and had been financed on the grounds of providing scenes of low-grade sex and violence for non-discerning audiences – as well the BBFC knew. Deke was employed for that reason but Tenser, in particular, needed as much nudity as possible for the 'continental' cut (sometimes referred to as 'the German version'). This footage would also be used to push the envelope with the BBFC, testing the boundaries of acceptability. The main nude scene would be in the tavern, and the main sex scene would be between Richard and Sara. While the latter was to be handled with sensitivity, the former was an opportunity to get as much exposed flesh in the can as possible. Some of Tenser's actresses arrived and Jack Lynn, playing the Brandeston innkeeper ('More ale, sir?') took uneasy, improvised directions from Mike for the 'tame' tavern scenes; he was to nuzzle a wench's exposed cleavage for as long as possible. When Jack asked 'Any dialogue?' Mike answered 'No – just enjoy yourself.' Mike loathed the experience, and would try and reduce the sequence in the cutting room, including Jack's nuzzling.

Mike was not present during the filming of the alternative nude take. This was restaged 'from memory' by other members of the crew the next day, overseen by Tenser, acting as director. He had ordered Mike to take a break, dispatching him to London where he saw the just-opened *Bonnie and Clyde*. Mike would have been very impressed with the blood – or, rather, with the redness; the only colour that stands out in the sunned-out, hallucinatory reimagining of a dusty 1930s Deep South. The sudden and brutal ending demands a response from the viewer. Just as Mike had left

Kwai with a checklist of things he would do differently or better – he would have left *Bonnie and Clyde* with a similar list, heading back to the set to do just that. *Bonnie and Clyde* undoubtedly informs the bloody climax of *Witchfinder*; Mike returned with a dozen ideas about bullets and flesh, stopping off first to visit the Barretts at King's Mead.

During Mike's absence Tenser had brought some models down from London, organised a raucous evening for the night before with them, and then had them brought on to the set the next day. Euan:

> We were to re-shoot a couple of scenes with Bob Russell plying a couple of bawds in a bar that Mike had previously shot. But Tony was no director: 'Just set it up the way he shot it,' he told Johnny Coquillon. So we relaid tracks as for the original shot, which dollied out from behind a medieval chimney breast to reveal Bob and the two girls in the 'nook'. The rushes were hilarious. No sooner had the camera started to move than this huge nipple hove into the frame ...

Some of the nude footage may have been for Tenser's private use since more seems to have been shot than could have made any cut of the film. Perhaps nude out-takes from *Witchfinder* appeared with the usual fare at the Old Compton Cinema later that year.

Mike understood that he too needed to render a pound of flesh. He had anticipated the sequence in the script with optimism ('They kiss and laugh and fondle each other. Their laughter ceases as they become more passionate ...',[42] prompting Ogilvy's new wife to the set) but not with the details that would see him through an awkward experience. For *The Sorcerers*, Mike was able to skip over the sex, or veer it into violence – embarrassed groping and kissing giving way to manageable physical occurrences. Now, however, there was no escape. Ogilvy recalls it as slightly more breezy: 'Mike said "Right, we're coming into the permissive age so off with all your clothes." I refused point blank.'[43] Deke remembered the event as tense, and offered to play the 'the bad guy' if it would help facilitate the filming.[44]

Hilary, as the fresh-faced Sara, was finding the shoot stressful. She was only 21 at the time, but with three years of television experience and a new contract with Tenser and AIP:

I lurched from not frightfully good film to not frightfully good film, playing someone's girlfriend and trying to differentiate which ... The bane of my experience on [*Witchfinder*] was an old make-up artist, as they were trying to save money absolutely everywhere. She was frightfully old and couldn't see an awful lot. I think I was a bit spotty and all I wanted to do was cover my spots up. And she would dab at me with this wretched brush. I can remember feeling awful, because I held it all up because of the wretched spots on my forehead and this woman dabbing at me with this brush saying [shrill Scottish accent]: 'A little more Light Egyptian, dear.' I can remember bursting into tears and saying 'I look an absolute mess.' I was so self-conscious and worried about myself. There was no time or money for me to be bursting into tears and Mike was just wonderful. He had words with her. Mike was tremendously understanding, for one so young I think he had a great maturity. He was really inspiring to work with. And because it was my first film I didn't know how lucky I was.

As Sara, Hilary's role also called for some brazen wenchery as she teases her fiancée into bed. Philip understood her presence as 'an AIP starlet' ('We couldn't afford much in the way of stars, and Michael had seen something she had done. We all believed she was a good actress') even if Hilary was a little more uncertain of her role ('I don't think I realised that I was the star'). Part of the deal was that she would be expected to duly disrobe (as the poster had it, 'And introducing Hilary Dwyer'), 'as they become more passionate'. Tigon was pipping Hammer to the post in respect of nipples by a couple of crucial years at this point (it took until 1970, with Hammer's *The Vampire Lovers* and *Lust for a Vampire* rapidly making up for lost time). The role of Sara was reasonably ground-breaking in terms of what could be shown, much in the manner of *Repulsion*; Tenser's policy for filming as much as possible and then cutting back just to the point of acceptability worked well. This, coupled with all the usual bustle, meant that Hilary was nothing less than 'absolutely petrified': 'I was very shy about doing that. Mike said "Don't worry, we'll just use a dark blue filter ..." Was it hell! All I could think was "My God! What's my mother going to think?"' Once things were in place, Mike kept filming until enough exposed flesh was in the can. The acres of footage from this sequence, shot at Tenser's bequest, would allow him to edit together an extensive montage.

The days lengthened as shooting progressed. The overworked crew needed extra lubrication, to make the most of the few hours they had free after each day's shoot. Mike would sometimes join them for a beer in evening at the Angel in Bury St Edmonds. Vincent Price ('Mr Price' or 'Vincent' depending on the level of acquaintance) had more time to spare for socialising. Euan:

> Back at the Angel, Vincent would walk into the bar and order drinks for any of the cast or crew present – except I had to shout out the orders; 'Pint of Adams ... John Bull ... Black and Tan ... bottle of Worthington ... Bitter Shandy ...'
> 'What the hell are all these?' he would shout.
> 'Beers'
> 'Why don't they just say "beer" for Chrissakes?'
> 'This is England, Vincent'
>
> I remember one occasion when he was sitting in the restaurant at the Angel Hotel, surrounded by a coterie of sycophantic young actors, giving a very amusing running commentary on the progress of a young waiter struggling with a tray of glasses. 'Will he? Won't he?' Sure enough, he did drop them.

Everyone bar Mike seems to have loved Vincent. He would have arrived on the set with bluster, warmly greeted and wildly regaled the company with stories of his early years on the London stage, would cast aside the star persona with the same effortless grace with which he had flipped his cloak over his shoulder in the Poe horrors, revealing the true man beneath ... and what a pleasure it was for him to be back in England, how he had missed the restaurants, the art galleries, the camaraderie of the theatre culture, and how he looked forward to treading the boards again, very shortly, as soon as the shoot was done. And what a pleasure and an honour it was to be surrounded by such a cast and crew. Wasn't there just something so quintessentially *English* about all the best horror films? Even the Hollywood ones! He had worked with James Whale after all (wonderful director, delightful fellow), and AIP was as nothing compared to *Hammer*. The English do their horror with so very much more – ah – *panache* than we do (and with so very much more *sex*). When one day the catering truck failed to materialise, Vincent and driver sped to Bury St Edmonds, bought up vegetables, pasta and shrimp and whipped up a meal for sixty in the hotel's kitchen. Euan remembers that:

> A kinder, more thoughtful and genuinely modest man you couldn't hope to meet. One day he asked me in an embarrassed tone if I could advance him some money. He hadn't received his expenses from London. None of us had been paid – it was that kind of production. I lent him a tenner and drove him to the Natwest branch in Bury. 'But nobody knows me here,' he protested as I bundled him into the manager's office. The manager was, of course, delighted to open an account and advance him any amount he liked. He was genuinely bemused that his credit seemed good, even in this 'hick town in England' ... I saw him once after the shoot, on the set of *The Oblong Box* at Shepperton. He introduced me to Christopher Lee and asked 'What happened to that pretty young lady who came down to see you in Suffolk?' 'We married right after the shoot and we've got a 2-month-old baby.' He did a quick count on the fingers of both hands. 'You just scraped in there, boy.'

Yet this easy friendship was just another facet of the Price performance that Mike objected to, cloaking both Price's inability to act any role other than that of Vincent Price and his secondary agenda (not unrelated to being back in England). Mike wanted to pull off the cloak and the actorish behaviour (which he loathed per se). It was essential for the film; the violence and madness needed to be rooted in a convincing and realistic central presence. To achieve this, Mike seemed determined to minimalise Price's input – he would have wanted Price to do only what he asked him to do, leaving it to the director to oversee the rest. Mike would have read about Antonioni's 'odd' direction on *Blow-Up* the year before – autocratic and dictatorial auteurship – and taken inspiration from that. But any benefit of the doubt that Price might have afforded Mike was soon thrown right back at him; Price was now out of the comfortable studio, on wind-swept moors somewhere outside London, and confronted by young Mr Reeves's audacity as a director and flippant direction. Ogilvy recalls 'he was faced with this kid actually telling him, "Could you take it DOWN a bit?"'[45]

What was the matter with the boy? Corman wouldn't have thought twice ... and his films were very well received. For a veteran to receive notes, undoubtedly mildly condescending in tone and content, from a 24-year-old was bad enough ... but for the 24-year-old to try to tailor his performance to a one-note sadistic psychopath (and Price would have raised an eyebrow at the amount of nudity and Mike's liberal splashing about of blood) was not at all Vincent's cup of tea.

A further problem relating to Price's off-set performance was that it concealed something Mike would have perceived to be the hidden agenda for the friendliness and familiarity that was wowing everybody else; Price's sexual designs on him. In this, Mike saw crystallised everything he disliked about Price and everything that Price represented: ultimately, what irked Mike beyond the suggestion of a sexual dalliance was that this itself illustrated a great lack of seriousness and professionalism among (as he described AIP in a letter to Trevelyan), 'that bunch of ponces'.

Had Price considered the talk of a young public school fellow – *very* keen on film – in the light of his early years in London (at the Courtauld Insistute, studying German art, and then the Gate Theatre) and his time with Charles Laughton, in terms that suggested that Mike was part of the deal? Like many Hollywood types of his generation, Price's homosexual side was skilfully concealed and all operations were covert – even to the point of a show-business marriage later in his life with Coral Browne.[46] Price had been through the McCarthy era and seen the hounding of decent and honest men from Hollywood; subterfuge was more about survival than hypocrisy. Would Price have talked of Mike's great future, of moving to America for the next film? Naturally, he knew some senior AIP people he *must* introduce him to, it was all a *marvellous* opportunity. After all, Price was more than used to getting his way. The sounding-out, by the then-standard technique: the hand would have been placed on the knee ...

Mike undoubtedly would have overreacted, angrily distancing himself from Price, reading the subtext not as an invitation but as a take-it-or-leave-it instruction. The mask had finally fallen, and Mike's anti-AIP prejudices were seen to be well founded. Price would have moved quickly and the incident would have occurred fairly early on during the shoot. Mike was soon certainly convinced that Price was after his body, and told a few trusted members of the production. Rumours circulated around the lower end of the film industry about a botched come-on; one such had it that the reason for Price's fiery performance in *Witchfinder* was that he was 'besotted with the director'. Thereafter all professional interaction would take on a further dimension; the avoiding of eye contact, cold distance on Mike's part, or ignoring Vincent outright, overcompensation rather than embarrassment on Price's part, and then slight, humorous, scorn. After direction, Price would reply 'Thank you, young man'[47] to Mike. '"Oh, my gawd, I think I'm getting typecast," Vincent hit his forehead with the palm of his hand and made everyone laugh as he lined up for the first shot. I was standing holding the reins of his frisky white charger as Mike painstakingly described the reaction he wanted. "You mean my No. 6 look?" – staring angrily into the distance.'[48] The tension was so palpable that even Philip's photographs capture it. Like married royals, barely able to conceal their loathing for each other, Mike and Vincent strain to look in opposite directions. Soon Vincent had had enough and disappeared, and was later found, with his packed bags, at Bury St Edmunds train station. Tenser, picking up the bad vibes, simply felt that Vincent should have more confidence in Mike. The scorn would have found endless other reasons for justification throughout the rest of the shoot; Euan:

> In one scene he had to fire his flintlock between the horse's ears. Mike wanted to put a blank charge in the breach so you could see the puff of smoke. 'What? You want the gun to go bang between the ears of this fuckin' nag? How do you think he's going to react?' There was a long discussion with the wranglers before Mike finally prevailed. Predictably the white stallion reared up, sending Vincent sliding down its arse in slow-motion. We all held our breath. He wasn't hurt, but he was very angry ...

Price would have retreated back into the warm embrace of the rest of the cast and recovered himself: 'He didn't want to be there. He absolutely didn't want to do it. But as we went along he got jollier and jollier; I think he realised that it was actually going to be quite good fun.'[49] Once Vincent was out of the way of Mike's camera, he was free to camp things up as usual; Ogilvy:

> I got myself all kitted up for my first morning's work, which was a riding shot. I had a huge horse, who was very fast and almost uncontrollable. I was trying him out, cantering him down the driveway to the vicarage. I noticed a black shape sitting in a ditch ... As I rode past, I heard, 'Oh my God! Look at *her*! She's so damned *pretty*! She rides that damn horse so *well*! I *hate* her!' That was my introduction to Vincent. He could be very funny, in a 'queeny' sort of way.[50]

Philip recalls another incident along not dissimilar lines; after a tumble from a horse on the first day of shooting (despite Vincent's prior advice that he was an able rider), Vincent retired to the hotel to recuperate and refused to see a doctor or talk to Tenser or Arkoff, calling from Hollywood; the insurers may need to be alerted. Tenser persuaded Philip to try to talk to him:

> So I went down to the Dickens Suite again and knocked on the door. Vincent asks 'Who is it?' and I say 'It's me again – Philip.'
> 'Come in – the door's open.'
> So I went in and there he was, in the big four-poster bed, wearing a long nightgown with a pointed tassel cap with this enormous book in his lap – reading. I said: 'Vincent, we've got to call a doctor for insurance purposes.'
> 'I'm not seeing any goddamn British quack!'
> 'Well, Vincent, at least let me see if your back's okay.'
> So he climbed out of bed and knelt on the floor, bending over the high bed. I lifted up his nightshirt, and gently began feeling his nether region, saying 'Does it hurt here?'
> 'No, that's fine, dear boy' Vincent replied.
> At that moment there was a knock on the half-open door and the young wardrobe mistress swept in, carrying Vincent's costume freshly ironed for the next day. Imagine the look on her face!

With Vincent off his case, Mike was able to concentrate on the set pieces and action. Gillian Aldam, then only a few years older than Hilary, had been hired by Tenser as Maggie Kimberley's double (as Elizabeth Clark) and to cover other, miscellaneous stunts: to be semi-drowned in the moat, to 'sit on the cellar floor with rats running over me, and chained to a wall', to be hanged, and then lowered into a blazing pyre as a witch. For the moat scene she was to have been filmed bound by a rope and struggling underwater during the ducking – but the moat, full during the location scouting, had only eighteen inches of water during the shoot. Mike despaired.

The burning represented the central set piece of the film; the culmination of Hopkins' reign of terror and a complete expression of the world of the film (onlookers, fire, execution, death: the justice of yesteryear). It was to be the major spectacle, not least in that a fair proportion of the budget had been earmarked for it. The few villagers who are initially seen helping Hopkins have been joined by many more, and they all gather to watch Hopkins burn suspect witches alive in the Lavenham village square. For the high-angle shots, Philip had hired a cherry picker (cheaper than a crane) and a camera crew was packed into it. For extras, Euan had liaised with the local press (who were happy to oblige – they would get a good run of stories in exchange for discretion) and an ad was to be run – 400 extras needed, to be auditioned at the Angel Hotel. Alas, a misprint transformed it into a call for 4,000, resulting in an enormous queue that wound around the entire hotel. The full 400 were needed for the Lavenham scene. Costumes consisted of grain sacks, bought from a local farmer and dyed red, blue, green or yellow the night before, to be worn over discreet clothing. Some extras would surreptiously sneak into the background of every shot while the pyre was being built and primed, necessitating retakes.

Gillian worn a protective plaster of Paris mask, with eyes holes but no mouth (a last-minute decision) and fire-proof clothing (that is, clothing soaked in a solution; these were still the days when 'we put our necks on the line') and was tied to the top of a ladder. Unbeknownst to her, six gallons of petrol were to be thrown on to the fire, in keeping with *The Sorcerers* production. One-take wisdom informed this all-or-nothing approach; good or bad, there was no time or money for retakes. Tension was high. Mike silenced the entire square: if something went wrong, Gillian would call out – and she had a free arm to wave – so it was essential that she could be heard. Hilary: 'I can remember some old man coming out of his front door and everybody screaming at him and me thinking "God how awful – all he's doing is coming out of his front door and he didn't know"'. Members of the Parish Council and the Lavenham Preservation Society looked on as the pyre was lit. The £30 fee paid for the use of Lavenham would not go too far in the event of any mishap.

Those in the cherry picker were already cooking when the explosion, which rocketed straight past Gillian's head, almost ignited them too. It was only when the fire had died down that Gillian could be cautiously lowered towards it, entirely dependent on those who had lowered her down to pull her back out again. In the event, their judgement was a minor arm burn and two eyebrows short of completely correct. As soon as she was out, the fire brigade began to dampen down the edge of the pyre and the area around it with a view to slowly working their way into the main blaze. Unfortunately, a fireman with a hose slipped, doused the fire directly in water, and engulfed the entire scene in smoke: 'It was quite horrendous!' But a visiting Arkoff, sucking on a fat cigar, was 'over the moon with that scene'. He told Mike so too, and good terms were established between the two. The next day, Lavenham residents complained of a night of spectacular supernatural disturbances.

As the production moved into its final phase, Tenser announced that there was to be another redrafting of the script. It had transpired that the ending, as written, could not be filmed. An inferno in Orford Castle was impossible both to the Ministry of Public Buildings and Works and on budgetary grounds; Mike's special Fire-FX unit joined the helicopter battle shots – vetoed by a realistic Tenser, aware that some of these costly sequences may not get past the BBFC during the post-production round of negotiations. In addition, the production was behind schedule, and the time was no longer available to shoot the complicated inferno sequence. With only a couple of days before the end of Price's contract, a new ending was urgently needed. Since procrastination was also out of the question, Tenser locked Mike in his hotel room and instructed him to rewrite the end as quickly as possible.

Philip, accustomed to working in live environments from his days as a radio show producer, stood by the typewriter and the brainstorming began. For Philip, the 'problem' of a well in the middle of the Orford Castle dungeon, which would hamper or block action and severely limit the camera, was no problem at all: it could be covered and transformed into an altar of sorts – Sara could be tied to it and tortured as a chained Richard looks on. Mike agreed; he's going mad, after all – this is the *drama* of the scene – this is what the sequence adds to the film at this point: let his madness run riot, run over, run into death lust as he sees his beloved in agony, the harrying of the one pure facet of the base world of the film. Richard has become Hopkins, and so no wonder Sara then goes mad herself. This is why Richard must be killed. Violence breeds violence: the downward spiral concludes with both good and bad dead. God has fled in the revised version – even the cross to be burned into Sara's flesh is replaced with a pagan 'W' for 'Witch'. No hope, no peace, no love and unity, but annihilation, madness, nihilism. The summer of love is obliterated by an ice age winter. Between Mike and Philip, this ending was completely and rapidly redrafted.

Although the rush must have precluded much in the way of thinking out new strategies to counter the BBFC, Tigon and the budgetary and acting constraints, the fact remains that the revised ending is considerably darker than second or third drafts. As it stood, it would have come under considerable BBFC fire had it been that way in September, during the inspection of the script. It would have conveyed an overwhelming sense of pointlessness to the entire film, allowing the BBFC to question the *reason* for the film in the first place. Redrafted, the film is defiantly without a 'moral'.

In the BBFC-invited redraft script (the third draft) Sara is jabbed then branded (a cross burnt into her back), a bound Richard desperately deliberates over whether to falsely confess to save her from further torture. Then, in a typically ill-advised eleventh-hour lapse in judgement, Hopkins has Richard (still down as 'Margery') released so as to better see Sara's agonies in up close – his face next to hers. He breaks loose, seizes a pike, slaughters Stearne

and moves to do thes same to Hopkins who turns Sara from witch
to hostage – a ladle of 'flaming liquid' as his weapon:

330. Int. Dungeon. Master Three-Shot
MARGERY stands poised as does HOPKINS, ladle held over SARA's
back. A completely still tableau. The sound of running footsteps
from outside as SWALLOW and HARCOURT approach.

331. Close on Hopkins
His attention distracted for a second, he glances up.

332. On Margery
Seizing his opportunity, he flings the pike as hard as he can.

333. Master
As the pike embeds itself in HOPKINS' chest. With a cry, he clut-
ches at it. He staggers back, knocking over the flaming vat,
sending its contents running all over the dungeon.

334. On Margery
Dashing forward, ripping SARA free from her bonds, dragging her
from the table back towards the doorway. Flames all around.

335. On Hopkins (double)
As he sinks back on his haunches right into the flames, trying to
pull the pike from his body. His cloak catches fire. In a moment he
is a mass of flames.

336. On Doorway
Almost simultaneously with the arrival of SWALLOW and HARCOURT
outside. MARGERY flings back the bolts, dragging SARA outside.
CAMERA MOVES IN ON THE GROUP as they watch HOPKINS in horror.

337. Their POV to Dungeon (Hopkins' Double)
HOPKINS, with a last frenzied cry, collapses forwards into the
flames; they engulf him entirely ...
There is no sound bar the crac[k]le of the fire.

CUT BACK TO:

338. On Group At Door
SARA sobbing in MARGERY's arms. The other[s] watching, transfixed.
the CAMERA MOVES IN TIGHT ON MARGERY's face. After a beat –

MARGERY:
(very softly)

May God forgive him. And us, too ...[51]

339. On Dungeon
A holocaust, the bodies of HOPKINS and STEARNE no longer visible through the flames.

BRING UP END MUSIC

ROLL FINAL CREDITS[52]

The last-minute revisions implemented by Mike and Philip make much less of the elaborate torture. Richard (now Marshall) still breaks free and this time grabs an axe and kills Stearne ('Stearne staggers back, crashing against the wall, trying to scoop his dangling guts back into his split stomach'[53]). He warns Hopkins to drop the red-hot iron he now brandishes; once Hopkins has done so ('he does as he is told'[54] – was he hoping for mercy?) Richard then grabs the iron and blinds Hopkins with it ('You've watched death too often ...'[55]) while Swallow and Harcourt finish off the sentries. They enter the inner dungeon:

336. Int. Dungeon
ON DOORWAY, the stairs stretching up out of sight. SWALLOW and HARCOURT come running down them, CAMERA MOVING in on them as they come to a halt by the door. An expression of horror comes over their faces – overscene we hear the sound of shrieking, crying, babbling ...

SWALLOW:
Oh God ... Oh God in Heaven ...

337. Their POV into Dungeon
HOPKINS is crawling about the floor, hands clutching at his seared eyes, moaning and screaming. He is covered in blood. SARA has her head turned away, sobbing hysterically. MARSHALL, the axe once again clutched in his hands, is walking along beside HOPKINS. Each time he tries to rise, MARSHALL swings the blade down, biting it into HOPKINS' torn limbs again and again. He, too is crying, tears pouring down his face, but never for a moment distracting his savage attention from the pathetic, half dead figure of HOPKINS. Suddenly a shot rings out. HOPKINS crashes over on his side in a bloody heap.[56]

That Swallow kills Hopkins denies Richard the complete revenge of methodically hacking Hopkins to death, as if to prove that the great witchfinder is no more than the sum of his severed parts – a symbolic castration writ large for Hopkins' defilement of Sara (she had offered her body to save her father's). For this, Richard moves to kill Swallow – at which point Harcourt guns Richard down ('The *slowed down report of the gun* echoes on the S/T as MARSHALL's body sinks down to the floor'[57]) and the film ends with a screaming Sara. This version eliminates any sense of those in the right prevailing, and any sense of narrative closure from Hopkins's demise is eclipsed by the death of Richard and madness of Sara: no one has won, nothing is finished, settled or satisfied. It is all a far cry from 'May God forgive him. And us, too ...' and the sense that a vestige of normality has been restored.

In the actual film, Richard breaks free once released by Stearne, blinds him, allowing for a split-second POV shot of the descending boot (perhaps easier to shoot than with Price, since the make-up would have added another complication) and rapidly has Hopkins on the ground and defenceless, repeatedly applying the axe. When Swallow, surveying the scene, mercy-kills Hopkins, Richard repeatedly screams 'You took him from me' (an addition that had been made in the final draft) and collapses. Swallow involuntarily murmurs 'May God have mercy on us all' while crossing himself, a sentiment mocked by Sara's insane screaming, which echoes around the empty corridors of the castle (shots taken from the beginnings and ends of takes during the editing). Richard is left alive and with the burden of the events portrayed – his anguished accusation indicating that something has gone forever; perhaps, like Sara, he has also descended into madness. If anything, this is even more pessimistic, defying every expectation, in the manner of *Bonnie and Clyde* – but less the mythologising and doomed romanticism. Nicky Henson (Swallow) remembers Ogilvy's life as being ultimately spared as a matter of mathematics; too many shots had already been fired from their one-shot flintlock pistols.

On the morning of Vincent's final day of shooting, Thursday 19 October, a seemingly impossible task lay ahead: thirty-five set-ups would be required for this crucial final sequence. Price was to play the lead in the musical *Darling of the Day* (a bit of frivolousness that would have enraged Mike further, Vincent was looking forward to it), due to begin rehearsals in New York the next day (his contract for *Witchfinder* expired at midnight). He could not be held over – missing shots, scenes or otherwise. And even this last day was restricted; permission had been granted to shoot in Orford Castle (a twelfth-century, Henry II-built keep) but the staff imposed limitations on its use, only allowing shooting from 6 p.m. to midnight. This meant that Mike only had six hours to shoot all the Price shots in the climactic scene – thirty-five set-ups in all – itself dashed out in screenplay form only three days before. The crew rallied around; Philip: 'That night was one of the most fantastic experiences I've ever had on a set – the crew were amazing; the Lee Electric "sparks" put socks over their shoes and were silently moving the big lights around one area of the confined space while the camera crew were shooting in another – it was all so incredibly professional'. With barely enough time to get the basic shots in the can, complicated stunt coordination was a luxury – and since it was all one-take the action could be as realistic as possible. Euan wound up running a shuttle service to the local hospital's casualty room. Back in the castle, Mike was busy manufacturing the gore. Tenser, wary of the spiral of violence, decided to rein in the director's bloodlust:

> He wanted the baser part of human nature. And he wanted to show this, so he wanted to show some of his guts coming out in close-up so you would be able to see it. And he contacted a local farmer in Bury St Edmunds where he wanted to buy some pig's guts which they were going to use under his cloak, right. And then when the time came, the farmer didn't have the pig ready for it, so they used string, pieces of string. When I came on set there was one of [Hopkins's] men – and he had this string [with] some Max Factor blood and he was bloodying it, getting it all ready, making it look like guts. I can't remember – it was Philip or Michael or whoever, and I said "Look – why are you doing this?" "Well, to be real ..." And I said "Well, it's all very well but Mr Trevelyan will not pass this. I know that." I mean, I knew Mr Trevelyan better than most people ... I knew exactly what was in his mind. He wouldn't

pass that. In his opinion, the audience wouldn't realise why it was being shown, it looked like gratuitous violence.

In the midst of all this, Vincent arrived on set in his limo the worse for drink; the end-of-shoot celebrations had begun prematurely ... and maybe Vincent needed some fortification for the final spat with young Reeves. Half an hour in, Mike cottoned on and tore over to Philip: 'He's drunk – how dare he be drunk on my set! I'll kill the bastard!'

It was last orders for revenge. Philip spotted Mike whispering to Ogilvy in a conspiratorial manner. Fearing that the game was afoot, Philip located some foam insulation pads and placed them inside Vincent's costume. His hunch was right; Ogilvy had been instructed to 'really lay into Vincent' with the stage axe and Vincent told that, in the name of realism, these blows would not be faked. It was a parting shot from a film-maker at the end of his tether, and it would have been a hung-over and bruised English Edwardian painter in New York the next day for the *Darling of the Day* rehearsals. Filming went on and the production wrapped on 13 November, a week over schedule. The crew pulled out of Lavenham leaving a flurry of unpaid bills in their wake, and marker on the walls of Orford Castle that has remained there to this day.

Mike moved straight into post-production, which was well underway. During the shooting, editor Howard Lanning had been assembling a rough cut from the footage as it came in. Mike had only had the opportunity to check the dailies occasionally, at a local cinema hired for that purpose (Price had initially refused to join him). Howard's brother Dennis was the dubbing editor, and it fell to him to build an almost entirely new dialogue soundtrack; the only scene with usable sound was the meal with Hilary, Ogilvy and Rupert Davies. This had also been pieced together while Mike was still shooting, not least as Vincent's time was so limited. Mike had been 'very upset' that he had lost control of Vincent's post-synching and, fearing that Vincent would lapse back into camp, took an off-the-cuff decision: would classically trained actor Jack Lynn accompany Price to the studio in Covent Garden and act as dialogue director for the three days of post-synching with Price? 'And Jack – you know that I don't want him to lapse into

melodramatic readings. I want it to be very natural. His performance is looking so good that I don't want it to sound like one of the
horror films.'[58]

By the time Mike got his hands on the rough cut, the soundtrack was sufficiently precise for the editing to continue, unham-
pered by ropey post-synch dialogue. The rush was over, and Mike
was able to work on the cutting at something more like his own
pace. Howard was impressed with the amount of time Mike spent
on the editing, even though the rough cut, sticking closely to the
script, needed little more than fine tuning rather than a process of
'finding' the film:

> He wanted it very, very fast. You don't dwell on a line for a reaction,
> you just go bang-bang-bang-bang. That was the way he shot it.
> Certainly he had a very definite style – the minimum of reaction
> time. It's very, very quick cutting, much faster than I was used to.
> Invariably I may have left certain frames in, after a particular bit of
> dialogue. He would actually cut on the dialogue ... He based his
> work on Don Siegel, his idol. He didn't chop and change too much
> after he got what he wanted ... he had a talent, a feel for it.[59]

Parts of the film are as fast as possible – unbroken dialogue is
used as a soundbridge across a cut to another scene. For Howard,
it was a relief to sink his teeth into a film that was perceived to
matter, unlike *The Blood Beast Terror*, the previous Tenser film
that he, and a fair number of the *Witchfinder* crew, had recently
finished. He felt *Witchfinder* represented the best work he had
done. Instincts and the original intentions, rather than dissemb-
ling, determined the cutting, and as a result the film remained
remarkably organic and real – the strong narrative drive uninterrupted. One of the few occasions where the cutting is not invisible,
and not entirely subservient to the narrative, is the love scene.
Mike was keen to polish the sequence, particularly after he had
whittled down the tavern scene as much as possible, setting up the
love scene as a contrast to the horror to come – and so that it did
not come across as out-and-out exploitation. Howard and Mike
worked on making it 'gentle': multiple images on the screen, slow-
motion, long mixes and lap dissolves, all to the point of abstraction. The montage was prepared twice to avoid the jerky camera

movements in the majority of the takes. After the experience of *The Sorcerers*, Mike was still aware of his own relative inexperience, and so sought opinions from all those involved in the post-production, and relied on Howard's diligent eye for detail (breaking chases involving the same horse into shots where this was not apparent, for example).

By the close of 1967, a rough cut was nearing completion. It was time to make good on the earlier promise, and call up John Trevelyan.

Notes

1 Tenser, BOUM interview. In fact, Price's films by this point were closer to seventy-five.

2 R. Bassett, *Witchfinder General* (London, Herbert Jenkins Ltd, 1966). Pan Books reprinted the book in 1968 with a still from the film on the front and approving copy on the back: 'A catalogue of horror' (Eastern Daily Press); 'There is a degree of authenticity that makes the blood run cold' (Cambridge News).

3 Tenser, BOUM interview.

4 Published in facsimile in M. Hopkins, *The Discovery of Witches* (Norwich, H. W. Hunt, 1931). A commentary on the book, with a facsimile, can also be found in M. Summers, *The Discovery of Witches: A Study of Master Matthew Hopkins, commonly call'd Witch Finder General* (London, Cayme Press, 1928). Hopkins's book begins with a quote from Exodus 22:18 – 'Thou shalt not suffer a witch to live.' For a fuller discussion of the historical figure, see A. E. Green, *Witches and Witch-Hunters* (Yorkshire, S. R. Publishers Ltd, 1971), pp. xiii–xvi.

5 Pirie, *Heritage of Horror*, p. 156.

6 Philip's Roundhead officer is the first to congratulate Cromwell.

7 It was only during the post-production, while shooting the opening credits, that Philip discovered that Tenser had officially upgraded him to Producer, and wanted him to take solo Producer credit; Philip modestly pointed out that the contracts for Arnold Miller and Deke Heyward meant that they had to be afforded a producer credit, despite negligible contributions.

8 Weaver, *Interviews*, p. 168. Emphases in the original.

9 When a package of their first five Poe pictures, rereleased as a 'Dusk to Dawn' drive-in extravaganza took a fair amount of rental money, there was some talk of selling all the films together to television, as a Poe series.

10 McGee, *Faster and Furiouser*, p. 274.

11 Weaver, *Interviews*, p. 33. Arkoff also claims credit for the title; Kelley, *Filming Reeves' Masterpiece*, p. 42.

12 S. Arkoff and R. Trubo, *Flying Through Hollywood by the Seat of my Pants: From the Man who Brought You 'I Was A Teenage Werewolf' and 'Muscle Beach Party'* (New York, Birch Lane Press, 1992), p. 143.

13 The US video and laserdisc releases used a Kendall Schmidt synthesiser score rather than the Paul Ferris one; some parts of the film, previously scored, have no backing at all. This was supposedly instigated by Orion Pictures in 1983 when they acquired AIP's back catalogue but neglected to obtain the musical rights as well. This resulted in the rescoring either to avoid paying royalties, or simply because the music could not be used. It has also been suggested that this was an attempt to 'update' the AIP films for their initial video releases. Ferris's score has since been licensed elsewhere, turning up in a variety of commercials. At the time of writing, a legal stalemate in terms of releasing a US version of the film with the correct score remains. The alternative title and Poe readings also remain on US versions of the film. The Schmidt score is far from as bad as it is reputedly to be, but it does not belong in the film.

14 Who was being taken advantage of in this deal remains in dispute; see R. Grey, *Nightmare of Ecstasy: the Life and Art of Edward D. Wood, Jr* (London, Faber & Faber, 1994), pp. 61–2.

15 Weaver, *Interviews*, p. 18.

16 A Supreme Court decision to separate exhibition from production had led to a trade war breaking out between the studios and the exhibitors – and this was at a time when half the US cinemas were failing to break even. Television stepped into the breach as each began demanding a higher percentage of the box office take. Republic and RKO went out of business, leaving AIP, with its minimal overheads, in an exceptionally strong position. For further discussion, see McGee, *Faster and Furiouser*.

17 S. S. Prawer, *Caligari's Children: The Film as Tale of Terror* (Oxford, Oxford University Press, 1980), p. 206. Emphasis in the original.

18 Weaver, *Interviews*, p. 163.

19 Weaver, *Interviews*, p. 161.

20 Weaver, *Interviews*, p. 144.

21 Elsewhere he claims to have rewritten half the script; Weaver, *Interviews*, p. 178. Ogilvy recalls that Mike inserted the 'Additional scenes' credit as an in-joke, a stab at Deke; Kelley, 'Filming Reeves' masterpiece', p. 43.

22 Erika Bond, interview with author, 2 October 2000.

23 Letter from Louis Heyward to Vincent Price, 12 August 1967.

24 Jack Lynn, interview with author, 20 April 2002.

25 Svehla and Svehla, *Vincent Price*, p. 239.

26 Letter from Michael Reeves to John Trevelyan, 7 April 1968. Held in the BBFC Archives. Emphasis in the original.

27 Svehla and Svehla, *Vincent Price*, p. 223.

28 Ogilvy, BOUM interview.

29 Pages 119–21 most probably detailed the final sequence, Hopkins's torture and death, in the original draft of the script.

30 Armstrong, interview with author.

31 T. Baker, M. Reeves, from the novel by R. Bassett, '*Witchfinder General*

final screenplay' (unpublished, Tigon-Global Productions Ltd, 1967), shot 66, p. 27.

32 Baker, Reeves, Bassett, 'Final Screenplay', shot 302, pp. 113–14.

33 Quoted in D. Petrie, *The British Cinematographer* (London, British Film Institute, 1996) p. 85.

34 Laurie Shane, interview with author, 12 June 2001. All subsequent remarks are taken from this source.

35 Hilary Dwyer, interview with author, 15 June 2001. All subsequent remarks are taken from this source.

36 Alf Joint, interview with author, 5 June 2002. All subsequent remarks are taken from this source.

37 Gillian Aldam, interview with author, 7 June 2001. All subsequent remarks are taken from this source.

38 William Maxwell, interview with author, 29 May 1998.

39 Euan Pearson, interviews with author across 2001. All subsequent remarks are taken from this source.

40 Swires, 'And now the screaming stops', pp. 16–17.

41 Kelley, *Filming Reeves' Masterpiece*, p. 40.

42 Baker, Reeves, Bassett, 'Final screenplay', shot 54, p. 21.

43 Anon, 'Ian Ogilvy', unnumbered.

44 Weaver, *Interviews*, p. 169.

45 Swires, 'And now the screaming stops', p. 19.

46 Benshoff quotes Parrish and Whitney on the nature of the marriage; H. M. Benshoff, *Monsters in the Closet: Homosexuality and the Horror Film* (Manchester, Manchester University Press, 1997); J. R. Parrish, and S. Whitney, *Vincent Price Unmasked* (New York, Drake Publishers, Inc., 1974), p. 136. Benshoff, who cites Laughton and Price (at length) as doyens of the 'homohorror film', does not mention Price's portrayal of Hopkins: a measure of the extent to which Reeves had altered Price's screen persona for the duration of the film; Benshoff, *Monsters in the Closet*, p. 14.

47 Tenser, BOUM interview.

48 Pearson, interview with author.

49 Dwyer, interview with author.

50 Swires, 'And now the screaming stops', p. 19. Emphases in the original.

51 These words appear in Bassett's ending too; Bassett, *Witchfinder General*, p. 250.

52 Baker, Reeves, Bassett, 'Final screenplay', shots 330–9, pp. 116–17.

53 T. Baker, M. Reeves, from the novel by R. Bassett, with final scene revisions by Reeves and P. Waddilove (uncredited), '*Witchfinder General* final screenplay' (unpublished, Tigon-Global Productions Ltd, 1967), shot 326, p. 120.

54 Baker, Reeves, Bassett, Waddilove, 'Final screenplay', shot 328, p. 120.

55 Baker, Reeves, Bassett, Waddilove, 'Final screenplay', shot 329, p. 120.

56 Baker, Reeves, Bassett, Waddilove, 'Final screenplay', shot 336–7, p. 121.

57 Baker, Reeves, Bassett, Waddilove, 'Final screenplay', shot 343, p. 122.

58 Lynn, interview with author.

59 Howard Lanning, interview with author, 12 June 2001.

Ultimata

6

When Trevelyan saw the rough cut on 5 January 1968, he noted 'I do not think this films is likely to give us much trouble.' John offered some informal advice and Mike made a number of careful cuts to the violence, happy that censorship would not be an issue thereafter. Once the fine cut was ready, the soundtrack and music were laid down. Both Mike and Philip had attended the recording of Paul Ferris's *Greensleeves*-esque score, principally 'The Legend of *Witchfinder General*' and 'The Love Theme from *Witchfinder General*' at Olympic Sound Studios with the noted sound-recordist Keith Grant. Ferris used part of his fee to pay for the extra time he needed to get his score completely realised. The music would be used to counterpoint continually the brutalities of the film – most particularly for the end credits; screams cutting across the gentle theme. Ferris, who had also scored *The Sorcerers* and was a friend of Mike and Ogilvy and, with Henson, had written songs for Cliff Richard and the Shadows, took a screen credit for his role as Paul Clark as 'Morris Jar' (a joke at the expense of David Lean's operetic composer, Maurice Jarre).

Post-production was complete by the late morning of 17 March 1968. Mike hurried off to the demonstration that would become the Battle of Grosvenor Square, outside the American Embassy, although had he thrown any bricks they would have been in the opposite direction – towards the AIP offices. The apolitical scene of early 1967, that had informed *The Sorcerers*, had turned into a highly politicised and furious rabble, united in disgust over

American action in Vietnam. Mike, watching the chaos unfold around him, the police beatings, provocations and intimidation, would have understood the context for his study of violence and society and that, more importantly, this context would be understood by those who would soon see the film. Just as Mike had done in *The Sorcerers*, the protestors were refusing to allow the violence to remain distant and abstract; they had brought something of it to the heart of London. The palpable shock that many felt over the level of violence meted out to the protestors would be reprised in the level and nature of violence in his film, shortly. Tigon officially submitted *Witchfinder* to the BBFC on 29 March and Mike, exhausted, prepared to go on holiday.

Yet despite Trevelyan's initial approval, the examiners now recommended half a dozen substantial instances of 'minimum cuts' that were required for an X certificate – that is, required for the film to be released at all; these were not requests, but ultimata. Lowes was to be jabbed only once, his screams reduced; the duckings and the burning of Elizabeth Clark were both to be 'reduce[d] to a minimum', with no shots of Elizabeth screaming and only a long-shot of her and the fire; there were to be no shots of Sara's torture and Richard was only to hit Hopkins once with the axe. A woman also tortured (strangled and slapped, face bloodied) in a cell next to Lowes was to be removed entirely.[1]

Mike met Trevelyan on 3 April. The usual arguments were rehearsed and Mike agreed to make some further cuts. Trevelyan noted: 'He agreed to make a few cuts, but only a few. I then said that I would like to show the film to the President since this raised a policy question. Michael Reeves will be away in the West Indies for six weeks. If work has to be done on the film, he would like to await his return rather than have it done by the editor, Howard Lanning. I think Mr Tenser will want to get the film passed without delay.' This could be interpreted along the lines of Trevelyan acknowledging Mike's refusal to cut the film to the specifications – hence the raising of a 'policy question'.

Mike arrived in Jamaica with all the frustration and anger over the continual interference that he had endured, the snipping away of his idea of the film on all fronts, and his fear for the print, back

in England with Tenser and the BBFC, intact. Embattled, he telephoned Trevelyan on 6 April, but the conversation was abortive,
so Mike then wrote at great length to Trevelyan on 7 April – three
pages of near stream-of-consciousness prose, banged out on a
portable typewriter, handwritten notes added in the margins,
from the Bay Roc Hotel in Montego Bay. The letter expresses the
desire to have his say, and demonstrates how personally involved
with the film Mike had become. Crossings-out indicate that the
letter was written without notes or a previous draft. It comes to
represent more than Mike's engagement with Trevelyan (keeping
within the parameters of the argument that Trevelyan had set in
relation to the specific cuts required), or a condemnation of AIP,
or the director's commentary on the film, or a demonstration of
Mike reliving the film fully in the knowledge of what he was trying
to achieve and why; it is Reeves's manifesto for film-making:[2]

Dear John,

First of all, please forgive the various lapses of spelling, grammar and typing that will occur in this letter; for like most writers I
am proficient at none of them.

Anyway, with regard to WITCHFINDER: I am sorry our talk the
other day was so brief; to be honest, I was so damned nervous, I
have a feeling that I probably made no sense at all. There were so
many things I wanted to say about the picture, and there was so
little time, that I in all probability made a complete idiot of myself.
In any case I thank you for your forebearance, and hope that a little
of what I was trying to say permeated through my sea of
incoherence! I thought I'd write you this letter to try and make
plain to yourself and Lord Harlech what I was a) trying to do with
the film, and b) my feelings on your particular problems with it
with regard to cutting.

First of all, let me say that I fully appreciate your difficulties, and
realise what they are: 1/ it is a film that, by very fact of starring
Vincent P., and being distributed by the firm that it is (I am not in
any way knocking Tony – I like and respect him) it may get seen by
sections of society that <u>maybe</u> (though I must add that in my
opinion, a mere 25-year-old though I may be, it won't) it might have
some detrimental effect on; 2/ whilst I myself may have certain
admirers amongst our illustrious press corps, I have the overall
image of a maker of cheap horror films – and this is not going to

help matters (by the way, this is said in the probably conceited assumption that I have *any* image as a film maker at all (!)

So – to the film itself, and by the way, you will certainly gather from what follows that I would like you to hold this letter in strictest confidence – please!!

Despite its pedigree, as outlined above, WITCHFINDER is a serious picture; that is not to deny its legion of faults – I am only too well aware of them, believe me. However, I think the end result is pretty powerful, as you yourself said – more so even than I thought it was going to be, and I knew what I was aiming at, despite the multitude of AIP inspired iron manacles that were perpetually descending vice-like on my shoulder. Its overall message (though I loathe the word) is as anti-violence as it can be. Violence breeds violence, and that end-violence in itself is insanity. To put that over to a paying audience, particularly one who is paying to enjoy a vicarious thrill from once-removed sadism, surely this cannot be anything but moral? And for what it is worth, I think this is what WITCHFINDER does, whether that audience is consciously aware of it or otherwise. If, as AIP wished me to do, I had dissolved from the final close-up to a shot of Marshall and Sara riding blissfully into the sunset, I would agree with you that the film should be cut – and to be honest I would have had a troubled conscious for quite a while at having made it. However, its present ending, I feel, is salutory, moral, highly depressing (it may even cause the film to lose money, and knowing this, and allowing me to keep it, is one of the reasons I admire Tony: AIP I never consulted, so thats their hard luck – in fact, feeling as I do about that bunch of ponces (and I mean that almost literally) I hope devoutly that it will in the States!

From the point of view of actual cutting, I have as you know, voluntarily made three cuts myself in the places where I feel the film in fact does descend into merely gratuitous sadism; (I ask you to excuse their initial inclusion on the grounds of directorial nerves, a desire to keep the film up to feature length by including all dramatic impact of any value at all in the cutting stages, and the usual problem of not realising one's mistakes till one sees a fully dubbed, colour, consecutively projected print.) Literally the cuts I have made are as follows: the cell scene: I have shortened it by half, removing the two most obviously vicious blows to the woman's face. The burning scene: I have cut the final C.U. of the Elizabeth Clark character's bleeding face – in fact, in terms of dramatic cutting rythm, this makes the whole sequence better constructed! Apart from these I am <u>not</u> willing to make any further cuts, and from what I remember of your office's rejection slip, I will try and outline why below.

<u>Generally</u>: in order for the film to retain its point, there <u>must</u> be a level of brutality throughout; thus, by seducing the audience into accepting it, we prime them for the ending, where the stool is whipped right from under their feet, and they are left looking at themselves, and their involvement with the foregoing violence, with, I hope (and am in fact sure) the sense of self-loathing one invariably receives when one has been momentarily involved in a flash of sadism – however slight it may be, no matter be it verbal or physical. If the film is cut to an "acceptable" level of violence, this ending will lose all point and become merely "horror-comic", and that is what both you <u>and</u> I so desperately wish to avoid. If the picture is "reduced" it could well become just an exercise in gratuitous violence (assuming you did'nt cut about 35 minutes in which case we are all wasting our time, and a lot of Tony's money!), and would have exactly the reverse effect it is intended to have, i.e. an audience having a lovely time reveling in their nice censor-protected "safe" brutality. (I am of course admitting that it is an extremely brutal film whatever you, I, or the projectionist at the Rex, Solihull, do to it!)

<u>In particular</u>: the torture of Lowes – one only sees the pricker (don't laugh, thats what they used to call it apparently …) actually go into his back twice, and on both occasions extremely briefly. If this is removed, the scene will become nonsensical, as well as dramatically ill-constructed, and thus point us on our way to the drastic error of moral judgement outlined above. As far as screams go, what is he supposed to do? Surely this would nullify the point that suffering is horrible, degrading and as far from what one could call "Hollywood glamourous" as it could be?

The beating up of the girl in the cell: as I said, I have already halved it, but it must remain in order to keep up the <u>vital</u> level of brutality, which for reasons mentioned earlier, has to permeate the whole film.

The moat-drowning sequence: same thing applies, though at this point I in all honesty cannot see where the objection to this lies. In my opinion, and due to lack of time, weather problems etc., this scene is so undershot that I only just managed to cut it together at all, and in fact, with reference to my whole thesis with the film, is what I would consider a regrettably tame sequence. For the record, apart from one extreme long shot there are only four cuts to the victims in the water, and each of these is only 18" long. The fact that anyone should even consider cutting the scene at all seems to me incomprehensible – but a considerable tribute to Paul Ferris' music and my editing! (For which, thank you – or [C], or whoever even envisaged the idea of even partly cutting the sequence ...!)

The burning scene: as I said, I have cut one of the shots of Elizabeth Clarke sans eye, and it improves the scene a lot. It was gratuitous in the first place, and destroyed the momentum. As for the rest of the sequence, there is only one other really horrifying shot, that where she actually catches fire: this is a) necessary for the "level of violence" thing, and b) occurs in a very fast long shot. The rest of the scene is entirely built in terms of effectiveness by the girl's fear, and Paul, and the crowd, and Hopkins' reaction to it. I do not see either how or why it should be cut, to be honest, scaring though it may be. (By the way, though this is obviously not an anticutting ploy, did you know this scene is entirely factual? Tom Baker and I reconstructed it from, I believe, a New Statesman article about witchcraft in the Middle Ages).[3] As far as level of screams go, the same comments apply here as to the torture of Lowes. This girl is suffering horribly, and I want the audience to suffer with her – not enjoy the sequence for its meretricious thrill value (if it has any).

The final sequence: this pertains particularly to my general remarks about the aim of the film. If cut, and just "suggested" it will just be an exciting (though probably nonsensical) finale of "Will the dashing hero escape and kill the dastardly villain rescuing the fair maiden on the way?" department. Then, instead of deeply disturbing the audience at the finish, the whole thing will merely become ludicrous, enlivened by some suggested sadism – and as I said earlier, I don't want my name associated with anything of that order, any more than I understand you and your office would. Marshall's madness at the end must be motivated, and strongly motivated, to have any effect; so also must the final image of Sara screaming hysterically. And if the sequence in the castle is cut down, this will not be the case. As I say, the morality of the film lies in its whole content; and the fact that in the final 90 seconds the violence explodes utterly in the face of the "sympathetic" protagonists (by their own participation in it) is the core of all that is good (morally good) in the film.

Destroy the film and you render its denouement of complete despair meaningless: do <u>that</u> and you might as well ban the whole thing, for it would become just another exercise in 'terror for kicks'.

I don't want that to happen; financially, 'artistic' or career considerations apart. Surely you have to agree with me on this?

I'm sorry this is so long and involved. I trust it makes some kind of literary sense – I'm afraid I can get a bit involved when I feel fairly deeply about a difficult subject. When I get back from here, I'd like very much to talk with both you, and, if you wish, David Harlech about the situation. Believe it or not, I have lots more to say! (Particularly regarding advertising, Tony's probable hostile attitude towards your office – which I beg you to disregard, though as you certainly know better than I do, with him it is just a manufactured phase! – and the best way to generally cope with this situation. Believe me, John, I have tried to be as honest as I can in this letter; I hope none of it sounds rude or unreasonable; I hope also you'll believe one thing about WITCHFINDER; whatever its demerits, it has at least one or two things going for it – its an honest film, and the audiences I have tried it on have all emerged from it well shaken, and with the overall <u>point</u> of the movie embedded in their not always too-sensitive brains. I think it will do the same for general audiences too, whether or not, as I said earlier, they are all able to put it into words.

Yours – Michael

NB: Please – also – forgive all the underlinings etc in this – I write better screenplays than letters, tho' that may not be saying much!

Despite the compromises and problems throughout its making, *Witchfinder* had essentially remained true to Mike's intentions. His initial conception of the film – defining it in terms of what the film would not be rather than remaining a discontent within the generic 'horror' framework – is entirely reiterated in his letter. The letter argues that Trevelyan cannot view the film in any context other than that of the film itself, and Mike's reading of the potential BBFC tampering is along the lines of the will to reduce the film to the level of any other horror. Mike perceives imposed happy endings, a facet of a reluctance to engage in an absolute realism, as essentially hypocritical. The implication is that, more often than not, adherence to generic expectations is at the price of a marginalisation of realism. What Mike needed was a sense of truth – in Jameson's description: 'the "truth content" of art, its claim to possess some truth or epistemological value'.[4] For Mike, this represents a moral position – and it is with a moral outrage too that he seeks to justify the film as presented to the BBFC. The letter suggests that an underlying process of the rejection of generic types and expectations informed his making of the film – and that such things are rejected on the grounds of their inherent compromise of an absolute realism. Exactly the same thoughts informed Godard, then making *Le Weekend* – an equally upfront portrait of societal breakdown, a parade of grotesques with a similarly pessimistic conclusion. Like *Witchfinder*, *Le Weekend* was shot in the last months of 1967, and released once the civil unrest of 1968 was well underway. But whereas Godard's Brechtian sensibility turned the contemporary surroundings into a caricatured, alienating reading of bourgeois Paris and Parisians, Reeves had found that, though the adoption of a western framework and extensive location work, his film had recorded the texture of English countryside with similar truthfulness in its realism. The alienated 'truth' of the violence would be contextualised in the recognisable truth of a sense of place and history; a powerful combination. The reactions that the film provoked in the BBFC examiners are essentially defensive; they acknowledge the achievements of the film (as Mike notes) and deem that film itself must not speak in such a way. This clashed with Mike's perception of film as, ultimately, a moral enterprise; an art form that must speak of the condition of man – free from any considerations that would hamper this. But unlike Tariq Ali, whose friends had clustered around to prevent the Grosvenor Square police getting to him, Mike was entirely exposed.

With this, Mike resisted any further cuts and hoped to persuade and pressurise Trevelyan, in person, to think again. Meanwhile, cuts were also listed for the trailer. Upon Mike's early return, he and Philip met Trevelyan at the BBFC; Mike had clearly been brooding – Philip recalls:

> Michael looked as if he were about to assault his cousin. I asked John if he was making his cuts 'to protect the British public or to protect the office of the Censor?' His reply was along the lines that 'I made the cuts to protect both the public and the office!' I then asked John if he would be prepared to repeat that statement publicly. He said he would gladly do so!

Philip recounted the incident during a BBC Radio interview. Shortly afterwards, he and Trevelyan were invited to appear on BBC television to discuss censorship, but Trevelyan declined. Behind the scenes, Trevelyan had brought the full staff of the BBFC to an examination of the uncut film. An internal note written by two of the examiners, dated 25 April, reports:

> <u>Nobody</u> thought that these scenes were tolerable in their present form. [A] considered that the original minute of exception(s) was well-founded, and [B], while recognising that the setting is important, could not visualise <u>any</u> set up in which she would have tolerated this degree of violence and sadism for public exhibitions. [Trevelyan] said that he would treat the film in accordance with our usual practices and that he thought he remembered the scenes well enough to pinpoint with the editor where the cuts should come.
>
> The President [Lord Harlech] has seen this film. It is understood that he feels less strongly than the original examiners about certain scenes, but [A] and [B] do not anxiously urge the Secretary not to [*sic*] give any ground beyond what the President thinks absolutely necessary and to represent to him the difficulties presented to us as a Board by being more lenient to this film than to other historical films representing forms of brutality and torture which ... to the public ... is made to look like just another horror film by the presence in a leading role of Vincent Price.[5]

Tigon submitted the film in colour for classification the next day. It is unclear whether Mike had implemented further cuts to the film at this point (those in relation to Trevelyan's noting that 'He agreed to make a few cuts, but only a few') but either way it would seem that the BBFC began to censor the print. Trevelyan wrote directly to Mike on 29 April:

I am very sorry that we had to make cuts in your picture *Witchfinder General*, and feel that I owe it to you to explain our reasons for this.

First. Let me say that I have no doubts about your integrity in making this picture, nor about the validity of the theme. You set out to show that violence is horrible, especially when associated with sadism. Unfortunately in doing so you presented us with serious problems, as follows:–

(1) We have for some years taken a strong line about scenes of violence, which we believe to be often harmful, and if we passed your picture without cuts this would, to many people, appear to be a complete reversal of this policy, which has been widely publicised in the Press and on television [...]

(2) We believe that, while many people deplore violence, there are some who not only accept it but actually enjoy it. This is something we do not want to encourage, and I believe that in passing your picture we would be taking a substantial risk of doing this

(3) There is reason to believe that the continuous diet of violence through screen entertainment, both cinema and television, may be conditioning people to its acceptance [...]

In conclusion I would like to express regret that I under-estimated the impact of this film when I saw an early assembly or rough cut. I now know the film well, and I believe that I am justified in saying that the impact was immensely heightened by the colour, sound effects and music. The picture in its final form was very much stronger that I had anticipated, and it will have the effect of making me more cautious in future in making preliminary judgements on films of violence.

In his memoir, *What the Censor Saw*, Trevelyan, writing about this period as one of being seemingly besieged by problematic films, does not hesitate to note *Witchfinder* as the occasion of a major battle. He sandwiches the film between Ken Russell's *The Devils* (which would also wind up calling in Lord Harlech)[6] and Sam Peckinpah's *The Wild Bunch* (with *Performance*, *Straw Dogs* and *A Clockwork Orange* following on shortly). This lapse in chronology suggests that Trevelyan automatically associated *Witchfinder* with the cycle of considerably more violent films of the early 1970s, marking the end of his time with the BBFC: 'Michael Reeves resisted our censorship of his film most vigorously, and eventually took no part in the cutting. I am happy to say that when eventually he saw the results he sent me a letter in which he said that the cuts had been very well made and had not harmed the film nearly as much as he had expected. This was generous of him.'[7] No record exists of this letter in the BBFC files and it may well have been that Trevelyan had misremembered Mike's letter of 7 April and the comment that some of his voluntary cutting tightened the film, repositioning this admission after the full cutting of the film. Nor is it likely that Trevelyan understood that the damage done to Mike's 1968 cut of the film would remain so for decades to come.

Notes

1 The continental versions have all this intact, and the additional nudity in the tavern. These scenes were restored to the UK Redemption video and Metrodome DVD release and they are intact in the US cut too. The film received further, unspecified cuts for its release in Ireland in October 1968.
2 The letter is reproduced with the emphases and grammatical and spelling errors unaltered.
3 This was probably one or more of his articles on the subject by the historian Hugh Trevor-Roper. In his review of *Witchfinder*, Austen alludes to a relevant Trevor-Roper article published in *Encounter*.
4 F. Jameson, *Signatures of the Visible* (London, Routledge, 1990), p. 74.
5 Emphases in the original.
6 Russell felt that *Witchfinder* was stronger meat: 'This is one of the worst films I have ever seen and certainly the most nauseous'; Ken Russell, interview with author, 27 September 1999.
7 Trevelyan, *What the Censor Saw*, pp. 162–3.

Commentary:
Witchfinder General

Of course, if I had a choice, I would not decide to make a film on a modest budget. However, in making films on a modest budget it has developed my style, which by necessity is taut, tight, and realistic. (Don Siegel)[1]

'I wanted this brutal and sensual film to have a profound reality and a point of view. I wanted one to feel the intelligence, the coldness and the cynicism of the killers ... (Siegel on *The Killers*)[2]

Sequence one (pre-credits)

Witchfinder opens in an appropriately startling way: the calmness of a pastoral scene is shattered by sudden and brutal violence.

A fade-in to the first image: sunlight shining through the branches and leaves of an oak tree. The light, refracted across the camera lens, forms a cross. The soundtrack is faded in seconds later – sheep, birds and a methodical thumping, the sound of wood hitting wood, as if a parody of that activity associated with such green pastures – English cricket. The camera pans down to frame grazing sheep in a movement identical to the opening of *Intrusion* before cutting to a second shot of the same, only this time a branch of the oak is across the frame, seen in silhouette, darkening the screen. The third shot reveals the source of the hammering: a carpenter driving in the final nails of newly erected gallows. It is a low-angle shot from the foot of a hill and the gallows and the carpenter are seen in silhouette against a vast sky, locating this image of death in the landscape, playing off the images of the gallows and the cross, the wood of the tree with the wood of the gallows.

Reeves cuts to village houses and an anguished scream. The drone of a priest's recitations fade in and a village mob comes into view. Reeves cuts straight into the scuffle – a dishevelled woman is being dragged towards the gallows. She is in rags and her hands are bound. Reeves uses a handheld camera for the medium close-ups, which fall in and out of focus, and so contrast with the smooth tracking shot of the intoning priest, his eyes fixed on his Bible. A cut back to the gallows offers the briefest of aural respites – the last nail is hammered home – before Reeves returns to the woman with a head-on medium shot which is also a shot from the POV (point-of-view) of Stearne, later identified as one of Hopkins's thugs. She collapses and is dragged along the ground. The sequence recalls the opening lynching of *Revenge of the Blood Beast*.

Reeves fades into a shot of the villagers at the foot of the hill. Grass sways in the foreground – the countryside is unperturbed by the lynching. A cut to the front of the group and a steady zoom back reveals a primed noose and two motionless hangmen, a device cribbed from Sergio Leone's *The Good, The Bad and the Ugly*. Within little over a minute of screen time the woman has arrived. We sense that the sentence was passed only minutes before. Leaving the zoom incomplete, Reeves tracks right, towards the approaching group. The sound of a biting gale is faded in. A cut to a low-angle shot catches the woman as she again collapses to the ground. A hangman calls for water and a crone, bucket at the ready, throws it over the woman. With such things, it becomes giddily apparent that this supposed horror film is re-enacting the crucifixion. It is an audacious ploy, lifting the Stations of the Cross, reinventing a primal scene of western society in such lowly surroundings. It raises the question: what on earth does Reeves think he is doing? It suggests that, ritual and the spectacle of violence aside, all executions are *the* execution. This can also be read, in Reeves's oeuvre, in relation to the similar strategy of time 'out of joint' in the opening of *Blood Beast*.

A cut to the priest shows his absorption in the text he is reciting, suggesting complicity with the brutal lynching and an unwillingness to face the suffering brought about at the behest of the church. Reeves then juxtaposes shots of the onlooking villagers with shots of the woman hoisted up to the gallows (including the low-angle shot from the foot of the hill). The villagers look on, impassive and weather-beaten. The priest nods to a hangman who kicks the stool from beneath the woman. The camera zooms back as the woman swings out, a stylistic lurch that mimics 'taken-aback' at the execution. Her screaming ceases immediately, leaving only the sound of the gallows wood creaking under the weight of the woman. It recalls the oak of the first shot and the unnerving sound of the cemetery trees creaking in the wind in the opening sequence of Lean's *Great Expectations*.

The camera now tracks left, taking in the departing villagers, led by the priest, and finishing with the slowly rotating corpse. A drum roll fades in on the soundtrack. Reeves fades to another angle on the body and unexpectedly crash zooms past the corpse to a cloaked figure on horseback, gazing at the scene from a distance. The zoom terminates with the freezing of the image into a blue lithograph and the credits roll, to suitably discordant music.

To zoom is considered bad film grammar, something born of economic necessity (the way to avoid a cut, the poor cousin of the tracking shot, the visual language of the television advert), but here the zoom is employed in an intensely cinematic fashion. It forcefully associates the hanging with the figure of Matthew Hopkins in a way that a comparable 'good' camera movement – a track-in or a whip pan – could not. Here the zoom functions in the same way as in frontline war footage, it tears the gaze of the viewer away from the foregrounded events and forcibly frames a significant detail – the gun that fired the shot; the ominous onlooking figure of the Witchfinder. The impact of the speed and suddenness suggests the hanging is a consequence of the presence of the silent figure – the zoom is accusatory. Milliseconds later this is confirmed with the opening credit.

In the shooting script, this information is conveyed in a more contrived and less cinematic fashion just prior to the actual execution:

4.   HOPKINS' POV. THE HILL
The gibbet standing silhouetted against the sky, a flock of sheep grazing peacefully around its base, and the figure of the CARPENTER standing-by.

5.   TWO SHOT: HOPKINS AND MAGISTRATE
HOPKINS' fishy gaze swivels round on to the MAGISTRATE.

> HOPKINS (statement, not question)
> You have my fee.
>
> MAGISTRATE
> Of course ...

He takes a small leather purse from his belt and hands it to HOPKINS, who takes it without examining the contents. The MAGISTRATE looks slightly surprised.

> MAGISTRATE
> The sum agreed upon is there.

HOPKINS nods cursorily; OS [off-screen] we hear the sound of incoherent cursing and screaming as it gets nearer. HOPKINS and the MAGISTRATE glance in the direction of the noise.[3]

This conversation does not appear in the finished film and its function – to connect Hopkins to the execution – is better expressed through the use of the zoom. In addition, the script has the woman attacking Hopkins ('she has lunged sideways and is at HOPKINS' throat, seemingly trying to tear it from him with her bare hands'[4]), which is also rendered unnecessary by Reeves's filming style. By keeping Hopkins as a wordless presence – focusing on his minions (the priest and a couple of heavies, all seen to be doing God's will at the instigation of this onlooker), he remains an unknown entity.

The zoom frames Hopkins in a medium shot and Reeves then prints the headline, the opening title emblazoned across a blue lithograph, precisely recalling the opening credit sequence of *The Killers*:

Matthew Hopkins

WITCHFINDER GENERAL

Abstract black and white lithographs follow, details from grim faces and blotchy countryside scenes are shuffled beneath the credits. The shooting script notes:

> Remainder of the TITLES over similar LITHOS, depicting HOPKINS, STEARNE, a selection of hangings, burnings, swimmings, etc. (There are some genuine lithos like this that could be found and photographed for these title backings.)[5]

The final credit – 'Directed by Michael Reeves' – appears alongside a Baconesque face, its features distorted into a silent scream.

This opening operates in two essential, narrative ways. Firstly, it fulfils the requirement of exploitation genre; Reeves cuts straight to the violence, vamps the star's entrance, and promises much more of the same (brutality, screaming women, inquisition-like church activity). Secondly, it sets the scene for later, establishes the timeframe, so that period details can now be fleshed out with gestures rather than laborious recreations. But beyond this, the opening thematically presents the harsh world of the film in microcosm and introduces the clash that will determine the central tension of the film and colour the *mise en scène* – the juxtaposition of nature and violence and the suggestion that the two are interconnected, and that Hopkins resides at their intersection. It questions notions of the benevolence of nature, posits organised religion as an agent of destruction and – most importantly – illustrates the democratic nature of the execution: the violence comes from the mob, the blood-thirsty villagers, the small crowd of extras – the good people of England. Clearly, evil is no external or externalised force in *Witchfinder General* as it is in *The Sorcerers*.

Sequence two

Clipped tones and a slightly eccentric voice[6] – as if that of a favourite history teacher – meander through the only instance of voice-over in the film. This opening device creates a spiritual kinship with Siegel, whose films *Invasion of the Body Snatchers*, *Riot in Cell Block 11* and even the by-the-book Universal western, *Duel at Silver*

Creek, begin in identical ways; it is a secret *hommage* on Reeves's part.

> The year is 1645. England is in the grip of the bloody Civil War. On the one side stands the Royalist Party of King Charles, on the other Cromwell's Parliamentary Party, the Roundheads. The structure of law and order has collapsed. Local magistrates indulge in individual whims – justice and injustice are dispensed in more or less equal quantities and without opposition; an atmosphere in which the unscrupulous rebel and the likes of Matthew Hopkins take full advantage of the situation. In a time when the superstitions of country folk are still a powerful factor, Hopkins prays upon them, torturing and killing in a supposed drive to eliminate witchcraft from the country, doing so with the full blessing of what law there is. However, his influence is confined largely to the eastern sector of the country – East Anglia, which is held firmly in Cromwell's grasp, but not so firmly that the Roundhead cavalry patrols have everything their own way. There still exists an ever-present threat from the remnants of the Royalist armies, desperately foraging for food, horses and supplies.

Both Siegel and Reeves work from the same premise: the structure of law and order has collapsed. It is a device par excellence for psychological horror – the circumstances in which the ordinary becomes sinister without the outward appearance altering: Siegel's body-snatched town folk (or the inadvertent and unaware drug couriers in his *The Lineup*), and Reeves's country folk and countryside. Thus when Richard asks Hopkins who he is looking for, he is told 'A man who may not be what he seems to be.' This neat little socio-political thumbnail sketch also calms the viewer after the atrocities of the opening sequence, and plays the all-important card of emphasising that exploitational violence is not really exploitational if within a historical framework (something echoed in the 'quality' casting too; one day bit-parts by established English actors such as Patrick Wymark and Wilfred Brambell). Aside from the BBFC reaction to this strategy, it does seem to have worked; the film was attended by an eclectic mixture of hippies and retired military gentlemen during the 17/18 January 1970 all-night Reeves retrospective at the London National Film Theatre.

The voice-over also works to define the historical period setting and paints the norms of the world of *Witchfinder* with broad strokes.

During the voice-over, the camera executes a steady tracking-shot around an ancient oak. The camera pans as it tracks so that the trunk remains in the centre of the frame. The sunlight, filtered through the leafy canopy, is given a green tint and a restless wind sways the foliage. The attention paid to the oak defies the viewer's expectations of establishing shots, which ordinarily would simply illustrate the information conveyed in the voice-over. Where is the devastation of the Civil War? Where are shots of Royalists and Roundheads? Where are the peasantry, fearful of witchcraft? The viewer demands interesting faces, wide-angled landscapes; an expositional montage. Reeves displays a tree instead – and the effect is both subtle and astonishing. This privileging of the tree lends a corporeality to the 'naive' aural attempt to conjure up 1645; the history itself is written into the knotted wood, the creaking branches. The leaves rustle in 1967 just as they did in 1645. Such a parallel between past and present has already been made in the opening execution. The voice-over is rendered a superfluous lull. It is the texture of the voice and the texture of the oak that concern us. In this, no low-budget philosophy of spartan scenery 'and the eye will paint in the rest' is in action; Reeves demands and elicits imagination instead. The oak has become some sort of aesthetic time-machine and Reeves's 1645 is suddenly credible – a complete evocation. Melding past and present in such a fashion is a mainstay of European art cinema, but here it seems more a tendency that is peculiar to English eccentrics; Alan Clark's recorded vision of a Lancaster bomber, for example ('I entered the mind of others, the ghosts of former times, who must have looked upon the same view ...'[7]) or, closer to home, the lecture in Powell and Pressburger's cranky *A Canterbury Tale*. In this, another eccentric history teacher, Thomas Colpeper (Eric Portman), delivers a public lecture to a motley crew of soldiers and land girls camped in a village outside Canterbury in 1944. Camaraderie palpably abounds among these thrown-together people. To provide a foundation for the imaginings of life after the soon-to-end war, the film moves backwards in time to make sense of the present.

Colpepper engages in this, and understands its importance too. Surrounded by darkness and in silhouette, his words transport his audience (and Powell and Pressburger's) back to the time of Chaucer's Pilgrims:

> There are more ways than one of getting close to your ancestors. Follow the old road and as you walk, think of them and the Old England. They climbed Chillingbourne Hill just as you did. They sweated and paused for breath just as you did today. And when you see the bluebells in the spring, the wild thyme, the broom and the heather, you're only seeing what their eyes saw: the same rivers; the same birds are singing. When you lie flat on your back and rest and watch the clouds sailing, as I often do, you're so close to those other pilgrims that you can hear the thrumming of the hoofs of their horses and the sound of the wheel on the road and their laughter and talk and the music of the instruments they carried. And when I turn the bend of the road, where they too saw the towers of Canterbury, I feel I only have to turn my head to see them on the road behind me.

The spell has been cast; the listeners catch their breath. Powell and Pressburger have achieved in feeling the equivalent to the audacious opening cut: a pilgrim follows a hawk in the sky with his eyes, a cut, not matching, replaces the hawk with a bomber, and the pilgrim-actor is now seen in army uniform. *Witchfinder* closes with a reprise of such 'in-camera flashbacks'; shots of the empty corridors leading down to the dungeon, echoing with Sara's screams; the location retains an invisible history of the events it has seen.

The camera stops panning and the tracking continues so that a parallax shot is created – revealing, in long-shot, a troop of mounted Roundheads behind the oak's trunk. Now the trunk becomes a stage curtain, sweeping back out of frame to reveal the characters and, as in theatre, there is a sudden sense of present-ness. As the camera tracks, foliage remains in the foreground. This will be a consistent aesthetic strategy throughout the film – up to the establishing shots of Orford Castle at the end, 'framed' by swaying branches. It is as if nature is encroaching on the world of the film, threatening to swamp and overrun civilisation – another front in the battle of primitivism and civilisation.

A cut to a steady tracking shot of the handful of parliamentary soldiers breaks the spell. Bright early morning sunlight, birdsong and breath in the air lend a sharpness to the scene. The camera frames Richard (Ian Ogilvy) to introduce him as the film's protagonist. He is thinking, as lost as the film is in ideas of absent presences. Richard's reverie is broken with the intrusion of earthy banter from a fellow soldier, until both soldiers are hushed by the paternal captain. The scene dissolves to a two-shot of the troop arriving in the woods, the foliage and trees are foregrounded and a third shot reveals a hidden sniper silently rising from the foliage, Vietnamesque.[8] He immediately aims, shoots and a troop soldier, busy with his horse, falls to the ground. The others take cover for some expositional dialogue from the Captain: 'Royalist snipers. Probably only a few of them after food and horses. We'll flush the bastards out in no time.'

Richard is left behind to guard the horses. Time passes and he hears cries, a gun shot and a scream. The woods screen the violence. His eyes move as he imagines the hidden slaughter; he licks his dry lips, seemingly in anticipation. The licking is marked by a cut – back to the soldier's corpse. As if his imagination gets the better of him, there is a sudden rustle in the undergrowth. Richard draws his gun and calls out – the camera alone taking in the bloodied hand of a wounded sniper – but dismisses the suspicion once the captain and others return. The snipers have been killed – all bar one, who got away after being stabbed. With a cry of 'Look out, Sir!' and before the others can react, Richard draws his gun and instinctively kills the sniper in the undergrowth (who has risen on cue). The sniper flies backwards with a cry. Richard freezes with a look of shock at the rapidity of his own gut reaction – the dominance of the instinct that automatically kills over thought. The captain thanks him in a business-like fashion, acknowledges that Richard came close to shooting the captain himself with his hasty discharge and Richard claims it was a lucky shot, a stab at shirking the moral responsibility. But he remains aghast: 'He was trying to kill you, Sir!'.

The camera zooms in on the second corpse. The birdsong is heightened and, as in a western, the sound of flies is introduced. A

rapid fade-in reveals a camp fire and cuts back to reveal a boisterous evening meal. Richard has been promoted to cornet and
the others tease him about his forthcoming leave which he will
use to visit his fiancée. In this way, sex and death are more than
linked: sex becomes Richard's reward for killing – a double
deflowering.

The shock that Richard registers indicates a new function for
violence. This film was made in the same year as *The Sorcerers* and
both place Ogilvy at their centre (and Ogilvy remains physically
unchanged; the same haircut and, to a certain extent, the same
type). Ogilvy's violence remains at the behest of others (here in his
role as a soldier, during time of war; a more diffuse reason than
that of *The Sorcerers*) but this time does not come to fill the void
that Reeves cites as at the heart of the London counter-culture and
the desire for 'kicks' – rather, the violence assails young Richard's
idealism. Idealism, as expressed in his will to marry and aspirations as a soldier, will come to be seen as the motivating force
behind the character. In a way, Richard is as possessed as Roscoe,
and also by a disinterested force (that is, one that does not
consider Richard's response to the violence he perpetrates). The
idealism is rapidly perverted in the bizarre religious ceremony
Richard and Sara engage in (swearing marriage and vengeance)
and, by the close of the film, this instinctive tendency to kill,
coupled with the remnants of his idealism, has become more than
just a quick draw; axe in hand, Richard will disembowel Hopkins.
His idealism will ultimately be at the service of his blood lust. This
paradox makes for the ambivalence in the film towards the protagonist. It is societal breakdown that allows for the ascendancy of
Hopkins, as noted in the voice-over, yet the notion of society and
of what is 'good' (as indicated in the kind of aspirations and
idealism that Richard represents) comes to seem to be little more
than a sham to begin with. Society is seen as a device to keep in
check, or channel, man's capacity for violence, which is already
present. After all, the nodes of society (in the small communities
of sheep farmers, villagers and so forth) are initially introduced
here as lynching their own.

Sequence three

Another classic western motif: a fade-in reveals a field and Richard galloping to Brandeston – the steeple of the village church visible above the trees. Richard refers to it as 'home'. In this sequence Reeves assembles sincerely felt images of a near-perfect rural existence: the countryside, the church, a warm welcome, the family meal – 'good food ... and ale', the beautiful 'country girl', the protective uncle. It is a utopian vision and remains as strong as the horrors that will shortly, and inevitably, follow.

The texture may be entirely English, but the narrative strategy is, as Tom Baker and Reeves envisaged, that of the western. This film plays with notions of heroism, dishonour, revenge and the law of the gun across sequences in taverns, travelling shots of riders, the outskirts of a civil war, drawing the drama against the background of rolling plains, mounted soldiers in tattered uniforms, rape and vengeance.

The uncle, John Lowes, the pacifist vicar of Brandeston now troubled by the anti-Catholic sentiment in the village, which could come to target him, talks of 'a lack of order in the land [which] encourages strange ideas'. He will give Sara to Richard – 'farm boy into soldier' – a marriage that will take her away from the village. His mock-serious chastisements to Sara urge her into Richard's bed to seal the agreement. Once he has retired, Richard jokes, 'And will you make a proper wife and mother, Sara?' And Sara, brazenly running her hand up Richard's leg, replies 'I still have much to learn, Richard.'

Sara embodies this utopian vision of 'home' in her downcast eyes, golden hair and smooth skin, her bound chest, her talk punctuated by giggling – refined virginity. She has something of the studied and not-entirely-convincing innocence that photographer David Bailey saw in Hayley Mills in his portraits from the 1960s. Green-blue light colours their skin as they make love in the darkness of a four-poster bed. Reeves uses multiple mixes until limbs become indistinguishable – an abstraction of flesh dissolving into flesh, and the love-making is presented as shared pleasure (much at odds with such scenes in films from this time, made on the cusp of the feminist movement). The *Greensleeves* variation strums on the soundtrack. But the final dissolve of the montage reveals Hopkins and Stearne, reversing the maxim suggested in Sequence two; now sex is to be followed by death.

Sequence four

Hopkins and Stearne bicker, behaviour far from the notion of harmonious Puritanism. Reeves shoots them with a deep-focus tracking shot, the flat countryside rolling by behind them, and cuts to close-ups. The wind returns on the soundtrack and they raise their voices above it as they each accuse the other of sadism and profiteering. Their talk establishes the interdependency of Hopkins's ministry and Stearne's brutality; simply put – brain and brawn. Such a jarring juxtaposition between Hopkins and Stearne and Richard and Sara hints at the similarities between Richard and Hopkins. Both are accused of murder during the time of Civil War (Lowes flippantly refers to Richard's 'silver [which] you get for killing good Christians' and Stearne quips 'the good Lord paying in silver for every hanging' and is told not to blaspheme) and both will make love to Sara. Their destinies are entwined.

Hopkins prissily holds on to his hat in the wind. His white gloves and white horse are equally disconcerting. The importance he evidently attaches to his appearance suggests that his reputation is something he works to maintain. Stearne chews on a clay pipe and is dressed in studded leather – the uniform of the dungeon torturer. Without a second thought Hopkins talks of 'a priest ... one who gives worship to Satan and calls him Lord' as ominous music swells. Reeves cuts to the priest as he and Sara bid Richard farewell the next morning. Hopkins's language is that of the New World puritan; for him, the surroundings, historically beset by religious fervour, are ripe for an Essex–Suffolk theocracy – of which he is the harbinger and his form of other-worldly justice the model.

The day-for-night aesthetic bolsters the foreboding feeling of the following scenes; the darkness on the ground against bright blue skies reverses the natural order. Richard meets a local drunk and others on the outskirts of the village, awaiting Hopkins's arrival. He gallops on and meets Hopkins himself. They exchange polite but guarded words and Richard remains oblivious to Hopkins's status and mission, believing him to be just a lawyer. It is made-to-order irony; the chance of a chance meeting in the calm before the storm.

Hopkins is now surrounded by the waiting villagers, reciting accusations against Lowes. He refutes them and promises to find out the truth, walking past the church towards the house. The dissonant music clatters on as Reeves cuts to a pastoral scene of Sara, walking by a river, the sun in the trees. Lowes is alone in the house and the mob approach the door, shot head-on; the homestead under siege. Hopkins's black cloak and hat and disgruntled look are now palpably ominous, his face flashing short temper and quick brutality. Yet when he finally greets the uncle – 'John Lowes?' – his voice is warm, resonant and thrilling.

There is a school of thought that holds that Price's screen persona undermines the absoluteness of the realisation of Matthew Hopkins. Wood writes

> The film has, unfortunately, a central flaw. Vincent Price does not really belong in it. It is not just that his accent repeatedly jars in an otherwise all-British cast: one can persuade oneself to overlook such incidental defects. He gives a very accomplished performance, but he remains always Vincent Price in costume. *Witchfinder General*, while certainly horrific, is not really a *genre* horror film, and it is the *genre* that Price's presence continually evokes.[9]

Perhaps this was more keenly felt when Wood was writing; Price's 'typical' roles have since faded somewhat from the collective consciousness. But Price's physical screen presence is a little jarring; he dwarfs some of the rooms in which he is seen (particularly in Lavenham, when talking with Stearne, for example). In the film, Price comes across as an English Civil War Lee Marvin – efficient, deadly, single-minded and charismatic. The Hopkins of Bassett's novel is more thoughtful – clichéd psychological profiles and formative experiences of violence that hardened his heart. Donald Pleasence would have fitted such a characterisation perfectly, feeling his way into the role of a witchfinder, uncertainty transforming into a taste for violence. It would seem that with Price in front of the camera, Reeves modified the characterisation – a streamlined narrative of violence replaces the pop psychology. This was a lesson learned from Siegel and his hair-trigger screen killers, and Reeves had reimagined the film along these lines in trying to accommodate Price. The camera constantly films Price from a low-angle, grimace on his face – an unstoppable bringer of death, looming across the screen, a character defined solely by his function, suggesting the logic of the film's full onscreen title – 'Matthew Hopkins Witchfinder General'. With Pleasence, also went the scripted idea that Hopkins would gain a sexual thrill from the torture – and a new 'reason' was not inserted. This results in a much more open reading of Hopkins; he now tortures and kills for reasons other than a simple hedonism, recontextualising, even if by default, the witchfinding as a facet of the socio-historical portrait of the time of upheaval. When Hopkins later notes that it has been suggested that he should be promoted to the primary witchfinder in England (in a film full of promotions) this indicates that witchfinding, by the close of the film, is now not so much a facet, but a possible model of the society to come.

After another shot of Sara, Reeves cuts straight into the inter-rogation of Lowes, now in full swing. In the shooting script, the shots of Sara are presented as moments in which she recalls her night of love, oblivious to the events in the house. Intentionally or otherwise, in the film, the shots of Sara are from too great a distance for her revelry to register – and the cacophonous music plays over them in the Reeves cut, dispelling any serenity. In this way, the shots function more like cutaways and so work in an entirely different way, clashing with the events in the house, continuing the juxtaposition of pastoral and violent scenes in Sequence one.

In no time, Hopkins has issued the order – Stearne is to look for 'the Devil's marks'. The villagers hold Lowes while Stearne, a look of anticipation on his face, digs a steel needle repeatedly into Lowes' back, and his prayers give way to cries.[10] Hopkins listens to a villager outlining the catch–22 logic of witch hunting to another. Sara is alerted now, by another villager, running towards her – their urgent talk drowned beneath the music. Removing scripted dialogue in this fashion makes for a more cinematic and less wordy approach.

Hopkins sees the meeting from the house but does not register alarm. He seems to have an unreal power – a master of the situation, both inside and outside. He steps up the torture; Lowes is made to run around a table (the camera pans with him, background blurred, Lowes groaning, barely conscious) and Hopkins waits outside. Sara runs towards the house, straight into Hopkins's arms (another moment akin to the opening of *Great Expectations*: Pip running into Magwitch). Both Sara and the tracking shot slam into Hopkins. 'You must be his niece' he casually remarks. Price's calmness here is a direct contradiction to the frantic cutting, movement and action of this sequence – he remains a still, magnetic centre. Sara automatically begins to flirt with him, denying that she is his niece but a 'foundling'. A bargain is struck: Hopkins will release her uncle in exchange for Sara's euphemistic promise of 'help' – 'You may come to my room tonight, Sir.' She has the same lust and forwardness she applied to Richard.

There is barely the pretence of 'actual' witchfinding despite all the outward signs of Hopkins's religious zeal and mission (the clothes, the rhetoric, the single-mindedness). The blunt modus operandi seems more akin to some South American police state, and is quite in contrast to the film's immediate predecessors, the clinical torture of Dreyer's *Days of Wrath* and the quasi-legal proceedings of Arthur Miller's *The Crucible*. Hopkins returns, Lowes collapses into a close-up for the low-angle camera shot, and Stearne is told to cease the torture and jail the 'Papist bastard' since he has yet to confess. He shrugs and orders the villagers to do as Hopkins has instructed.

A sound-bridge of a woman's scream suggests further tortures but, with a cut, a tavern scene with a naked woman is presented. This sound-bridge connects violence with sex in the manner of Sequence two. She screams as Stearne strips her of the last of her clothing. He boasts of his exploits, his hanging of women – one of whom, he claims, seemed to desire the execution. Hopkins passes through, takes in the scene disapprovingly, and ducks into his room. Stearne empties his ale over the screaming woman.

Sequence five

A long establishing shot of the vicarage, dark against the dusk sky, marks a change of rhythm (it takes twenty-two seconds for Hopkins to reach the door). The film has become enshrouded in shadows, and Hopkins is the bringer of this darkness (his cloak dissolves his figure into it, rendering him almost invisible) as much as the onset of the night. His presence has now wrested the narrative from the glaringly absent Richard; the film follows him, the plot evolves in tandem with his movements, machinations and actions. With 'Sara, I've come to question you,' Stearne's drunken revelry is replaced with the cautious parlour words of Hopkins and Sara as they work towards an implicit understanding.

Once inside, Hopkins picks at the buttons of Sara's clothing, his voice lilts as he talks of men's 'strange motives,' blue moonlight freezes his face. The beauty and modulation of Price's voice, offset against Dwyer's English tones, wrests control of the soundtrack too, teasing Sara into submission, setting the tempo of the exchange. Hopkins hedges all bets – there will be no deal, in the name of justice: 'he is an idolater ... he must confess and die' he says with mock simplicity. Sara seems to soften, offering herself to him once it becomes obvious that siding with 'the priest' will indicate guilt on her part, and that her body is all she has left to bargain with. Hopkins makes no reply but automatically moves to embrace her.

The bile returns immediately as Hopkins kicks a snoring Stearne awake – 'you unkempt lout' – the next morning. Stearne in turn kicks a wench off him, who squeals like a startled cat. Stearne stumbles outside and throws up. Hopkins instructs him to leave Lowes in the cell. Stearne understands what has happened and accuses Hopkins of 'a-wandering' – the alliance of mutual blackmail expounded in Sequence four. The scene's awkward cutting and post-synch sound seems to originate in attempts to cover for continuity faults or technical errors.

A dissolve to a rat. The camera pans up and frames a half-conscious Lowes, chained to a cell wall, dried blood on arms. A guard strolls by and calls in; Lowes will be interrogated no further, but kept in the cell. The prison is a claustrophobic sewer, anonymous cries and groans underscore the ominous rumblings on the soundtrack. Bright light reflects off the damp stone walls, rendering the image almost black and white. More eerie day-for-night shots follow as a moody Stearne searches for Hopkins in the church grounds, intercut with Hopkins's second liaison with Sara. As he follows Sara up the wooden stairs, the shadows from her candle renders the scene momentarily expressionistic – darkness sweeps across the room. Stearne climbs up the ivy and gazes into the bedroom.

A piercing scream, another sound-bridge, returns us to the dungeon. In these ways, the connection of sex and death has evolved into the dominant factor in the film. Stearne, left to his own devices, takes out his frustration on a woman, slapping and strangling her, ranting about her 'foul iniquity', as her bloodied forehead is battered back and forth. A villager and Salter, the jailer, look on. In the next cell, Lowes babbles incoherently. Hopkins drops by to inform Stearne that he will be working elsewhere for the night – to which Stearne makes the usual taunts before returning to the cell. Hopkins is seen riding off against denuded trees and a watery autumn sky – a landscape drained of life.

The next image is of Sara in the open, her eyes cast down, morning light and the sun in her loose hair, strands of which blow against a graceful neck – a jarring vision of beauty after the grime and brutalities of the previous few minutes. It indicates the imminent further violation of the character, an ongoing sullying of the utopian aesthetic. The camera zooms back to reveal her feeding chickens with grain – then crash zooms back in to capture the shock on her face when she detects Stearne's presence off-screen. Again, the zoom functions in a provocative way. The contradictory movements back and forward contrast with the predominant tableaux-like compositions of the previous scenes. It also mirrors Sara's shock and surprise – a flurry of 'psychological' film grammar, surprising in light of Sara's increasingly and enigmatically emotionless behaviour – and recalls the shock-zoom back after the hanging of Sequence one. As with Siegel, the film language is prompted by the suddenness of the action.

Stearne strolls towards Sara as she asks about Hopkins's where-abouts with mounting desperation. When she learns that he (and her 'protection') has gone, leaving Stearne in charge, she runs and the camera tracks with her. He knocks her down and rapes her, shouting into her face that he is aware of her relationship with Hopkins. A grinning village idiot looks on from a field; Stearne grunts and Sara screams.[11]

This sequence anticipates the rape of another fresh-faced blonde – Susan George in Peckinpah's *Straw Dogs*, complete with village idiots and violent inbreeds. Peckinpah had seen *Witchfinder General* on the advice of Siegel and hired Coquillon on the strength of it for *Straw Dogs*. Peckinpah's vision of rural England contained the same bloodiness and sense of violence in the brooding landscape. The essential difference between Peckinpah and Reeves, however, is that while Peckinpah saw the ensuing battle as a rediscovery and reaffirmation of masculinity, for Reeves it leads only to insanity.

Hopkins returns and learns from the village idiot about Sara's 'infidelity'. The camera tracks with Hopkins, from the usual low-angle but, by framing his face in a medium close-up, it discon-certingly reveals his inner turmoil – more unexpected psychology. It is as if, having first streamlined the film for Price, Reeves now lets those elements tailored for Pleasence seep back in, discover-ing in Price his abilities as an actor. A blast of sunlight illuminates his face and moist eyes as he walks purposefully towards the tavern. He tells Stearne that he has changed his mind about Lowes's interrogation and Reeves cuts straight back to the dun-geon, with Stearne belting Lowes and yelling 'Confess!' Lowes's murmurs are taken by Hopkins as a confession and Stearne ensures that Salter will be a witness.

Sequence six

A cut brings us back to the content of the pre-credit sequence – a lynching – only this time Lowes is the victim. The hand-held camera returns as a bloodied Lowes is dragged past the church.

Sara looks on from the bedroom window of the house before throwing herself on to the bed she shared with Hopkins, sobbing. A zoom back reveals that the procession of victims is sizeable – more than just Lowes – and is headed by Hopkins. An overhead shot allows this procession to fill the screen, a steady pan up frames a large, moated country house. It begins to seem that the village lynch mob of *Revenge of the Blood Beast* has become an institution in *Witchfinder*. This sudden multiplication of the victims suggests both that time has passed and Hopkins's direction on the scale from individual persecutions to mass murder.

Hopkins stops at the bridge and says a few uninterested words to the accused, voicing the principle of the 'trial by water' test for possible witches – that witches float (the historical theological reason for this: the water rejects them), while the innocent drown. It is the inexorable logic (albeit not entirely historically correct) that thrills British schoolboys (the kind of market Bassett seems to have been writing for). From the low-angle of the shot, Hopkins's hat makes for a black halo against the summer sky. An old woman, local colour, calls out the defence that she is 'with child,' setting up Stearne's punch-line – 'And who'd want to make you pregnant, witch?' for the appreciative audience of villagers.

Three of the victims are bound by ropes and lowered over the side of the bridge into the moat. There is something horrific about this sequence – the brief flashes of details of the paraphernalia of torture: Stearne tosses out lengths of rope to the jailer and the willing villagers; the fuss of binding the legs; the fumbling carrying of the victims to the side of the bridge; the onlooking rabble; the weight of the bodies as they are awkwardly lowered into the moat; and all the while the battered victims babble incoherently, seemingly only half-aware of the procedure. These brief shots are intimate, framed in a way so as to lose the focus on Stearne (and Hopkins is out-of-frame) and to allow the collective nature of the lynching to come to the fore. It is nightmarish yet hyperreal – flashes of a kind of violence more associated with the latter half of the twentieth century; the mechanisms of mass execution that determine the position of Srebrenica in the collective consciousness. With an irony that undoes the BBFC censorship of this sequence, the British 'restorations' of the film retrieved the missing frames from uncut laserdisc releases – thus degrading the quality of the shots to the texture of the grainy Hi8 look of genocide footage from Bosnia or Rwanda. The 1990s video of *Witchfinder General* took on an added relevancy accordingly, in the manner of the latter-day crucifixion of Sequence one.

The isolated act of violence, which is the tendency in film, tends to imply that the perpetrator is only the embodiment of evil and that, therefore, the reality as presented is somehow structured on unreality, is a code appropriate for entertainment, is a caricature, and ultimately only a form of visual metaphor (and the tendency to stylise violence, which increases the unreality, could be said to be a reaction to the limited scope of such an approach). As Reeves suggests in *The Sorcerers*, this approach to violence creates a space from which the film audience can watch without feelings of guilt engendered by their vicarious enjoyment. However, the portrayal of collective acts of violence works against this structured implication. It rejects the notion of the visual metaphor and defiantly proclaims that the film is a rendering of villainy not villains, the violence in reality as known, that the film adheres to and is guided by a '"truth content"... [a] claim to possess some truth or epistemological value'[12] or, for Reeves specifically, something akin to the 'profound reality' of Siegel's 'brutal and sensual' film *The Killers*. As with the zoom in Sequence one, it forces the gaze of the audience, demanding a consideration of the nature of violence as something born of the crowd, of the nameless onlookers, be they these villagers or, by implication, the nameless onlookers of the cinema audience. Few films present violence in such a way – particularly those films which have come to be seen as 'classics' of violent cinema (underwriting their violence with the idea of the effects of alienation specific to their times and places). Generally, the exceptions are those that have sought to document specific wars, such as Miklós Jancsó's films from the 1960s, or Elem Klimov's *Come and See*.

A slow zoom in on Hopkins's face, eyes narrowed, registers his initial disinterest turning to agitation. Reeves then begins to intercut shots of Hopkins's face with that of the drowning victims.

One woman drowns but the remaining two are winched back to the bridge, with a painful slowness. He orders that they be taken to 'the tree'. Reeves cuts again to reveal Lowes's corpse, swaying at the end of the hangman's rope. The tree creaks and the camera tracks back to reveal Hopkins looking on – an image which is, by now, a motif. Stearne hands Hopkins 'the money from the magistrate' as the silent procession leaves the country house, Hopkins and Stearne shoring up the rear. Their work is done and they prepare to depart. This represents the culmination of the first half of the film – another circle of executions completed, the moment of the greatest despair, and the moment before the arrival of the belated cavalry, in the form of an avenging Richard.

Sequence seven

Richard, upon hearing of the commotion in Brandeston, returns to Lowes's house at a frantic gallop. He finds the house deserted, the church desecrated and Sara initially reluctant to talk in a kind of momentary denial; the horrors have been too much for her to now articulate. Despite Richard's role, he has singularly failed to be her protector – robbed of his phallic status in this fashion and in that, as Sara indicates, Hopkins had exacted her as a price too.

This sequence is a reworking of another primal scene – but this time a cinematic one – as in the opening of *The Searchers* and, still good a decade later, it sets things in motion in *Star Wars* too. Beyond the material destruction, the murder of Lowes and the knowledge of his torture and Sara's rape, it indicates that the utopian ideal has been annihilated; Hopkins has laid waste to Richard's future and his sense of home and well-being – the smile that is first seen, as he is lost in 'ungodly thoughts of ... Sara', cannot now return; his idealism has been wrenched away as has any idea that the brutal world can accommodate idealists. So Richard initiates a new *raison d'être* in an impromptu marriage ceremony in which, swearing on his sword, he promises to avenge the murder of his Lowes and rape of Sara. This pact with God replaces the earlier association of sex and death made in the final cut from the love scene; now Richard and Sara's being together – that is, life itself – is dependent on Hopkins's death.

Richard rides through night and day, across open plains, to locate Hopkins. After a well-choreographed (and very contemporary) brawl in a tavern, Stearne, pursued by Richard, leads him to Hopkins. Reeves shoots the riding with the same distance and speed in his tracking shots as in *Duel at Silver Creek*, and in addition twice match-cuts Richard and Stearne as they gallop (a risky stylistic flourish; they are both using the same horse). As Stearne catches up with Hopkins, their conversation reiterates the nature of their relationship – he remains intellectually aloof and unruffled by the threat of a bloodthirsty Richard, joking and invoking his powers as a witchfinder; he believes in his own myth. This is why Stearne will remain nothing more than a thug, a footnote to Hopkins's historical–mythical status (despite their common base motives: money and women), whereas Hopkins, aware of the way in which his power is founded on his symbolic status, holds on to it. Writing about another such general, Slavoj Žižek notes: 'how did General Pinochet's arrest in the United Kingdom [in 1998] affect his symbolic status? The untouchable all-powerful *éminence grise* was all of a sudden humiliated, reduced to an old man who, just like any common criminal, can be interrogated, has to invoke his bad health, and so on. The liberating effect of this mutation in Chile itself was exceptional: the fear of Pinochet dissipated, the spell was broken ...'.[13] The seventeenth-century rumours of Hopkins's lynching at the hands of those he once terrorised (even if wishful thinking) would seem to operate in this way; a desire for the news that the aura has finally been broken. In the film, Hopkins's symbolic status has comparable strength to Pinochet's – but it has a supernatural foundation in conjunction with his political role; he proclaims himself as a God-appointed witchfinder (the very title suggests that he exists at the intersection of the divine and the worldly), that his status is God-given, and he continues to talk of his engagement in 'God's work' right up to the end. Therefore there can be no earthly stripping of Hopkins's power (that is, the destruction of his symbolic status) that can render him ineffectual, since he locates his authority in the heavens. This makes sense of Richard's vowing to God, in the desecrated church, to avenge Lowes's death by executing Hopkins rather than proclaiming it directly to Sara; he is addressing the source of Hopkins's authority. He later says 'They'll be no magistrates involved' in talking of the mission to his baulking colleagues, and informs Hopkins, once captured, 'I'm going to kill you, Hopkins' on more than one occasion; Hopkins invokes the power of his symbolic status – 'I don't think you'll find that easy; the law is with me, remember.'

In this ceremony, Hopkins is not the 'sacrifice' offered for Richard's marriage to Sara; Sara is the sacrifice in the vow to destroy Hopkins. Since it is only by killing Hopkins that his symbolic status can be dissipated, Richard must cast himself as someone who views the world in absolutes of good (those who may live) and evil (those who must die) – that is, he himself must become like Hopkins to achieve this. This parallels Marcus Monserrat's/Karloff's 'becoming' Roscoe/Ogilvy, and it also suggests that Hopkins, with his obscure motivational reasons, is already the Roscoe to whom Richard must aspire. The ceremony also connects Sara's fate with that of Hopkins; for Hopkins to be finished off, Sara, as sacrifice, must be accepted (and nor does Richard 'confess' to save her as she is tortured – she is not even worthy of a bargaining-chip status here; indeed, Richard inadvertently sends her straight to Hopkins with his instructions to her to flee to Lavenham). Richard unknowingly invokes a process that, once complete, will place him in Sara's position; inarticulate after the horrors that have been seen. When a colleague later tells Richard that this planned revenge is 'madness' he replies 'It's justice; it's my justice' – suggesting that madness may be the price that will be exacted for this form of justice. At this moment, mid-point in the film, a new philosophy is introduced and, with it, Richard becomes another figure in the Roscoe–Hopkins axis; driven to murder at the behest of external forces – beckoning on the psychic destruction that will go with it. The evil here is not cinephilia, or the desire to seek kicks from vicarious thrills, as in *The Sorcerers*. The actual 'kicks' of sex and violence are now readily available – and young Richard is well placed to experience both. Ultimately, the problem that is manifest in Richard's bloodthirsty new philosophy is the very same thing that he initially represents in the utopian aspects of the film: idealism, and daring to believe that the world could be a just and free place. The swagger and self-satisfied aspects of the early Richard, in Ogilvy's performance, resonate with such an assumption, and the problem of idealism, thematically, is particularly apparent as Sara is tortured; Richard will not confess to prevent this on principle. Idealism is the reverse side of the coin to the youthful trait of *The Sorcerers*, complicity. Yet both idealism and complicity denote the failure to engage with the world as it really is.

Sequence eight

Richard rejoins his unit, receives a half-hearted dressing down for his temporary desertion, and talks to his colleagues on the eve of the Battle of Naseby. Hopkins encounters soldiers, is unflustered by the prospect that Richard would have briefed them to look out for him, and Stearne is left behind in the ensuing scuffle (one soldier unintentionally falls off his horse before the cut to Hopkins galloping away). Stearne breaks away from his captors but in doing so sustains a shot to his shoulder. As he operates on himself, Reeves pans and dissolves across the woods, Stearne's screams echoing on the soundtrack. It is as if the countryside itself is tortured; the montage recalls that of the love scene – the screams now replacing the love theme that played earlier. This is another example of Reeves removing the scripted detail (where the camera was to move to Stearne's sweating face and bloodied bandages are glimpsed) during the actual shoot and adding subtlety, generic details replaced with a response to the open rural settings. As a result, the amount of time that the film spends surveying the countryside is substantially stretched out too when compared to the provisions for this in the shooting script.

This is the key to the distinctiveness of the film – something that all critics have mentioned,[14] and something which, if accepted, questions why the film remained absent from the majority of

critical writing on the British cinema if it is so intimately connected with the rural English environment from which it is drawn.
The expected use of surroundings in a film made at this time
would be in terms of 'psychological realism'; in a modernist fashion,
the language of the film would suggest an exploration of the
psyches of the protagonists, so that the brutalities of the world of
the film would be predominantly presented as visual metaphors
for the disharmony of their minds. This is achieved through compositions that tend to place the protagonist in the foreground of
the scene so that, whether the background is stylised or expres-
sionistically presented, or just reproduced 'straight', the nature of
the surroundings reflect the nature of the protagonist's mind. In
such compositions, the viewer remains primarily aware of the
protagonist's circle of concentration and so this determines the
function of the surroundings (or, in the case of stylisation, offers
the 'alibi' for their alteration).[15] The work of 'modern' film-makers
in the West from this period, such as Polanski, Antonioni or
Losey, is typified by such a strategy, itself determined by the then
preoccupation with reproducing the psychological condition of life
under late capitalism – that is, the creation of a filmic expression
of alienation.

Reeves, who removed a stylised 'psychological realism' sequence
from the initial screenplay of *Terror for Kicks* (Roscoe dancing with
a Soho prostitute, his POV vastly at odds with the tatty reality), dis-
pels any such ideas from *Witchfinder* too, until the final moments
of the film. This can be accounted for both in terms of Reeves's
'anti-intellectual' stance[16] (psychological realism, with Polanski,
Antonioni and Losey, was the domain of the art film) and the
desire to achieve the same 'profound reality' he found in Siegel's
films, particularly the art-free *The Killers*. The result is that the
countryside of *Witchfinder* is just countryside, and Stearne's
screams, bridged across a brief montage, do not create the effect
that the countryside and the slaughter somehow reflect Stearne's
mind (after all, the shots are completely unassociative; the countryside remains unperturbed by Stearne, with the same stillness and
indifference here as elsewhere). The result is the impression that
the countryside itself is awash with slaughter, has become a

killing ground, and this is present in the very woods and foliage of the location – it is the material world of the film that is in agony. In this poetic way, the process of psychological realism is reversed; the countryside draws its 'psychology' from the protagonists. This accounts for the sense in which the past and the present are seen to converge in Sequence two – the 'psychology' of the landscape (denoted by the concentration on the foliage in the foreground of the screen, animated by the wind) remains the same across the years, despite human evolution. This is why, in the film's continual contrasts between the idyllic and the brutal, the connection between the two is made in a materialistic way – the wood of the gallows and the wood of the tree. In Sequence one, it is the *ritual* of the crucifixion that is re-enacted; the characters are not themselves baying for blood (indeed, their passivity is what disturbs – it suggests an understanding and so acceptance of the brutality) but merely repeating an execution as if this ritual itself is in harmony with their surroundings. The indifferent birds who will feed on the carrion indicate as much too.

Reeves's preoccupation is therefore not so much the evil in man, but man lost in an evil world. Yet, in that the world is both evil and beautiful, and that the film spends time in the timeless evening fields, watching the breeze through the branches of trees, with the texture of a Suffolk autumn in which the whole English *mise en scène* is that of a magic hour (light, late evenings; the dying of the light patterned on the clouds; uninterrupted rural horizons; the stillness of the countryside; the hegemonic rhythm of the wind, the grazing sheep and the swaying grass), a sense of order is profoundly upset. The protagonists and the world of the film are united in disgust at the brutal reality they find, surrounding them and in themselves, yet this is continually offset by the pervasive beauty of the world. This 'offsetting' remains absolute; the hyperrealism of Reeves's arresting violence does not allow the viewer to consider the violence in terms of a sense of a brutal Mother Nature – the violence remains repulsive and literally unnatural, not contextualised or to be understood in terms of the surroundings. This determines the film along the lines of the biblical metaphor of the Fall of Man (in the story of the exile from the Garden of

Eden); the post-idyll, unceasing battle between good and evil is written into the landscape of the film. This alone makes sense of Hopkins's behaviour; his theocracy will be a device to banish the evil from the surrounding world in order to save those who live in it, and this is to be achieved only by eliminating those who have been infected by this outward evil – that is, to purge those who actually are of the 'wrong side' so as to establish a new Jerusalem. In terms of attaining such a greater good, his methods transcend ethical and moral considerations; they are perceived as God-given, and Hopkins does not doubt this, right to the end of the film – it is a 'war on evil' that recognises no boundaries. Even his use of Sara is incidental to this greater reason. Hopkins's ministry is a way of intervening in the world, drawing from the same brutality that colours the world to do so. He reverses the binary distinctions to intervene against the ongoing reverberations of the Fall of Man; what is 'good' in the world is, in fact, evil (the innocuous-looking women, all potential witches) and what is 'evil' (his torture and murder) is thus translated into the 'good' (the purging of evil). Hopkins's world is that of the actual battle between good and evil – there is nothing 'psychological' or transcendental about it. Reeves's film is equally materialistic. He is also concerned with the 'meaning' of reality as he finds it, albeit drawing different conclusions. Psychological realism, and the stylised portrayal of violence, and the notional idealism that drives Richard, are all based on readings of reality 'at one remove' from encountered reality. Like Hopkins, Reeves doggedly goes after the 'true' reality, interrogating it with his camera in the hope that a 'truth content' will be yielded, that the world itself will 'confess' and admit a tallying with evil.

General Cromwell (Patrick Wymark) is introduced with a moment of 'chicken leg' period acting – something typical for British films. He appreciates his food, and the picturesque quality of the setting also recalls the last time in the film food is enjoyed; the meals with Lowes, Sara and Richard. This scene is another such moment of calm and another reordering: Richard is promoted to Captain and sent off with his colleagues to track a supposedly fleeing king.

A lengthy sequence, unfilmed, was cut from this point. In it, Richard and his colleagues spend the night in a farmer's barn. Stearne also meets the farmer, and is also offered food and lodgings by him. When he learns of Richard's presence, he flees. The next morning, as Richard and the others talk to the farmer and hear about the night visitor, they assume that it was the king, incognito. This chance encounter parallels the earlier one between Richard and Hopkins, but does little to advance the action. Nor does the potential intertwining of the mission to find the King and the hunt for Hopkins have space to develop; the King has already long gone.

Wilfred Brambell's horse trader provides some camp comic relief and, like the fisherman who tells Richard that the King has fled, is another of the locals who pass off key information as by-the-by chatter. Once Richard learns that his short-lived mission is over, he is free to pursue Hopkins. Reeves zooms into a crashing wave on the Dunwich coast and dissolves (via a pink tint, so as to smooth the transition) to the roaring flames of the Lavenham pyre. The wild elements underscore Richard's overpowering emotions, and the extremities that will mark the final scenes in the film.

Sequence nine

The mass of anonymous onlookers has now swelled substantially, but they still remain impassive and emotionless at the tortures they behold. Reeves's cutaway use of extras is similar to Pasolini's and his 'ethnographic aesthetic' (full-screen shots of real people, found at the locations of the production), cut into the fiction of his films with a neo-realist impulse. They both avoid the 'central casting' school of extras, and the films are rendered all the more effective for it (although Sinclair notes, with justification, that Ferris is out of place in this context[17]).

Elizabeth Clark is pulled from a pigpen, bound to an improvised ladder, and lowered into the fire (an in-joke: 'Siegel – fetch the rope!'). As she screams, Reeves uses the same disconcerting sound technique familiar from *The Sorcerers*: cutting to the crowd and interrupting the screams on the soundtrack. Her husband,

Paul Clark, is restrained; Sara and, cantering in, Stearne, also look on. Reeves spares us the other assembled victims. The village children cook potatoes in the dying embers of the pyre, prodding them with sticks – an unnerving moment that Peckinpah would borrow and rework for the opening of *The Wild Bunch*, along with the litho credits.

Hopkins and Stearne agree to continue their work, despite Stearne's feeling of betrayal. Spying Sara in the crowd, and realising that Richard may not be far behind, Stearne tracks Sara down and alerts Hopkins and his willing Lavenham assistants. This time, as a reunited Richard and Sara begin to make love, Reeves cuts to Stearne running in the opposite direction to Sequence four – no longer the hunter, now the hunted. Prior to this, when he match-cuts from Hopkins to Sara, lying on a bed, a zoom accentuating her as lost deep in thought, the suggestion is that she is thinking not of absent Richard, but of Hopkins. The previous match-cuts between Richard and Stearne suggest that such parallels are being made by the film, but whereas the connection between Richard and Stearne is incidental, the connection between Hopkins and Sara will prove to be terminal. Richard's arrival interrupts this reverie.

Richard and Sara, captured and bound, are led out. Paul Clark is gunned down trying to exact a revenge for his incinerated wife – a classic double bluff; the film had only just suggested that he would join in the fight against Hopkins with his own vendetta. But, dying, he fulfils the role of a local who passes on key location information – sending Richard's colleagues to Orford Castle to rescue him.

Orford Castle is introduced in ominous near-silhouette; this is the location for the moment of reckoning. As the party penetrate into the recesses of the keep, Reeves uses low angles and hand-held shots; there will be intimacy to this spectacle, unlike the Lavenham pyre. Once the torture has begun, both protagonists slip into extreme versions of their personas; Richard, crazed by his impotence, literally climbs the wall as Sara screams, while Hopkins exudes control through a disarmingly fey and untroubled exterior, reciting the familiar mantras. As Richard breaks free and attacks

Stearne and Hopkins, intercut with Richard's colleagues battling their way in, Reeves begins to cut to Sara's anguished face between the moments of violence. This belated concentration on Sara's psychological state, indicated twice before, both with the zooms, means that the horrors (a writhing, blinded Stearne, a screaming Richard, axing Hopkins) are seen to impact primarily on her – establishing the genesis of her madness. The same approach (violence and onlooking woman) also occurs at the end of *Intrusion*, but without any clear narrative reason. This readdresses Sara's status from the moment of the match-cut and zoom in, denoting her thought as dominated by Hopkins. While the violence goes on around her and the conflict winds its way to its conclusion without her participation, her isolation and immobility at the literal centre of the sequence, bound to a stone slab, is telling[18] – and the belated introduction of her into the narrative in this psychological fashion (this is more a psychological 'note' than 'psychological realism' but it is still vastly at odds with the 'profound reality' of the film) is, after Estelle in *The Sorcerers*, a second 'return of the repressed' in relation to a female sensibility. It means that she has no possibility of exacting her revenge, of exorcising her ghosts through conflict – that is, of engaging in the evolving events to extract Hopkins's internal presence (in her mind) while all others work on extracting his actual presence (his execution). She has effectively been abandoned by Richard once again in his idealism-founded pursuit of Hopkins – and therein is her fate; she is exposed to the horrors around her and they prove too much. Hopkins may have been killed, but his presence as torturer lives on in Sara's screams as the end credits roll. The invasion is over, but she has been body-snatched in the process.

Sara's downfall is that she is chosen by Richard to embody his idealism; she represents the type of existence to which he aspires. The film goes along with this, shows her in this way, and then puts her through the same process of beauty and horror that the landscape is also subjected to. Clearly, the lesson is that idealism must only ever be understood as an abstract, it cannot be located in anything material, even if those things appears intrinsically 'good' in themselves; that idealism is a trap, a false religion much more subtle in its calamities than the one that Hopkins sports. The profound ambiguity of such a sentiment in a film that offers vistas full of idealist–utopian scenery and sensibilities (another aspect of the way in which the film is often noted as almost uniquely 'about' the English landscape) is unsettling. The suggestion is that the Fall of Man landscape – a vale of tears, in which possibilities that could have been are now glimpsed and denied – offers no way back, no redemption. The crucifixion re-enactment indicates that humanity is content to remain in such a fallen state.

The film opens with the breakdown of law and order cited as a reason for the anarchy. But law and order, in the light of the film, seems to function not to keep man's bloodlust in check (the forces of law and order initiate the killing), but to provide the space for idealism to exist (that is, to offer a framework to support such aspirations). The civilisation of the film sustains itself by allowing for such idealism (from Hopkins's puritanism and desired-for English theocracy to Richard's absolutes and desired-for married life) – the hope of something better and pure, that is seen to be 'of' and in harmony with the idyllic surroundings. Indeed, in the early months of 1968, as the film opened in the UK, the breakdown of law and order was galvanised by notions of idealism (underwriting 'revolutionism' in many guises). Had society denied the dissenters the possibility of idealistic dreams of the opportunity to change the system from within, ultimately in harmony with it, on its own terms? The one thing that united the decaying bourgeoisie of both the West and the Soviet Union in 1968 was that they no longer believed in their own myths and authority, so the power they held was up for questioning – the institutional symbolic status had been effectively jettisoned, suggesting the possibility of overthrow in the name of idealism. The first stage of the revolution was to discover that the democratic means within the state apparatus were not sufficient for complete change, justice and freedom – and so the actual revolution (which did not occur) comes with the realisation that the dissenters must move out of and beyond the parameters of the state apparatus. Idealism underpins the naive assumptions of the first stage; Reeves's concentration on idealism as a form of self-delusion which debases action, and is founded on an unengaged response to reality is, in the context of the times, in keeping with a wider revolutionary perspective on this tumultuous period.

Notes

1 Lovell, *Don Siegel*, p. 38.

2 Lovell, *Don Siegel*, p. 4.

3 This sequence was shot, but did not make the final cut. An image of Hopkins collecting money from this unseen sequence was used in publicity for the film. Baker, Reeves, Bassett, 'Final screenplay', shots 4–5, p. 1.

4 Baker, Reeves, Bassett, 'Final screenplay', shot 8, p. 2.

5 Baker, Reeves, Bassett, 'Final screenplay', shot 22, p. 5.

6 In fact, it is Patrick Wymark, who also plays Cromwell in the film.

7 A. Clark, *Diaries* (London, Phoenix, 1993), p. 116.

8 The shooting script chronicles an equally voguish skirmish – the ambush (even with the optimistic direction 'helicopter shot').

9 Wood, 'In memoriam Michael Reeves', p. 6.

10 An intertextual in-joke; ever thrifty, Tenser used this gruesome prop for his next film. It makes a cameo in the 1968 AIP/Tigon production *Curse of the Crimson Altar* which opens with an antiques dealer explaining that it was used to prick falsely accused witches in the seventeenth century.

11 The shooting script has Sara talking her way out of the rape, threatening to tell Hopkins she is a witch and taking her orders from Stearne. Stearne decides 'you're not worth the trouble' and leaves. Baker, Reeves, Bassett, 'Final screenplay', shots 118, 118a and 118b, pp. 47–8. Reeves was going against BBFC advice in altering the scene during production.

12 Jameson, *Signatures of the Visible*, p. 74.

13 S. Žižek, *Did Somebody Say Totalitarianism? Five Interventions in the (Mis)use of a Notion* (London and New York, Verso, 2001), p. 169.

14 *Time Out* gives the standard line; '… [the film] remains one of the most personal and mature statements in the history of British cinema … no film before or since has used the British countryside in quite the same way.' J. Pym, *Time Out Film Guide* (London, Penguin Books 1997), p. 912.

15 Psychological realism conforms to Pasolini's outlining of the filmic language of *Soggettiva Indiretta Libera* (Free Indirect Subjectivity). His essay on this subject, 'Il Cinema di Poesia', is reproduced in B. Nichols (ed.), *Movies and Methods Volume One: An Anthology* (London, University of California Press, 1976), pp. 542–58.

16 Iain Sinclair, interview with author, 30 August 1998.

17 Sinclair, *Lights Out For the Territory*, p. 295.

18 Hutchings notes her 'exclusion and objectification' at points throughout the film, and by all the main characters within the film in relation to his gender reading of *Witchfinder*; Hutchings, *Hammer and Beyond*, p. 149.

Via dolorosa   8

Perhaps cinema is the most personal art, the most intimate. In cinema only the author's intimate truth will be convincing enough for the audience to accept. (Andrei Tarkovsky)[1]

Witchfinder General opened in the UK to considerable business, bolstered by a slew of letters in the press damning the violence in the film, and one local banning.[2] For some, such as Bernard Levin, who stormed out of a screening within minutes, it was perceived to be a watershed in this regard – a new low. But May 1968 was not a time for considered opinion; as with the serious civil unrest across the Channel, British protestors were preparing to further shake the dormant British government. In *Witchfinder* was a refraction of the same dying struggles of imperialism that were also manifest in the onslaught against South East Asia and the Cold War audacity of western powers in their contempt for life. *Witchfinder* was an index to those elements that fired the outrage and swelled the protesting crowds across 1968. The film was an exposé of the Establishment interconnectedness of high moral righteousness, political power, slaughter in God's name and corruption. Such things were too close to home, and their proponents then on the defensive in an unprecedented manner. And out of this chaos, the first two of many subsequent witchfinders were soon to be apparent in the ascendancy of Dr Henry Kissinger under President Richard Nixon, who himself had made his career witch hunting for the House Un-American Activities Committee.

And what was Matthew Hopkins other than – in today's parlance – a war criminal? It was safer to dismiss the film on grounds of exploitation. However, from a contemporary European perspective, the film sits comfortably with the other well-attended films of those riotous months: Bertolucci's *Before the Revolution* (which had first been released in Paris in 1967), a film also about the death of idealism, Leone's *Once Upon a Time in the West* with its comparable 'deconstruction' (to use the then freshly minted term) of Hollywood codes, and Anderson's *If...* which, along with a new print of Eisenstein's *October*, provided more uprising against the established order.

That a condemnation of *Witchfinder* became a facet of *The Listener*'s then highly reactionary stance would hardly be worth noting – except that the polemic drew in Mike, Austen and Trevelyan. In his regular column, eight days after the film opened, the playwright and satirist Alan Bennett first complained about BBC news reportage in relation to a perceived spin towards anticipated violence, and then over the emphasis on gossip, and then went on to write with (as it was termed at the time, and even then perceived to be something of a put-on) a 'splendidly prissy academic voice':[3]

> Still on violence, this time in the British film *Witchfinder General* ... [which] included the following:
>
> 1 slow drowning
> 1 double hanging
> 1 burning at the stake in which the victim was lowered slowly on to the pyre
> 2 scenes in which a knife is pushed repeatedly into the backs of screaming victims
> A man's eye kicked out
> A man hacked to death with an axe.

These highlights apart, there is a ground bass of beatings, shootings and torture, all weltering in blood. Of course blood and guts is the stuff of horror films, though, as with Victorian melodrama, what makes them popular and even healthy are the belly laughs which usually punctuate them. For these one can generally rely on the film's star, Vincent Price. But not here. There are no laughs in *Witchfinder General*. It is the most persistently sadistic and morally rotten film I have seen. It was a degrading experience, by which I mean it made me feel dirty. I would not have wasted space on such a shambles had not the film received serious and favourable critical attention in several quarters. Mr John Russell Taylor in the *Times* emphasised its subtlety, imagination and camera-work over three columns. Mr Tom Milne in the *Observer* commended it for showing intelligence and talent, real style and presence. This seems to me pernicious rubbish. The world of film is not an autochthonous world: sadism which corrupts and repels in life continues to do so when placed on celluloid. It is not compounded by style nor excused by camera-work. Hitler had a film made of the death throes of the plotters of July 1944. I wonder what Messrs Taylor and Milne would make of that. Purely, of course, in terms of film.[4]

Four letters were published over the next two weeks. Mike set forth his ideas, as initially expressed (and sharpened) during the interaction with the BBFC, and replied partly emulating the clipped style of Siegel's writing, and partly setting out his case in the manner of the Radley Debating Society:

Sir: In last week's issue of the *Listener*, there appears a somewhat vitriolic condemnation of my film, *Witchfinder General*, and of two of the critics who were kind enough to praise it. Mr Alan Bennett takes the film to task for 'making him feel dirty' due to the extent of the violence presented in it. I have no desire to quarrel with him over the film's merits or demerits as 'art' (whatever that may mean); but would like to make a couple of my own points in answer to his review. First, I think Mr Bennett and I are at least in agreement over one thing – that violence as such is more horrible that can be adequately described on paper. However, Mr Bennett implies that violence on the screen is perfectly acceptable so long as it is 'punctuated ... by belly laughs'. Not only does he state this, but also indicated it may even be healthy in such circumstances. With this I would quarrel most vehemently.

Surely the most immoral thing in any form of entertainment is the conditioning of the audience to accept and enjoy violence? Is this not exactly the attitude that could lead to more and more *casual* indulgence in violence, spiralling nauseatingly upwards to a crescendo of international blood-letting? To sit back in one's cinema seat and have a good giggle between Mr Bennett's bouts of 'healthy' violence, as he so strangely advocates, is surely immoral to the extent of criminality. Violence is horrible, degrading and sordid. Insofar as one is going to show it on the screen at all, it should be presented as such – and the more people it shocks into sickened recognition of these facts the better. I wish I could have witnessed Mr Bennett frantically attempting to wash away the 'dirty' feeling my film gave him. It would have been proof of the fact that *Witchfinder* works as intended.[5]

Both Mike and Bennett had furnished expected reactions. For Mike, Bennett's wrong-footed response only confirmed the success of his initial intentions for the film. Bennett's 'made me feel dirty' exactly fulfils Mike's stated strategy to Trevelyan, that the film's violence must cause a 'sense of self-loathing'. Mike's reply demonstrates a clear vision of the moral burden of film, even as entertainment, in relation to what is shown, and how, and why. His reading of Bennett's tendency to marginalise film as an instrument capable of an engaged realism, through the somewhat hyperbolic context of 'international blood-letting', pits a sensibility of 1968 internationalism against Bennett's limited view of the role of film. Bennett's cultivated cynicism would be swept away with the dawn of Thatcherism, and nudge his moral position closer to Mike's. But in 1968, Mike aptly casts him as one of the bores of *The Listener*, then partial to voyeuristic condemnations of student protests. To be a young contender for such a position is even worse.

Austen, who in his *Films and Filming* review likened the film to Bertrand Russell's writing on fear,[6] delivered a counterpunch:

Unless [Bennett] has sat through the uncensored version, he did not actually *see* 'a victim being *slowly* lowered on to a pyre' ... The audience's laughter for nervous release, from Hitchcock to Hammer films, I would consider healthy and indeed necessary, but I would feel extremely uneasy about the belly laughs experienced by Mr Bennett in other recent horror movies, unless it was directed, for example, at those Grand Camp performances of Vincent Price ... It is obviously too uncomfortable for him to be faced with truth in a commercial film. What is most frightening is that it appears that Mr Bennett advocates the censorial attitudes which can create the climate in which Hitler and Nazism, to use his example, can flourish ... it must be said that it is [Bennett's] opinion which is 'pernicious rubbish'.[7]

A non-partisan letter also attacks Bennett and a further letter praises Bennett's views on violence and television news. Critic Eric Rhode, an exponent of 'quality cinema', leapt to Bennett's defence in his film review column, and questions the priorities of the BBFC:

> My heart warmed to Alan Bennett when he trounced *Witchfinder General* in the *Listener* last week. What he did not make plain, though, was that most of the victims in the atrocities he mentioned were women. Two sequences were especially sickening: one, of a lovely girl being lowered slowly into a fire while her lover shrieked and implored for mercy; the other, of a torturer gradually knifing open the heroine's back. Our Film Censor cannot keep his scissors off the chaste nude in a masterpiece, *The Switchboard Operator* – and yet, unaccountably, he allows this sort of thing a general release.[8]

Rhode has a point, of course, but the use of the word 'lovely' somewhat gives the game away. Nor had he noticed that the film also rhetorically accounts for its misogyny; Hopkins comments, after asking about the witches in Lavenham, 'Strange, isn't it, how much iniquity the Lord invested in the female ... the foul ungodliness of womankind.'

The following week, Bennett was more concerned with the attack on his views on broadcast news and replied in the letters section,[9] and in doing so distanced himself from Mary Whitehouse and her censorious campaigns, then consolidating into the organisation that would deliver a direct challenge to the BBFC 'liberals' in the form of the Festival of Light. Ironically, Bennett would be subject to the Whitehouse complaint factory only a month later.[10] Sometime Reeves producer Arnold Miller would also be caught in the crossfire ushered on, in part, by the *Witchfinder* controversy and the renewed calls for censorship: he had drifted off into 'education' shorts, forming Global-Queensway Films, which turned out the 'notorious sex education short *Growing Up* (1971) which, to the horror of moral reformer Mary Whitehouse, showed children how to masturbate'.[11] In addition to feeling the need to shake the idea that he was a champion of censorship, Bennett was perhaps also stung by the Reeves–Austen moral indignation and wary of making an issue out of BBFC procedure;

Trevelyan had written in to state the film was far from the explicitly violent 'sadism' of Bennett's claims, and that perhaps Bennett had seen the pre-BBFC cut (difficult to imagine the circumstances in which this would have occurred; Trevelyan was mischievously muddying the waters and illustrating that he had cut the film): 'It would be fair to the film-maker, Michael Reeves, to say that it was his intention to show that violence was repellent, but the Board did not feel that his intention justified the exhibition of this film in its original form.'[12]

In June, Mike left for North America with Annabelle, to travel down the continent and visit AIP as they were about to release *Witchfinder*. He hung out with film students in UCLA, and then they pressed on to Southern California to meet Chuck Griffith, then working on a cycle of Hell's Angels films. The three drove down to Mexico. Chuck remembers a raucous night in a Mexican saloon, a sozzled cowboy giving head to a go-go dancer on the bar, and Mike screaming with laughter.

Mike was calling on AIP to cement his reputation. The executives had been astonished when they viewed a print of the uncut *Witchfinder* in April 1968. First, their contribution to the budget had been a tax write-off (and done for ulterior motives at that), and so the quality of the film was completely unexpected, and second, some were unable to comprehend how the tiny budget had been stretched to cover the construction of an authentic period village square. But once this was cleared up (and why were they making films in England, after all?), they soon realised that, as Jim Nicholson told Deke, 'it is one of the best we have gotten from England. Everybody also thinks this is about the best production in the Poe series for the past few years.'[13] Arkoff later recalled: 'Michael Reeves brought out some elements in Vincent that hadn't been seen in a long time. Vincent was more savage in that picture. Michael really brought out the balls in him. I was surprised how terrifying Vincent was in that ... I hadn't expected it.'[14] Price got wind of AIP's delight too. For him, this was the culmination of a belated realisation of the film's worth. When Price first saw bits of the film, during the post-synching, he seemed 'crestfallen' and told Lynn that he would have to let Mike know that he had been in the wrong during their disputes. He wrote to Mike:

> a very impressive, moving and exciting picture! Congratulations! The contrasts of the superb scenery and the brutality, the action of the hero forces against the inexorable almost pedantic inaction of the forces of evil make for a suspense I've rarely experienced. I'm sure you have a big success and a long feather in your cap ... So, my dear Michael, in spite of the fact that we didn't get along too well – mostly my fault as I was physically and mentally indisposed at that particular moment in my life (public and private) – I do think you have made a very fine picture and what's more I liked what you gave me to do![15]

Mike, who reputedly cabled back a reply which consisted of 'I told you so', carried Vincent's letter around with him in his wallet, showing it to friends and associates. It was more than just a boast; this letter, like Bennett's review, was a form of confirmation. Legend has had it that the letter was a long mea culpa, but in fact it consists of two hand-written pages, seemingly prompted by a missed phone call from Mike to Vincent, and could be said to read, congratulations aside, as a formal 'thank you' note, perhaps even written with one eye on the looming *The Oblong Box* production. It was one of a number of such letters Vincent fired off during this period. But maybe he should be taken at his word. Once safely back in the USA and with windswept East Anglia as only a bad memory, had Vincent seen the film with objectivity he might have realised that Mike really had, by whatever methods, drawn from him a performance that would subsequently be hailed as his best. Like Arkoff, had Vincent Price seen, in the Vincent Price up on the screen, something that he had not quite seen before in himself either? A measure of defensiveness, also present in this gracious letter, would later inform Price's misleading talk of Mike in interviews. In his fumbling come-on to Mike, Vincent had not realised that, in reality, it was Mike who would be taking Vincent into new territory, not vice versa. It is difficult to think that Vincent, who frequently talked about Mike, was left anything other than troubled by his memory and legacy.

AIP implemented the title and voice-over alterations, placed a fire-breathing skull and burning witches on the poster and em-blazoned 'Leave the children home! ... And if YOU are squeamish, stay home with them!' across the top.[16] As *The Conqueror Worm*, the film was double-billed with, among other AIP films, another Euro shocker, *The Young, The Evil and the Savage* and the home-grown *Psych-Out*. The latter – bad trips in Greenwich Village – would have made the connection between *Witchfinder* and the contemporary counter-culture even more apparent. In the USA, *The Conqueror Worm* grossed $10,000,000 in its first run.

In West Germany, Tenser's 'Continental Version', *Der Hexen-jäger*, was an equally big hit. Deke recalled that within weeks of prints arriving, 'a bootleg company came out with *Conqueror Worm II...*'.[17] In due course, the film gave rise to a number of derivatives, some not without merit, that played up the torture and nudity: Michael Armstrong's *Mark of the Devil* (an impressively single-minded 'ninety minutes of solid violence'[18] with the distinction of garnering a complete ban from Trevelyan) and Jess Franco's *The Bloody Judge*, a film lacking the lightness of touch of Franco's erotic horrors from this period. Piers Haggard's unfairly forgotten *Satan's Skin*[19] is also often cited as made under the influence of *Witchfinder*, but despite the surface similarities (another Tigon location production), the film heads in quite the opposite direction; the supernatural becomes manifest within a rural community and the film charts its subsequent collapse at the hands of the forces of law and order. The theme, the horror and the hysteria would find its fullest expression in Ken Russell's *The Devils*, and a contem-porary reworking in Robin Hardy's *The Wicker Man*. This marks the formal limit of the influence of *Witchfinder* on a short-lived horror sub-genre and films that, like *Mark of the Devil*, may not have been made under the direct influence of *Witchfinder* but were understood, at producer level, to be attempts to cash in on its success. Beyond this, Leon Hunt sees in the film the shape of future torture movies – the women-in-prison flicks and the Nazi death camp 'nasties'.[20]

Maybe Mike also saw the potential for such things, since he decided straight after *Witchfinder* to move on from Tenser and exploitation productions altogether. He began to court those in

'respectable' areas of film-making, soliciting for introductions
then arranging for lunches over which to discuss his ideas. The
praise for *The Sorcerers* and *Witchfinder* meant that it was time to
implement the second phase of the 'well-made rubbish' strategy
and look for producers and studios to impress with his track
record. Mike was not the only one to think that he had finally
earned his spurs; as Robin Wood noted, he was waiting for news
of the next Michael Reeves film so as to arrange an interview for
the prestigious *Movie* – quite a jump from Tenser's favoured film
magazine, *Cinema X*.[21] Mike and Michael Armstrong began
talking about setting up a production company of their own rather
than continuing to battle with the frustrations they had to contend
with. It was a timely sentiment as more problems were in the
offing; tensions between AIP and Tigon surfaced in 1969 over
Armstrong's *The Haunted House of Horror*, a production in which
AIP had initially replaced David Bowie (cast as the serial killer)
with Frankie Avalon. The casualty of the spat was the release cut of
the film,[22] and a vexed Armstrong left for Germany to shoot *Mark
of the Devil* in early 1970 (a film for which Mike had also been
suggested as director). Meanwhile Tenser had sunk the *Witchfinder* profits into Norman Wisdom's comeback, the anaemic sex
comedy *What's Good for the Goose*, produced entirely by Tigon in a
hired Southport hotel, and the sci-fi sexploitation oddity *Zeta One*,
with Charles Hawtrey as a heavy. The former finished Wisdom's
film career and, sadly, represented the beginning of the end for
Tenser and film production. The era is enshrined in the 1975 film
Eskimo Nell. Armstrong fleshed out Stanley Long's idea for the
film, and took the role of a young, first-time cinephile film director
(spotted with the Cinema One books on Visconti, Godard and
Losey, and Alexander Walker's *Stanley Kubrick Directs*) who has
been given his break by one Benny U. Murdoch, head of BUM
Productions (played by Roy Kinnear), Tenser to a T. He winds up
directing various and vastly different configurations of a film
script (each to please the different financial backers – including a
brash, Deke-like American producer who, as with all the others, is
keen to cast a partner in the main role). McGillivray describes it as
'a vendetta against British low-budget film-making'[23] and, certainly,

many old scores are settled with near-libellous precision; it was rumoured that whole sequences were reproduced verbatim.

The year 1967 had been one of continual, frantic work for Mike – constant development, rushed periods of pre-production, impossibly tight shooting schedules, high stress post-production; a struggle on all levels. This was Fassbinder or Godard speed – working without the time to look back – yet fighting against anything that smacked of compromise. The 'final straw' reaction of Mike's letter to Trevelyan was evidence of the strain, and it is also, in its emphatic, apologetic, angry, self-interrupting, pleading, reiterating and fragmented tones, and the constantly switching perspectives, an insight into Mike's troubled mind. The endless fluster of work with which Mike surrounded himself, noted by others as perhaps masking something else, had somehow ceased to completely preoccupy him. Betty had been worried and it was at her insistence that Mike had taken a break in Jamaica, and then to North America. But Mike returned as exhausted as before – unable to sleep, reluctant to eat (he would order double portions of everything in the Carlton and pick at them, eating little or nothing) and depressed. His doctor, who had previously been keeping an eye on Mike's lungs, referred him to a psychiatrist. Betty suggested a move away from the house party in Yeoman's Row and, by July, Mike was installed in Flat 6, 19 Cadogan Place in Belgravia – a quieter area, with relatives nearby. Beneath the plethora of projects in development (and 1968 was a year in which everyone had films in development), and, despite a number of very real and progressive possibilities for 'the next film', things would begin, very rapidly, to unravel.

Tenser wanted to secure Mike for Tigon on a long-term basis and talked of an unprecedented five-year contract (albeit fee rather than percentage based)[24] for at least one film a year, hopefully two, and with conditions that would not prevent Mike from making other films. He offered Mike the *Kill Me Kindly* script, as he had done to all other Tigon directors; it was a script he had bought some years before – a mother and son, he topping girls while sporting black gloves, she covering up (the suggestion was made that it might be good for Joan Crawford or Bette Davis). It was a psychological horror, but with 'nothing psychological about it at all'[25] and a source of in-jokes for Armstrong and Mike. Tenser made moves to buy the rights to a subsequent Bassett book, *The King's Shilling*, with a view to Mike making it into a companion piece to *Witchfinder*, still a period war film, but this time centred on a woman who passes herself off as a male soldier so as to find her missing husband. But one potential project was particularly appealing – *O'Hooligan's Mob*, a *Bonnie and Clyde* in an Easter Uprising Ireland setting, told through the eyes of a young IRA man. The half-written script was from an idea by Tenser, 'completely non-political'. Although wary, Mike agreed to go into development on the film and was dispatched to Ireland to scout locations. Mike felt his way into projects by imagining key sequences; here it would be a figure with a gun staggering down a cobblestone street in moonlight, wet with the night rain. Even though Mike had promised Tom writing duties, he passed them on to Amos Powell, from *Revenge of the Blood Beast* days, without offering a reason and leaving Tom stung. But it was all academic; *O'Hooligan's Mob*, a film that Mike certainly could have made, and which would have given early 1970s Scorsese and Peckinpah a run for their money, was not to be. The reason cited was simply Mike's unwillingness to stick with Tigon, but the events of 1969 would have rendered Tenser's anachronistic vision doubly so – perhaps even impossibly so. Nor were the contracts with Tenser ever drawn up.

For Hammer, with Patrick Curtis, Mike planned a pirate movie to star Welch (as Anne Bonnie) and Ogilvy in the main roles, to be called *Mistress of the Seas*. This was to be shot in Malta and with a budget big enough to cover the construction of two galleons. Hammer immediately had a poster designed but, by that point, were themselves running aground.

Philip had moved straight from *Witchfinder* into developing a film based on Janice Elliott's free-love epic *The Buttercup Chain*, to be shot in Sweden, England and Spain doubling for Greece. Once Columbia Pictures expressed delight with the script, Philip's main consideration was ensuring that Mike would be acceptable to Columbia for direction duties (Columbia initially suggested Jack Clayton). A long period of consultation with Mike began, with

Mike pressing for Welch in a main role. For Mike, this script and company represented *the* opportunity to leave the world of exploitation film-making behind once and for all – it was a blueprint for his next stage and a film quite specifically about the shift from the dreams of youth to the compromises of maturity, mapped on to love, death and loss among a jetsetting quartet of carefree bohemians. Mike, to whom critics were now referring as a 'New Wave' director, would have brought a touch of Truffaut to it. Philip:

> Despite the fact that we persuaded their figure-crunching production department that our one million dollar budget with Michael Reeves directing was feasible, Columbia wouldn't agree. Their total film-making budget for the UK that year was ten million dollars, but they didn't want to make ten one million dollar films – they wanted to make five two million dollar ones for half the effort. More realistic than us, Michael finally told us that Columbia would never relent on hiring him as our director and that we should now accept the fact.

By early summer of 1968, despite his total enthusiasm for the film, Mike was no longer on the project. He had diplomatically informed Philip and his co-producer that he believed the film would never be made as long as his name was attached to it, and he asked his agent to inform Columbia that he now recognised this. Such a resignation from Mike was a new note. Previously he barely understood what 'no' meant in terms of film-making – it was only something to be overcome.[26] Schlesinger was the next director to be attached to the film but because of prolonged post-production on *Midnight Cowboy* he also withdrew. Polanski seemed on the verge of accepting, but then went straight to *Rosemary's Baby*. Eventually, after explorations into several other European directing talents, Philip and his partner were persuaded to screen *The Heart is a Lonely Hunter* to see the work of its director, Robert Ellis Miller. Even though Miller was an American and the film was meant to qualify for tax relief under the British Film 'quota', the two producers recognised immediately that, otherwise, he was an ideal candidate. Within a matter of hours, they persuaded Columbia to give the go-ahead to sign him, finally clearing the way for the film to begin production.

In between producers and meetings, casting and pitches, Mike had been working on his own initiative for a next film. His mind turned to film projects about loners, the misunderstood, the marginalised, those psychically oppressed. A little earlier, Sinclair, picking up on Mike's own identification with such preoccupations, worked on a script along these lines too, with the intention of Mike as its director:

> My man worked ... as a film lecturer. He had his leftist pretensions, constantly trying to push his students into collaborating on Brechtian fables. He's paid very little and lives on his wife's private income. To break out of this cycle of dependency, he takes a night job as a porter in a near-brothel in Finsbury Park. This is a dump where East End gangsters can hide out, or play cards, after killings or major hijacks; a convenient location for Trade Unionists to meet their mistresses, or be serviced by prostitutes.
>
> The man is taken up by one of the hotel's clients (who, he subsequently discovers, is also the owner). He's asked, for what he assumes are purposes of blackmail, to film an adulterous couple in one of the rooms through a two-way mirror. He agrees. The woman, of course, is revealed as his own wife. Very soon he is implicated in even murkier events. There's an accidental killing. A corpse to be disposed of, and – in the script's only prophetic aside – an elaborate gangland funeral in Chingford Mount.
>
> There probably wasn't enough pace, enough structured violence for Mike; too much ambiguity, too much chat. I meant to get the finished script to him, but, by then, the connection was broken.[27]

First Mike planned an adaptation of H. G. Wells's *When the Sleeper Awakes*, an idea that AIP had been keen on since the mid–1960s (they would go on to produce a short-lived cycle of Wells films); a protagonist who suddenly finds himself in a strange and terrible future. This could have been a straight adaptation (with a sufficient budget) or a new film in the spirit of Wells's vision, which offers the contemporary for Wells's future. Mike was taken with the idea of a Christ-figure in the London of 1968. A thriller, to be called *Razor*, was scripted. In the latter half of the year, Mike turned to the idea of an adaptation of Walker Hamilton's *All the Little Animals*, a book with which he was obsessed. In it, a couple of Steinbeckian misfits bury the wildlife killed on motorways and eke out a tramp-like existence. Arthur Lowe, with his ability to inject a very human aspect into figures that border on caricature and his willingness to experiment (apparent in *If ...* and *The Bed Sitting Room* respectively) was offered, and accepted, the role of the older tramp, a pitiable, alcoholic former bank manager. *All the Little Animals* could have been an extraordinary, heartfelt film, capitalising on the deep connection Mike felt with the world of the book. It would have been a world of pity to *Witchfinder*'s world of pain, but equally adrift in English foliage.

For American projects, there were also often-voiced thoughts of a Fitzgerald film, and an adaptation of John O'Hara's *The Instrument*. Mike's identification with O'Hara's novel is easy to spot; a writer trips back from despair and an attempted suicide only to be plunged into the world of Broadway intrigue, art, sex and differing agendas; the artist is besieged, and runs away, and then draws on things that first revulsed him for his art.

Like Tigon, AIP were also getting big ideas, and Mike was 'hot' enough to help implement them. Deke and Arkoff were keen to put Mike straight back into production. Deke claimed: 'We could easily see an output of several films a year with young Michael, whose work we much admired. We, on our corporate level, were comparing him to one of our stalwart directors, Roger Corman ... I had planned a long career for him, in order to utilise his extraordinary talents and visions. We spent hours and days together in my offices in London, planning future projects which I was prepared to produce with him as director.'[28] However, unlike Tigon, AIP overreached disastrously with one such project, Deke's *de Sade*, while bungling the chance to produce *Easy Rider*. Before he died, Coquillon wrote to a colleague and described a phone call from a wildly enthusiastic Mike in LA, outlining their next film – a biker film, to be shot on 16 mm, while riding around the USA, with a non-union crew and starring Peter Fonda. Coquillon believed that Mike was talking about *Easy Rider*, the film that would change everything. It may have been that a motorcycle picture had been discussed by AIP with Mike. It could have been akin to the Chuck Griffith-scripted Fonda biker film, the ugly *The Wild Angels* (Corman, 1966), which comes across as an apocalyptic future dystopia in the manner of earlier Corman films. This discussed film would have been a logical follow-on to *Witchfinder*: the landscapes, the violence, the nihilism, bikes rather than horses, the contemporaneity now explicit. However, the dates do not coincide for this to have been the *Easy Rider*, and no one involved has any recollection of a Michael Reeves attached to the project. But, while talking with AIP, Mike may well have thrashed out an outline that contained the *Easy Rider* formula. His acute sensitivity to the concerns of this period makes this much almost certain. AIP also discussed the projects that were to become *Bloody Mama* and *The Red Baron* and their forthcoming vehicle for lifting themselves out of the lower end of the market – classy period titillation in *de Sade*. Deke was overseeing the film and hoped to deliver a strong slice of European decadence. It would be shot in Munich and West Berlin and, during the early stages of pre-production, Mike was slated to direct. But once the budget began a steep ascent as expensive actors were signed and costumes ordered, and with Mike talking about writing the script himself, AIP decided to opt for someone with a longer track record; Mike was bumped in favour of Gordon Hessler. Mike's involvement, however, was only ever informal. Deke recalled: 'Reeves really was never in the picture 'cause there was no script when Reeves was alive. Just my concept of naked bodies and boots behind the opening titles – that's all that existed.'[29] Hessler was older than Mike and with experience in American television. He and Deke had both worked for Universal when Hessler was an associate producer for *The Alfred Hitchcock Hour*. Deke was hedging his bets, and Hessler had the ability to 'turn in a workmanlike job'[30] but, after even further escalation in the budget, Hessler was dropped ('fired, virtually'[31]) and shortly afterwards found himself back to London to produce an AIP Poe horror, *The Oblong Box*, with Mike down as director; a consolation prize for both. Panicking, AIP called in a gaggle of directors (Cy Endfield, Richard Rush, fresh from directing *Psych-Out*, and Corman), with Deke trying to use John Huston (hired as an actor) as a technical adviser once Endfield began to lose control of the production – with predictably messy, and long-forgotten, results.

Deke drafted another of his invites to Vincent, now for *The*

Oblong Box: 'hope we have another *Conqueror Worm* on our hands'.[32] The script had been written by Lawrence Huntington and, unsurprisingly for someone in his seventh decade, erred towards the literary and expositional rather than a framework that could buzz with cinematic invention. Despite having to rescind on all his post-*Witchfinder* ambitions, the collapse of *The Buttercup Chain* and *de Sade* offers, and the personal projects coming to nil put Mike in mind to take whatever was actually going into production. And AIP would get the film made, whereas doubt remained with Tigon and their *O'Hooligan's Mob*. Even half of the *Witchfinder* crew were lined up to work on it: Coquillon, Hilary Dwyer, now playing Price's wife ('He said that if I get to play his mother, we'd get married'), Rupert Davies in a supporting role, Deke as executive producer and – at long last! – the elusive Christopher Lee. So maybe the project could meet some of his hopes for *The Devil's Discord*. Mike suggested shooting it in Ireland, using some of the places he had found while scouting for locations for *O'Hooligan's Mob*. Nothing could be worse than to be incarcerated in a studio with such a script.

However, his good intentions aside, once Mike had accepted the job, the worry set in. The script was lifeless and would remain that way regardless of studio or location work. It was firmly jammed in the AIP–Poe mindset, from which nothing, not even extensive alternations, seemed able to dislodge it, and had a projected budget of less than *Witchfinder*. What had been the point of the Herculean effort Mike had put into *Witchfinder*, lifting it out of its tarnished genre, making it look five times the budget, fighting for it at every stage of the post-production – only to be back at the same starting point, but this time hobbled with such a lacklustre script? Nor, even more importantly, did *The Oblong Box* represent the opportunity for Mike to create a personal vision – something that remained an essential if he was to make films of worth at all. As Mike struggled with the script through long nights, making no progress, it became apparent that this could only be a step backwards. Implementing the uncertain dramatic arc could even give rise to an out-and-out disaster. While the *Witchfinder* script had offered endless possibilities, and those possibilities had made the film his own, the *Oblong Box* script was just a catalogue of horror clichés waiting to be fleshed out and was, in itself, profoundly un-Reevesian. Although the film begins with a lynching, it is diametrically opposite to his world-view; it posits evil as an external force, originating in the dark continent and a couple of uncomfortable racial stereotypes. The sexual politics were equally primitive. The prospect of more drunken wenches and another round with Vincent Price was too much to bear.[33]

With the principal photography date fast approaching, there was almost nowhere to turn. Mike called in the writer Chris Wicking, a former art student and film critic (and also a client of Andrew Mann at the William Morris Agency). Wicking would implement last-minute changes to the script, wedge in whole extra scenes, try to kick some vitality into it. Wicking: 'I think he just realised that he couldn't make a good picture with the material available. I remember he'd talked about printing some of the murders in negative, which was just a gimmick and a sure sign of fear on his own part, an awareness that the material was just not worth his while or that he couldn't think of anything in the material that would really make it work'.[34]

Mike gave Wicking a crash course in Siegel, but the script offered little scope for an implementation of the Siegel model. By mid-November and with one week left in pre-production, there were still five sequences that Wicking and Mike were struggling to redraft, with Wicking adding extra scenes to lend direly needed clarity. Mike inserted a voodoo chant of 'Namroc, Namroc, Namroc' ('Corman' backwards); perhaps he had decided that it was best to return to the *Revenge of the Blood Beast* mindset. But, window-dressing aside, it was not working. For Mike, *The Oblong Box* was no longer a film, but an intractable problem, wrecking havoc with the mental and physical exhaustion that he had been unable to shake after *Witchfinder*. His professional desperation turned to personal desperation, finding fertile soil in a by now precarious mental state. The film was a paradox; the only chance going to direct after a year away from a film set, yet also a film that Mike could not make. For someone who had only ever lived to film, to have found that he was losing control of the opportunity to make films, or had opportunities unfairly denied to him or, with his exhaustion and anxiety attacks, possibly over the very ability to make films, the blow was against the reasons for living. Mike's juvenile realm in which all things remained possible, was neutralised by the prospect of a film in which nothing would be possible. This was precisely not the way that Mike should advance out of this realm and into a mature 'second period' of film-making. It was for the sake of the possibility, and necessity, of subsequent films that *The Oblong Box* remained impossible.

Armstrong knew that *Witchfinder* was a film, for Mike, 'drawn out of his blood'. The experience of making it had revealed to him the vast extent of his personal involvement with the films he made, the emotional investment film-making demanded of him, and that he was willing to surrender. This was the high cost of leaving an imprint on his film. For all the talk with Austen of jobbing directors and action movies, Mike was assailed by his art on the one hand, and on the other still harboured massive feelings of insecurity founded on his perceived technical failings (something he had always feared, despite his on-set confidence). Perhaps, he would have felt, this failing would prevent him injecting something better into the film once on the set. Such a feeling may have been founded on a sense of guilt. From the beginning, Mike was not a studio-proven film-maker. He had used his considerable wealth to buy into all his films bar *Witchfinder*. At other times he disliked the idea of his money, was apologetic for it to those who knew, said that he felt that he did not deserve it, and did his best to make it collective by footing the bills for whatever meals a rapidly increasing circle of friends and hangers-on enjoyed on a daily basis. At times he would try to make incredibly generous financial gifts to friends (sometimes rebuffed), at other times he would ensure he was the first to point out whose turn it was to buy the 'round' – playing down his ready funds. Armstrong felt that Mike's wealth insulated him, leaving him particularly unprepared for the tribulations of his final year. Mike began to feel it stopped producers taking him seriously. Such insecurity became a theme of his increasingly self-obsessed conversations with friends during this dark period – continually putting himself down, claiming he was not up to the job. It was as if *Witchfinder* had not happened, and he was back at the emergency meeting one week into the *Sorcerers* shoot, feeling the burn of tears. The old arrogance had fled, leaving him battered by a sense of betraying the kind of films to which he had committed himself, terrorised by fears of inabilities, feeling that *The Oblong Box* was going to be the film that prematurely ended his career. Yet he was to be the director, and lacked the courage of his convictions to formally leave, despite his talk.

Such dead-end introspection during long, sleepless nights trying to rework the hated script as his concentration deserted him only deepened the depression, and something began to give way. Mike was now constantly agitated and stressed, at times histrionic, and assembled from his doctors (who began to implement formal treatment for depression) a regime of pills to help him sleep. To Hessler, 'serious nervous disorders' were apparent, and the insurance company were becoming increasingly uneasy. Huntington himself, then also in the final few weeks of his life, was sounded out as a possible director should Mike back out.[35] Hessler:

> I remember him tossing the script across the room in frustration. He was very nervous and impulsive and he must have been going through a very rough period. He was always talking of quitting. I tried to calm his fears about the project and how it could be made to work. One afternoon, during a taxi ride to the studios, he confided in me he was having electric shock treatments in a private hospital and did not think he could make the film. He appeared haunted by his own personal darkness. I was stunned. Nobody had confided in me the extent of his illness.[36]

One wretched night just prior to the shoot, drunk and despairing, Mike took four or five capsules of the anti-depressant Nembutal, and washed them down with alcohol. It was enough to suggest a suicide attempt, but not enough to really do any damage. Or perhaps it was simply an accident, or perhaps Mike was wilfully capitalising on his own forgetfulness as a way of attempting to shirk the moral responsibility for such an act. Mike was found unconscious in the hallway of his flat and wound up in hospital the weekend before principal photography. This was how Mike finally achieved the wished-for severance from the film.

So Hessler again replaced Mike for AIP directing duties, and the film was shot in Shepperton Studios and a field at the end of a Heathrow runway in three weeks from late November. It was only when Hessler called Wicking during the early stages of the shoot to request more scenes that Wicking learned that Mike was no longer on the project. Mike's agent had informed AIP directly: he could not direct the film. Austen tried to encourage Mike by ensuring that he kept in with Tigon, and kept *O'Hooligan's Mob* and *The Instrument* in development.

The Oblong Box turned out to be just what Mike feared – dull and redundant, in spite of the luminous cinematography of Coquillon, and despite the redrafting by both Hessler and Wicking. An air of indifference hangs over it, terminal for a film about a terrible secret. It begins with an odd day-for-night establishing shot followed by a scrappy zoom, and then moves into an overlit, creak-free manor as the convoluted plot kicks in, a Rider Haggard hang-over and Dorian Gray creepings around a period London underworld. It is a film of pacing performances and constant expositional dialogue, shot in jarring deep-focus. Confirming that the project was doomed from the start, Deke later commented 'Gordon saved my ass on that picture, because we didn't have the money to do it.'[37] The film is not the iceberg that sank Reeves, but it is of the same substance that was shortly to sink the British film industry.

Hessler seems to have reacted strongly against it too – going on to make the New Wave-esque *Scream and Scream Again* for AIP and Tigon in May 1969, an arresting hybrid of sci-fi, horror and police procedural. It was another film that Mike might have gone on to direct,[38] and it again included a number of his associates (Hessler, Coquillon, Wicking, Deke, Price, Lee). Even the title suggests a subliminal connection to *Witchfinder*: *Scream* (the closing moment of *Witchfinder*, and now) *Scream Again*, whereas *The Oblong Box* simply stole the final shot of *Witchfinder*. What is left of *Scream and Scream Again* after a producer hatchet job is sporadically brilliant and surprisingly hard edged – a defiantly contemporary vision, a million miles from the few good moments of *The Oblong Box*. This violent film of shadow governments and endemic paranoia denoted a new, post-Hammer British horror sensibility, one that anticipated the shift from a liberal society to an authoritarian one as the decade died. The dream of change that had underwritten the events of 1968 had vanished. In *Scream and Scream Again*, a psychotic clone, Keith (played by the reliably psychotic Michael Gothard), rampages through London nightclubs, part way to *A Clockwork Orange* or *The Final Programme*, the Amen Corner grooving through *When We Make Love* on a tiny corner stage like cut-price Stones. Keith drives the girls he picks up on to Hampstead Heath in his MG, where he rapes and murders them. He is a Frankenstein's creature, fascinated by his ability to squeeze the life from the human form yet, in his garb, this tendency is lent the ethos of no-holds-barred hippie hedonism. He possesses the same blankness in the face of violence as Richard Burton's lone Kray in *Villain*; a Hitchcockian visual metaphor – murder as sex, violence as sexual frenzy. The Heath shots are day-for-night – a jarring darkness at noon – and are oppressive and unreal; the light of his world repulses, as it might to a depressive. A near wordless police chase winds up in a disused factory, Keith sprinting up the collapsing vertical side of an abandoned quarry and then, once caught, ripping his own hand off to escape and automatically diving into a pool of acid to obliterate himself. In its pervasive hopelessness and nihilism, its corrupt state apparatus and constant brutality, the high-speed car chase and the rejection of any sense of freedom, it is a film haunted by Mike. Ageing German expressionist master Fritz Lang saw something in it too, perhaps an introduction to the new Zeitgeist, and outlandishly heaped praise upon it;[39] perhaps Lang felt a frisson of the Weimar Republic days in the death of the 1960s and the film connected the two in its distant echoes of Lang's own 1930s work – pulp Fascism, secret states and scientific progress for a new, madder God.

Mike's rejection of *The Oblong Box* was only one of many rejections. He felt that he had to go further, to free himself of people who would slow down his career. Now away from Yeoman's Row, it was possible to sever ties with that crowd, from his closest friends to the freeloaders (a fair few of whom Mike had been effectively financing). This, and the final, unhappy termination of his relationship with his girlfriend (and then avoiding her friends too), left Mike on his own. And Mike, who did not like living on his own, was now lonely, and periodically angry with them. But he understood all this in the same way that he had perceived *The Oblong Box*; he had no choice but to push away everything that was not working, to break the cumulative cycle of personal and professional problems. For periods, this even took him beyond his concerns for film-making. Perhaps he entertained the idea that he would not direct again. Tom was then working on rewrites for a Twentieth-Century Fox television series being shot at Borehamwood:

> It was suggested that Mike might be offered a segment to direct. Would I ask him? I was pleased to. For so long he had been my patron in film-making adventures, I welcomed the chance to offer something in return. Only TV, it's true. But as I recall each film had a budget much the same as *Witchfinder*'s. I was saddened and rather shocked when he showed no interest. Hardly seemed to hear in fact. So engrossed with himself and his press cuttings scrapbook did he seem to be. Backed down his own tunnel.

Yet, at the other end of a mood swing, Mike would lighten up considerably. He visited the *Oblong Box* set and, in January 1969, fired off a letter to Tim Kelly (who had prepared the screenplay for the next AIP UK-based horror, another *Witchfinder*-derivative, *Cry of the Banshee*) to say how eager he was to get started on the film.[40] Maybe he had changed his mind, decided to cut his losses and do one more low-grade horror for AIP with Vincent, just to be back behind the camera, to find a focus on things again. He bumped into Jack Lynn at the Empire Leicester Square after a screening of *Gone With the Wind* in late September 1968 (he would have noted a young Patrick Curtis in the film, playing Baby Beau Wilkes) and was enthralled with the *idea* of the film itself, epicism as another avenue of film he should try out: 'My ambition would be to make a film that had that marvellous quality – that it was considered so wonderful to have it reissued every several years or so.'

However, such flashes of the old enthusiasm were the exception. By the latter half of 1968, Mike had simply drifted off, fallen out of contact, and had managed to semi-disappear. Mike's horizons, and the shadows, closed in. No one seems to know with much certainly what Mikse was doing with his time once he left Yeoman's Row. Perhaps he paced the night streets, *à la* Mike Roscoe. At other times, he would sit up all night watching *The Killers*, or playing poker, drinking fairly freely, and taking the pills he needed to bring him down before he crashed. He spent hours reading, or poring over his clippings book, customarily lying on his back on the floor of the front room of his flat, wearing his pyjamas. Sometimes he would retire to bed early with a bottle of Scotch to accompany a volume of Fitzgerald short stories or the Nietzsche that *2001* had turned him on to. Mike did not 'need' the alcohol but it calmed him down, like the pills, and brought on the fitful rest he needed so desperately. Mike had always been something of a creature of the night and had a tendency to arrive at his family friend Diana's flat for conversation in the early hours, but by now it had become rare for Mike to be seen during the daylight hours at all.

Friends who called round were surprised and concerned at this change, and even the physical difference, and then found their welcomes cut short. The wider family became aware that Mike was in a 'very bad state'.[41] Don visited and later wrote, offering Mike advice, suggesting that he sought further medical help, and reassuring him that things were not as bleak as they seemed. Mel Welles visited Mike three times, and noted the same change (he was 'hyper and tense ... edgy ... troubled, but playing the affable guy'), whereas for Maslansky, when he visited, Mike was down and 'not the kid anymore'.[42] For less prestigious visitors, conversation was becoming impossible: it was either about Siegel or, mostly, about himself – for Tom, 'He was self-obsessed to a boring degree'. The Yeoman's Row crowd took the hint. Deke remembers: 'After the picture [*Witchfinder*] was completed, he'd come to my office in the penthouse there, and just sit on the floor. He'd say, "I just like being here. I like being with you. I like to be around. Is it all right? Am I bothering you?" It was sad.'[43] In an about-face Mike flirted with hippiedom briefly – donning the regulation clothes and horrifying friends who noted that, rags aside, something was clearly very wrong. He had 'gone pretty arty', 'hippie-esque', 'quite actorly': 'he's lost it somewhere ... he was not the same'.[44]

For his doctors, Mike was an awkward and uncooperative patient, constantly breaking appointments and unwilling to consult them other than when he felt inclined to. For a while, and behind their backs, Mike enlisted a further doctor and took his course of medication too. Mike understood his problems as stemming entirely from insomnia and claimed that the suicide attempt had been nothing more than an accidental overdose because of insufficiently powerful sleeping tablets. Stronger tablets were issued, which Mike added to his 'collection of pills' (as he referred to them, mostly prescription downers),[45] frequently disposed of by concerned friends when they saw the zombie-like state to which the pills reduced Mike. He even took to throwing them away periodically himself, and then resorting to drink to calm himself down. He resisted any set course of treatment. On one occasion, with his full consent, Philip flushed away some of Mike's pills. He also telephoned his psychiatrist to voice his concerns over the number of prescribed medications. Another gestural suicide attempt followed in December (as before, a small amount of pills and large amount of alcohol, fixed this time by Diana administering a quantity of coffee) and after Betty's intervention with his psychiatrist, Mike agreed to a programme of electroconvulsive therapy treatment in a psychiatric unit. After the first session of ECT, Mike contacted Diana; would she visit him in the clinic, and bring as much chocolate as possible? She did and recalls his pale face, demolishing a vast quantity of chocolate. Mike checked himself out after a week.

Betty had little concern for anything other than her son. Yet Mike would go back home frequently, for long periods, and would seem happy. He would eat large meals, and rapidly gain weight. Betty, like Philip, also persuaded Mike to throw away the pills that only seemed to be doing harm. Mike stayed with his mother over Christmas, spending most of the time drugged and asleep. Betty became convinced that the doctors were bleeding him for money, keeping him on unnecessary drug regimes. She also felt that a number of friends had deserted him at his time of need. She would go on to say as much to some too, likening them to 'rats leaving a sinking ship'.[46]

And then, in mid-January 1969, the newly formed Granada Films greenlighted *All the Little Animals.* Arthur Lowe would star and Philip Mackie would produce. Mackie, also a writer, would have been eminently sympathetic. Locations were scouted. This would be Mike's art film, and preproduction was initiated. It was the break he had fought for, and would not be a reprisal of his films or experiences with the companies he had sought distance from. Everything changed. Mike was back to his old form – script work, phone calls, potential actors invited out for working meals (Mike put on two stone), ideas. Thinking of catching the opportunity while he still had the time, Mike headed back to Suffolk with friends for a weekend at home at the end of January. He threw away whatever pills he had left, joking that there was enough to kill a dozen people and reassured his mother that he could never really commit suicide – he could not inflict such a thing on her, regardless of what he thought about it himself. She, and others, were overjoyed; she recalled 'I've never seen him so happy – so completely happy.'[47] Mike returned to his psychiatrist, who also noted the change, and they agreed to continue with the ECT with a view to establishing some mental stability. Hilary, who had lunch with Mike at the Carlton on Monday 10 February, remembers the 'round red imprints' on his temples from the treatment. She recalled him as chatty, jolly and upbeat, as did his cleaning lady on the morning of that day. He talked to Hilary about the ECT, and about the script he was working on that he wanted her to look at. Mike called Armstrong to cancel a meeting to talk some more about their planned production company.

Mike would have returned to his flat, perhaps to work some more on the script and certainly in time to watch a BBC2 documentary on Hammer at 10.55 p.m. ('On location with the celluloid shine-chillers who won the coveted Queen's Award to Industry'[48]). Then, later on, half changed into his pyjamas, took some barbiturates. Perhaps he had been restless, and unable to sleep. Maybe, newly unaccustomed to them, he took too many. He had not been drinking.

Was Mike reading Fitzgerald as he slipped into sleep? Mike would have encountered, in the long hours spent with Fitzgerald, a resonance of that problematic sense of innocence that concerned him too – and that would concern him, in *All the Little Animals*. And, in *The Great Gatsby*, a similar loose community of likeminded friends and family, Nick Carraway enjoying the new freedoms of early adulthood, soon encountering a world 'paralysed with happiness' and, like Mike Roscoe, freely abandoning responsibility for his own actions. And an economy of structure, and protagonists who are arrested adolescents, unwilling to mature, also remaining in the realm where anything and everything is possible, as Waugh and Brookman identified; on the surface it seems not to make sense, but Gatsby takes Daisy because he can, likewise Mike directed films because he could. And like Gatsby, Mike, in his depression and paranoia, would have felt that he, as a film director, could be seen as both great, and as something of a sham. Fitzgerald's ambivalence towards the ghosts of a bygone Eden would have made sense to Mike too – the child who initiates the lynching in *Revenge of the Blood Beast*, the lost idyll of *Witchfinder* with Sara at its centre and as its embodiment. For Fitzgerald, such moments had both tenderness and romanticism, and irony. For Mike, the tenderness was felt and palpable in the film, the irony was that, as in the horror genre, such scenes exist only to be decimated shortly thereafter, to become the yardstick against which the horror can be measured. The tragedy of *Witchfinder* is played out along such lines too; the final moments with the absolute annihilation of innocence, subsumed by bloodlust and madness. This altogether last shot is a final, secret corrective to the last shot of *Intrusion*. There, after the beatings and the burglars successfully thwarted, the couple embrace and Mike fades to black: the enemy has been repelled, order has been restored with the couple reunited. There is no price to pay, the world revolves around the omnipotence of what is right, and the restoration of that balance. In *Witchfinder*, the right prevails and the restoration is achieved, but now the couple are the casualties of the final playoff in the dungeon. The enemy has still been repelled but the price is absolute. For a split second, Mike is finally out of his enchanted realm in which all things are possible – a split second only since Mike freezes the screen, halts the film, stops time on Sara's screaming. The image is as much that of a crying new born baby as a crazed woman: a rebirth. The first period of Mike's filmography had closed at the moment of the onset of maturity. *All the Little Animals* would open the next period.

Perhaps he had fallen asleep, woken and, absent minded as usual, taken a second dose of barbiturates. Perhaps after throwing away so many pills a fortnight before and attempting to go without, while reneging on this abstinence, had decided not to do things in half measures. Maybe after work on the script, he simply desired a good night's sleep so as to press on the next day. His battered health and slim physique offered little resistance to, at some point that night, his inadvertent crossing of the narrow therapeutic index with barbiturate use, between the dose required for sedation and the dose that would cause death.

At 11.30 a.m. on the morning of Tuesday 11 February, his cleaning lady found Mike seemingly unconscious and tried to wake him; she had found Mike unconscious in November too. She called an ambulance. Betty, who had talked of little other than Mike for months, arrived at noon for lunch and was met by the traumatised cleaner. As Betty entered the room, she instinctively knew that Mike was dead. His body was on the floor by the bed, dressed in a green shirt and blue pyjamas. Two bottles of pills were by the bed. A doctor and policeman arrived, and the body taken away.

A little later, Diana called Mike's flat, to check train times for a planned visit to Betty, arranged for a few days later. Betty answered the phone. Diana gathered that Betty was now in his flat, on her own, and so Diana immediately headed over. Betty, on that day and thereafter, was convinced that Mike had died from the same 'rare illness' to which she also attributed the death of his father. Depression had created the circumstances in which some further mishap, a heart attack for Bungie, an overdose for Mike, had become decisive. Diana spent some time talking to Betty, leaving as night fell. The next day, Betty began to call friends and associates with the dreadful news, leaving many stunned, angry and upset. Others, who had encountered Mike over the last six months, were not surprised. Back in Wardour Street, those still besieged by Tigon–AIP took the news as yet another such disaster; Austen called Michael Armstrong, then editing one of the cuts of *The Haunted House of Horror* to break the news: 'You think you're having problems? If you really want to see [Tigon] suffer – Michael Reeves is dead'. They would have noted the irony that ancient Karloff had passed away only eight days before.

In the outer circles of associates, where rumours of Mike's troubles circulated, the death was perceived to be a suicide. It left the same sense of tragic, pointless waste and, for those who had known Mike, a persistent feeling of unfinished business. And, invariably, questions of what could have been. Many try to imagine Mike now, what he would be – or, rather, should be – doing (most conclude a status comparable only to Spielberg); for Tenser, he would 'still be making excellent films – hopefully with me'.[49]

At the inquest, Mike's doctors, on record, noted that an overdose of Carbrital and Largactil was the cause of death – 'there are not high levels and are consistent with injudicious overdosage ... [For] a good night's sleep he might take such a dosage.' After commenting on Mike's previous overdoses, his psychiatrist noted that 'It is possible that he intended to make another demonstration in his usual theatrical way and miscalculated the dose.' The officially returned verdict of 'accidental death' is only lent a further precision in the light of the psychiatrist's speculation. Mike, in a year of depleting and disabilitating depression, may have been periodically suicidal, but he did not commit suicide. Those who had known Mike well thought as much at the time, and continue to think so today, as do the wider family. However, in such circumstances, a fateful carelessness – a wilful challenging of the importance, to him, of his own life – had come to pass. He had found himself in a situation in which, consciously or otherwise, he had courted death.

Mike was cremated in a private service on 20 February at Ipswich Crematorium, his ashes scattered on the February Lawn in the Garden of Rest. Betty arranged the service to be dirgeless, and the church to be filled with the most colourful flowers. Later that year, the film critic Philip Jenkinson secured a print of *Carrion* and screened it during his BBC2 *Late Night Line-up* as a tribute. For the first anniversary, on 17 January 1970 (a Saturday night), the National Film Theatre staged an all-night tribute to Mike, showing *Castle of the Living Dead* and the three other films. Few would have known it, but Mike's Radley film *Down*, when it reach the finals of the National Amateur Film Festival a little less than eleven years before, had also been shown in the National Film Theatre. From teenage amateur short to complete retrospective in such a space of time is the bitterest of accolades.

Diana wrote to Don Siegel, hoping to fill him in on details that he may only have gleaned from the press. Don was isolated in Cocoyoc, Mexico, shooting *Two Mules for Sister Sara*, and had not heard. He replied on 25 February 1969:

> I am dreadfully shocked at the sad news ... It's extremely difficult for me to comment about Michael Reeves. He was so young, so full of promise. I always felt that he would have many fruitful and enjoyable years as a director of great potential. Of course, I was touched by his being a Siegel buff. He was so interested in my work and, naturally, I was very pleased with the many complimentary things he had to say about it. I had hoped that the letter I wrote him several months ago might calm him down a bit. I realize that his youth made him terribly strong in his demands for the future. I saw in Michael many of my own faults and I had hoped that, without being fatuous, I could be of some help to him.[50]

Don later elaborated on this sentiment: 'I think he was just terribly nervous about getting up to bat, as any person who's talented is. It's only the pods and the peasants who get up there and aren't afraid. I'm always very nervous. I always think each picture I'm going to do is the last one.'[51] From Siegel's perspective, Mike, along with the still-aspirant director Clint Eastwood, would have been just one of a dozen true disciples. But the death played on his mind (perhaps letting his nose for a good story get the better of him, he decided it was suicide)[52] and he talked of Mike's achievements with pride. He then decided to apply his film-maker instincts to that story. He arrived in London in August, booking in to stay at Mike's haunt, the Carlton, and arranged to meet Diana.

He asked her to investigate Mike's story, in a way that can only be seen in film-making terms, and confirmed this with a letter to her later in early September: 'I hope I haven't been too big a bore asking you to help me out in investigating the various people who knew Michael. If it disturbs you emotionally to pursue this line of investigation, please don't do it. I know there's a most interesting and touching story about Michael if we can find the key to unlock the true story. If you run into any expense in your efforts to help me out, don't hesitate to let me know as I can get the studio to defray whatever this cost might be.'[53] Diana, who had no connection to Mike's 1967 productions, could only offer tentative advice, but she provided Betty's address, and sent Don a copy of *All the Little Animals*. He bought the film rights. Don and Diana kept in contact until the early 1970s, but Don dropped the idea of an investigation of Mike's life. His response to Mike and the nature of their relationship came in his next, and arguably his greatest film, *The Beguiled*. The film represents the mirror image of *Witchfinder*. A lone soldier, also detached from his unit during time of civil war, now encounters a world of eroticism rather than a world of violence. Madness comes not from bloodlust, but from incest – both expressions of the same perversity Mike and Don saw within the human psyche.

The Buttercup Chain finally went into production in early May 1969 ('When two people are in love, they're a couple. When four people are in love, they're *The Buttercup Chain*') and Mike and Shaughnessy's *Appassionata* script followed in July. It had moved from one company to another, altered at every stop, and was now renamed *Crescendo* after being redrafted by Hammer's Jimmy Sangster. Hammer had attempted to get Joan Crawford for the part of the mother that eventually went to Margaretta Scott. Shaughnessy only belatedly found out that the script was being made, once the production was well under way, and he shared an on-screen writing credit with Sangster. Although the seed idea remains Mike's, he is not credited. The film retains his *Jane Eyre*-esque idea of a lunatic twin brother holed up in an otherwise idyllic villa to which a young American writing her postgraduate thesis unwisely strays. In a smart twist, the unfortunate visitor becomes the monster – reimagined as a bride risen from the dead in the deranged perception of the twin brother. The tight trajectory of the unfolding horror survives in the stagy, actorly rendition of the script. The film was enough of a financial failure to bring about Hammer's ill-advised late return to Dracula territory[54] and thereafter followed Dracula in some kind of Swinging Chelsea (*Dracula AD 1972*) and Dracula as the unacceptable face of capitalism (*The Satanic Rites of Dracula*). The films did for Christopher Lee as Dracula, and did for Hammer too.

As the British film industry fell into a terminal decline that would last decades, the few genuine achievements were pored over. Pirie wrote: '*Witchfinder General* – especially in its overpowering use of landscape – contains the seeds of something which could develop into an important cinematic idiom in this country, and one which is as intrinsically *native* to England as the western is to America.'[55] But it is possible that even more would have transpired in Mike's second period. The intimate connection between *Intrusion* and *Witchfinder* demonstrates that, even when fashioning commercial fare, the scenes he created were intrinsic to his whole being, only to be communicated through the very act of filming. The repetition of the final sequence is not obsessive but a declaration of intent: this is film. Despite the manifest commercial considerations, production restrictions, and the accommodation of the BBFC advice, and in spite of the pervasive Siegel influence, Mike has made a film that was entirely personal, entirely felt, and burns with the intensity of a unique understanding of what film could be, combined with an ability to speak to the Zeitgeist. It is little wonder that such an ability and sensitivity left Mike so unprotected.

It can be argued that all contemporary western mainstream cinema has been determined by the 1960s films of David Lean, Alfred Hitchcock and Sergio Leone. From these three European imaginations came the blueprints for everything, from the straight-up action film to the Oscar-laden epic, from the new lexicons of film styles to the idea of subversion from within genre. It is present in Leone in his casts of one-dimensional characters, who kill *because* they kill (which does not detract from the political critiques embedded in his films), freeing the films to advance stylistically rather than narratively; in Lean's epic eye and assemblage of history via his history-maker protagonists during the end times of the empires of the twentieth century (a model of filmmaking for the intelligent); and in Hitchcock's establishment and then destruction of small-town familiarities, etching the contours of sexual repression on the surfaces of suburban conformity (a model of intelligent film-making). Had Mike lived, he may well have been the fourth member of this group. In the constantly shifting interactions between landscape and romanticism, violence and tenderness, idealism and idyll, sanity and madness, corrupt authority and unchecked anarchy, and the tensions that arise from all combinations, comes a palpable sense of the fraying of contemporary civilisation behind his sleek action sensibility. This, more fully expressed, would have been his unique contribution – his blueprint for films to come. His brush with the *Easy Rider* milieu illustrates that he was in contact with those who were in the right place at the right time to make such a massive impact. After *All The Little Animals*, working in America would have allowed for a fuller expression, a complete consolidation of themes, rather than further innovation. The kind of films that Mike would have made or exerted an influence over are of the type that was the first to collapse, and the first to be revived as the model for Hollywood films in the era of Reagan and Spielberg, dampening the still smouldering remnants of the events of 1968 and the Watergate revelations with high-octane no-brain escapism, corporate-sponsored mass-forgetting, and the resultant shirking of a historical tendency to reflect and critique society.

But, in a brief filmography founded almost entirely on his work from one happy year, Mike had sketched out the essential elements of his vision. And, in the final analysis, that work is neither diluted, nor incomplete.

Notes

1 A. Tarkovsky and K. Hunter-Blair, *Time Within Time: the Diaries 1970–1986* (London, Faber & Faber, 1994), p. 101.

2 The ABC Regal at Sale (near Manchester) was prevented from showing the film when the local council banned it outright; J. Bamford, 'Bloodbeasts and witchfinders', *Films in London* (28 December–10 January 1969/70) 6.

3 A. Games, *Backing Into the Limelight: the Biography of Alan Bennett* (London, Review, 2002), p. 76.

4 A. Bennett, 'Views', *The Listener* (23 May 1968) 657–8. For a summation of reviews for *Witchfinder*, see L. C. Williams, *The Complete Films of Vincent Price* (New York, Citadel Press Books, Carol Publishing Group, 1995), p. 211. Taylor, who had made favourable comments about *The Sorcerers*, had compared the 'all-out passion' and 'intensity' in *Witchfinder* to Anderson's *This Sporting Life* and noted the 'obsessive Pre-Raphalite detail of the observation' in J. R. Taylor, 'Horror, and something more', *The Times* (11 May 1968) 39.

5 M. Reeves, 'Alan Bennett's views', *The Listener* (30 May 1968) 704.

6 D. Austen, '*Witchfinder General*', *Films and Filming* (July 1968) 36.

7 D. Austen, 'Alan Bennett's views', *The Listener* (30 May 1968) 704. Emphasis in the original.

8 E. Rhode, 'Films: Lorenzo baby', *The Listener* (30 May 1968) 713.

9 A. Bennett, 'Bennett and the beast', *The Listener* (13 June 1968) 775.

10 Games, *Backing Into the Limelight*, p. 86.

11 McGillivray, *Doing Rude Things*, p. 40.

12 J. Trevelyan, 'Censored', *The Listener* (13 June 1968) 775.

13 Letter from Louis Heyward to Vincent Price, 22 April 1968.

14 Kelley, 'Filming Reeves' masterpiece', p. 42.

15 Letter from Vincent Price to Michael Reeves, 18 April 1968.

16 AIP's US Press Book for the film made marketing suggestions around the idea of making the screening at event – nurses in attendance, local artists to 'duplicate the art work from *The Conqueror Worm*' and so forth, name-checking the Sears chain of stores, with whom Price was affiliated.

17 Weaver, *Interviews*, p. 169. This was most probably the Franco film.

18 McGillivray, *Doing Rude Things*, p. 104.

19 The title was later changed to *Blood on Satan's Claw*.

20 L. Hunt, '*Witchfinder General*: Michael Reeves's visceral classic', in A. Black (ed.), *Necronomicon Book One: the Journal of Horror and Erotic Cinema* (London, Creation Books, 1996), p. 127.

21 *Cinema X* was a grimy little 'photo-spread' rag whose existence centred on passing itself off as an illustrated magazine for the popular film enthusiast (perhaps one shelf down at the newsagents) and this would thus lend publicity, of a sort, to Tigon among others.

22 It opened in the US as *Horror House*, the lower half of a double-bill that included *Curse of the Crimson Altar*, retitled *The Crimson Cult*.

23 McGillivray, *Doing Rude Things*, p. 104

24 Tenser wrote to Price, by way of thanking him, 'If you weren't so damned

expensive I would give you a four-picture a year contract!'; letter from Tony Tenser to Vincent Price, 24 April 1968.

25 Armstrong, interview with author.

26 John Hall, interview with author, 22 January 2002.

27 Sinclair, *Lights Out For the Territory*, pp. 286–7.

28 Louis Heyward, interview with author, 24 June 1998.

29 Weaver, *Interviews*, p. 170.

30 Weaver, *Interviews*, p. 173.

31 Weaver, *Interviews*, p. 144.

32 Williams, *Complete Films of Vincent Price*, p. 216.

33 Price was seemingly unperturbed, pencilling 'Costumes. Mike Reeves' in his notes for 12 November; Williams, *Complete Films of Vincent Price*, p. 216

34 J. Petley, 'Chris Wicking interviewed by Julian Petley', *Journal of Popular British Cinema Issue 1: Genre and British Cinema* (London, Flicks Books, 1998), p. 145.

35 Williams, *Complete Films of Vincent Price*, p. 216.

36 Gordon Hessler, interview with author, 22 May 1998. All subsequent remarks are taken from this source.

37 Weaver, *Interviews*, p. 174.

38 According to Price, Reeves was to have directed it (French, *An Interview with Vincent Price*, unnumbered), although Hessler has no recollection of this.

39 Entry for *Scream and Scream Again*, in Hardy, *The Aurum Film Encyclopedia*, p. 211.

40 Letter from Tim Kelly to Tim Hodgson, 2 December 1991.

41 Huddleston, interview with author.

42 Paul Maslansky, interview with author, 2 July 2002. All subsequent remarks are taken from this source.

43 Weaver, *Interviews*, p. 168.

44 Armstrong, interview with author.

45 Mike was using Carbrital, Lagactil, Doriden, Triptizol, Phenergan and Nembutal. A side-effect of the ECT was a stutter, and the treatment may well have caused memory loss. From today's perspective, it could be argued that Mike was suffering from a bipolar disorder.

46 Baker, interview with author. This was not a criticism levelled at Tom.

47 Anon, 'Film director's drug death was accident', p. 1.

48 Anon, *Radio Times* (6 February 1969 and week following) 18.

49 Tenser, BOUM interview.

50 Letter from Don Siegel to Diana Tetlow, 25 February 1969.

51 Kelley, 'Filming Reeves' masterpiece', p. 45.

52 Kelley, 'Filming Reeves' masterpiece', p. 45.

53 Letter from Don Siegel to Diana Tetlow, September 1969.

54 I I. Maxford, *Hammer, House of Horror: Behind the Screams* (London, B. T. Batsford Ltd, 1996), p. 104.

55 Pirie, *Heritage of Horror*, p. 155.

Filmography

As director

Carrion circa 1958, 10–20 mins

8 mm, black and white; believed lost
Starring: Michael Reeves, Ian Ogilvy, Tom Baker and others
Camera: Tom Baker
Sound: Diana Tetlow

Down circa 1958/59

8 mm, black and white; believed lost
The Film Production Unit (Radley College)
With: Kenneth Brookman, possibly Alex Waye

Intrusion 1961, 10 mins

16 mm, black and white; sound missing
A Leith Production
Camera: Tom Baker
Production Manager: Paul Vestey
With: Sarah Dunlop, Desmond Bane, John Hardy, Martin Reid, Ian
    Ogilvy, Michael Reeves (uncredited)
Other, miscellaneous shorts; believed lost.

Revenge of the Blood Beast 1966, 74 mins

Alternative titles: *La Sorellas di Satana* (Italy), *The She-Beast* (US);
    Working titles: *Vardella, Il Lago di Satana*, '*Ruini Etrusci*'
Producer: Paul M. Maslansky
Second Unit: Charles B. Griffith
Camera: Gioacchino Gengarelli
Editor: Nira Omri
Script: Michael Byron (i.e. MR and Chuck B. Griffith, with contribu-
    tions from F. Amos Powell and Mel Welles)
Score: Ralph Ferraro
Initial distributors: Cineriz (Italy), Miracle Films (UK), American
    International Pictures (US)
With: Barbara Steele, John Karlsen, Ian Ogilvy, Mel Welles, Jay Riley,
    F. Amos Powell (uncredited: Paul Maslansky)
UK release print cut

The Sorcerers 1967, 87 mins

Alternative titles: *Im Banne des Dr Monserrat* (West Germany), *Los Brujos*
    (Spain), *Il Killer di Satana* (Italy), *La Créature Invisible* (France);
    Working title: *Terror for Kicks*
Company: Tigon-Curtwel Global Productions/Tony Tenser Films Ltd
Producers: Patrick Curtis, Tony Tenser
Executive Producer: Arnold L. Miller
Camera: Stanley A. Long
Editors: David Woodward, Susan Michie (uncredited: MR and Ralph
    Sheldon)
Script: John Burke, Tom Baker, MR (credited as: Screenplay by MR
    and Tom Baker from an idea by John Burke)
Score: Paul Ferris
With: Boris Karloff, Catherine Lacey, Ian Ogilvy, Victor Henry, Eliza-
    beth Ercy, Susan George, Dani Sheridan, Ivor Dean

Witchfinder General 1968, 86 mins

Alternative titles: *The Conqueror Worm* (US), *Le Grand Inquisiteur*
    (France), *Der Hexenjäger* (West Germany), *Il Grande Inquisitore (Italy)*
Company: Tigon British/AIP
Producer: Arnold Miller, Philip Waddilove, Louis M. Heyward

Executive Producer: Tony Tenser
Director: MR (alternative version: some tavern scenes by Tony Tenser, uncredited)
Camera: John Coquillon
Editor: Howard Lanning
Script: Tom Baker, MR from the novel by Ronald Bassett, 'Additional Scenes by Louis M. Heyward' (uncredited contributions from Philip Waddilove)
Score: Paul Ferris
With: Vincent Price, Ian Ogilvy, Rupert Davies, Hilary Dwyer, Robert Russell, Nicky Henson, Tony Selby
UK release print cut; US release print with additional voice-overs

Miscellaneous

The Ballad of the Battle of New Orleans circa 1959

8 mm, black and white; believed lost
The Film Production Unit (Radley College)
Producer, possibly director: Kenneth Brookman
Assistant editor/Assistant sound editor: Michael Reeves
Music: Lonnie Donegan, 'The Battle of New Orleans'

Some dialogue coaching for tests, possibly in preparation for *Flaming Star*; uncredited.
Director: Don Siegel, for Twentieth Century-Fox; 1960

Television commercials (various, unknown); as assistant director, circa 1961–64

Runner on *The Long Ships*

Director: Jack Cardiff, for Avala Films/Warwick/Columbia; 1963

Runner on *Genghis Khan*

Director: Henry Levin, for Avala Films/Irving Allen Productions/Columbia; 1965

Castle of the Living Dead 1963, released 1964, 90 mins

Alternative titles: *Il Castello dei Morti Vivi* (Italy), *Crypt of Horror* (unknown), *Les Château des Morts Vivants* (France)
Producer: Paul Maslansky
Production Company: Serena Films/Francinor
Director: Warren Kiefer (pseudonyms: Luciano Ricci, Herbert Wise, Lorenzo Sabatini)
Script: Warren Kiefer (uncredited: Paul Maslansky, MR)
Second Unit Directors: Frederick Muller, MR (credited on some prints only)
Camera: Aldo Tonti
With: Christopher Lee, Gaia Germani, Philippe Leroy-Beaulieu, Jacques Stanislawski, Donald Sutherland (uncredited: MR in a cameo)

Appassionata

Screenplay by Alfred Shaughnessy and MR, from an idea by MR; screenplay believed lost.
Made as *Crescendo*
Director: Alan Gibson, for Hammer Film Productions; 1970

The Oblong Box

Some script work by MR, unspecified and uncredited, before and with Christopher Wicking
Director: Gordon Hessler, for AIP; 1969

Out-takes from *Witchfinder General*

Possibly as director, with Tony Tenser; uncredited, believed lost
For Compton Cinema Club (possibly shown circa 1967–68 and thereafter)

All The Little Animals

Treatment, possibly screenplay, by MR from the novel by Walker Hamilton; believed lost

Attached as director to other projects formally in development

The Devil's Discord (Leith Productions/The Compton Group), 1966–
67
De Sade (AIP), 1968
The Buttercup Chain (Columbia Pictures), 1968
The Oblong Box (AIP), 1968
O'Hooligan's Mob (Tigon), 1968–69
All The Little Animals (Granada Films), 1969

Select bibliography

Anon, 'Film director's death from pills was accidental', *Chelsea News* (28 February 1969)

Anon, 'Film director's drug death was accident', *Chelsea Post* (21 February 1969)

Anon, 'Ian Ogilvy', *Films in London* (19 April/2 May 1970)

Anon, 'Obituary', *Films and Filming* (May 1969)

Anon, 'Programme Notes 17 January 1970', *National Film Theatre* (held by the British Film Institute)

Anon, *Radio Times* (6 February 1969 and week following)

Anon, 'Shows – horror clicks', *Penthouse*, 3:10 (UK edition, undated) 12.

Arkoff, S. and R. Trubo, *Flying Through Hollywood by the Seat of my Pants: From the Man who Brought You* I Was A Teenage Werewolf *and* Muscle Beach Party (New York, Birch Lane Press, 1992)

Armes, R., *A Critical History of British Cinema* (London, Secker & Warburg, 1979)

Austen, D., 'Alan Bennett's views', *The Listener* (30 May 1968)

Austen, D., '*The Sorcerers*', *Films and Filming* (October 1967)

Austen, D., '*Witchfinder General*', *Films and Filming* (July 1968)

Bailey, D. and P. Evans, *Goodbye Baby and Amen: A Saraband for the Sixties* (London, Condé Nast Publications Ltd, 1969)

Bamford, J., 'Bloodbeasts and witchfinders', *Films in London* (28 December–10 January 1969/1970)

Barr, C., '*Straw Dogs, A Clockwork Orange* and the critics', *Screen: The Journal of the Society for Education in Film and Television*, 13:2 (summer 1972)

Bassett, R. *Witchfinder General* (London, Herbert Jenkins Ltd, 1966)

Bennett, A., 'Bennett and the beast', *The Listener* (13 June 1968)

Bennett, A., 'Views', *The Listener* (23 May 1968)

Benshoff, H. M., *Monsters in the Closet: Homosexuality and the Horror Film* (Manchester, Manchester University Press, 1997)

Black, A. (ed.), *Necronomicon Book One: The Journal of Horror and Erotic Cinema* (London, Creation Books, 1996)

Boot, A. (ed.), *Fragments of Fear: An Illustrated History of British Horror Films* (London, Creation Books, 1996)

Brookman, K., '*Reflections on the 139th Psalm*', *The Radleian* (13 October 1957)

Brosnan, J., *The Horror People* (London, Macdonald and Jane's, 1976)

Cardiff, J., *Magic Hour: The Life of a Cameraman* (London, Faber & Faber, 1996)

Clark, A., *Diaries* (London, Phoenix, 1993)

Clover, C. J., *Men, Women and Chainsaws: Gender in the Modern Horror Film* (London, British Film Institute, 1992)

Dixon, W. W., *Re-Viewing British Cinema, 1990–1992: Essays and Interviews* (Albany, State University of New York Press, 1994)

Dixon, W. W. (ed.), *Collected Interviews: Voices from Twentieth-Century Cinema* (Carbondale and Edwardsville, Southern Illinois University Press, 2001)

Durgnat, R., 'Revenge of the Blood Beast', *Films and Filming* (November 1966)

Games, A., *Backing Into the Limelight: the Biography of Alan Bennett* (London, Review, 2002)

Green, A. E., *Witches and Witch-Hunters* (Yorkshire, S. R. Publishers Ltd, 1971)

Green, J., *All Dressed Up: The Sixties and the Counterculture* (London, Pimlico, 1999)

Grey, R., *Nightmare of Ecstasy: the Life and Art of Edward D. Wood, Jr* (London, Faber and Faber, 1994)

Hardy, P. (ed.), *The Aurum Film Encyclopedia: Horror* (London, Aurum Press, 1996)

Hogan, D. J., *Dark Romance: Sex and Death in the Horror Film* (Northamptonshire, Equation, Thorsons Publishing Group, 1988)

Hopkins, M., *The Discovery of Witches* (Norwich, H. W. Hunt, 1931)

Horovitz, M. (ed.), *Children of Albion: Poetry of the 'Underground' in Britain* (London, Penguin, 1971)

Hunter, I. Q. (ed.), *British Science Fiction Cinema* (London and New York, Routledge, 1999)

Hutchings, P., *Hammer and Beyond: The British Horror Film* (Manchester, Manchester University Press, 1993)

Jameson, F., *Signatures of the Visible* (London, Routledge, 1990)

Johnson, W., 'A walk on the wild side', *Sight & Sound* (spring 1986)

Jones, M., *Psychedelic Decadence: Sex, Drugs, Low-Art in Sixties and Seventies Britain* (Manchester, Critical Vision/Headpress, 2001)

Kelley, B., 'Filming Reeves' masterpiece: *Witchfinder General*', *Cinefantastique* 1 (1991)

Lachman, G. V., *Turn off Your Mind: The Mystic Sixties and the Dark Side of the Age of Aquarius* (London, Sidgwick & Jackson, 2001)

Lee, C., *Tall, Dark and Gruesome: An Autobiography* (London, Mayflower/Granada Publishing, 1978)

Lovell, A., *Don Siegel – American Cinema* (London, British Film Institute, 1968)

Maxford, H., *Hammer, House of Horror: Behind the Screams* (London, B. T. Batsford Ltd, 1996)

Mellor, D. A. and L. Gervereau (eds), *The Sixties: Britain and France, 1962–1973 – The Utopian Years* (London, Philip Wilson, 1997)

McFarlane, B., *An Autobiography of British Cinema* (London, Methuen, 1997)

McGee, M. T., *Faster and Furiouser: The Revised and Fattened Fable of American International Pictures* (London, McFarland and Company, Inc., 1996)

McGilligan, P. (ed.), *Backstory 3: Interviews with Screenwriters of the 60s* (Los Angeles and London, University of California Press, Berkeley, 1997)

McGillivray, D., *Doing Rude Things: The History of The British Sex Film, 1957–1981* (London, Sun Tavern Fields, 1992)

Murphy, R., *Sixties British Cinema* (London, British Film Institute, 1997)

Murray, J. B., *The Remarkable Michael Reeves: His Short and Tragic Life* (London, Cinematics Publishing, 2001)

Nichols, B. (ed.), *Movies and Methods Volume One: An Anthology* (London, University of California Press, 1976)

Nuttall, J., 'seedy jeff', *The International Times* (13–26 March 1967)

Parkinson, D. (ed.), *Mornings in the Dark: The Graham Greene Film Reader* (London, Penguin Books, 1995)

Parrish, J. R. and S. Whitney, *Vincent Price Unmasked* (New York, Drake Publishers, Inc., 1974)

Payn, G. and S. Morley (eds), *The Noël Coward Diaries* (London, MacMillan, 1982)

Petley, J. 'Chris Wicking interviewed by Julian Petley', *Journal of Popular British Cinema: Genre and British Cinema* 1 (1998)

Petrie, D., *The British Cinematographer* (London, British Film Institute, 1996)

Pirie, D., *A Heritage of Horror: The English Gothic Cinema 1946–1972* (London, Gordon Fraser, 1973)

Pirie, D., 'New blood', *Sight & Sound* (spring 1971)

Polanski, R., *Roman* (London, Pan Books, 1985)

Prawer, S. S., *Caligari's Children: The Film as Tale of Terror* (Oxford, Oxford University Press, 1980)

Pym, J., *Time Out Film Guide* (London, Penguin Books 1997)

Reeves, M., 'Alan Bennett's views', *The Listener* (30 May 1968)

Rigby, J., *English Gothic: A Century of Horror Cinema* (London, Reynolds and Hearn, 2002)

Rhode, E., 'Films: Lorenzo Baby', *The Listener* (30 May 1968)

Robinson, D., 'Case histories of the next renascence', *Sight & Sound* (winter 1968/69)

Savage, J., 'Turning into Wonders', *Sight & Sound* (September 1995)

Shaughnessy, A., *A Confession in Writing* (Cornwall, TABB House, 1997)

Sinclair, I., *Lights Out For the Territory: 9 Excursions in the Secret History of London* (London, Granta Books, 1997)

Street, S., *British National Cinema* (London and New York, Routledge, 1997)

Summers, M., *The Discovery of Witches: A Study of Master Matthew Hopkins, commonly call'd Witch Finder General* (London, Cayme Press, 1928)

Svehla G. J. and S. Svehla (eds), *Midnight Marquee Actors Series: Vincent Price* (Baltimore, Maryland, Midnight Marquee Press, Inc., 1998)

Swires, S., 'And now the screaming stops', *Fangoria* 112 (May 1992)

Swires, S., 'When the movies got tenser', *Fangoria* 128 (November 1993)

Tarkovsky A. and K. Hunter-Blair, *Time Within Time: the Diaries 1970–1986* (London, Faber & Faber, 1994)

Taylor, J. R., 'Horror, and something more', *The Times* (11 May 1968)

Trevelyan, J., 'Censored', *The Listener* (13 June 1968)

Trevelyan, J., *What the Censor Saw* (London, Michael Joseph, 1973)

Underwood, P., *Horror Man: The Life of Boris Karloff* (London, Leslie Frewin Publishers Ltd, 1972)

Watkinson, M., and P. Anderson, *Crazy Diamond: Syd Barrett and the Dawn of Pink Floyd* (London, Omnibus Press, 2001)

Waugh, A., *The Loom of Youth* (London, Cassell & Company, Ltd, 1929)

Weaver, T., *Interviews with B-Science Fiction and Horror Movie Makers* (North Carolina, McFarland and Co., 1988)

Williams, L. C., *The Complete Films of Vincent Price* (New York, Citadel Press Books, Carol Publishing Group, 1995)

Wood, R., 'In memoriam Michael Reeves', *Movie* (winter 1969–70)

Žižek, S., *Did Somebody Say Totalitarianism? Five Interventions in the (Mis)use of a Notion* (London, Verso, 2001)

Music

Amen Corner, The, 'When We Make Love', *Farewell to the Real Magnificent Seven* (Immediate, 1969)

Beatles, The, 'Tomorrow Never Knows', *Revolver* (Parlophone, 1966)

Lonnie Donegan, 'The Battle of New Orleans', *Lonnie Donegan Hit Parade* (Pye, 1959)

Pink Floyd, 'Astronomy Domine', *The Piper at the Gates of Dawn* (Tower, 1967)

Cliff Richard and the Shadows, 'In the Country', *Cinderalla* (EMI-Columbia, 1967)

Otis Redding, '(Sittin' On) The Dock of the Bay, *The Dock of the Bay* (Atco, 1968)

Frank Zappa and the Mothers, 'Cheepnis', *Roxy and Elsewhere* (Discreet, 1974)

Unpublished sources

Baker, T., and M. Reeves, from the novel by R. Bassett, with final scene revisions by M. Reeves and P. Waddilove, '*Witchfinder General*' final screenplay (unpublished, Tigon-Global Productions Ltd, 1967)

Burke, J., 'The Devil's Discord' (unpublished screenplay, 'original story and screenplay by John Burke')

Burke, J., 'Terror for Kicks' (unpublished outline, F. H. C. Productions Ltd, 1966)

Burke, J., 'Terror for Kicks' (unpublished screenplay, 1966)

Burke, J., M. Reeves and T. Baker, 'The Sorcerers' (unpublished screenplay, Tony Tenser-Curtwel Productions Inc., Vardella Film Productions Ltd, 1967)

French, L., 'An interview with Vincent Price', conducted in 1979 and 1985, unpublished

Index

Titles of films and literary works can be found under their authors' names where the names are also mentioned in the text. Numbers in *italics* denote illustrations. An 'n.' after a page reference indicates the number of a note on that page.